YOUNG MEN SURVIVING CHILD SEXUAL ABUSE

Research Stories and Lessons for
Therapeutic Practice

WILEY SERIES
in
CHILD PROTECTION AND POLICY

Series Editor: Christopher Cloke,
                  NSPCC, 42 Curtain Road,
                  London EC2A 3NX

This NSPCC/Wiley series explores current issues relating to the prevention of child abuse and the protection of children. The series aims to publish titles that focus on professional practice and policy, and the practical application of research. The books are leading edge and innovative and reflect a multi-disciplinary and inter-agency approach to the prevention of child abuse and the protection of children.

  This series is essential reading for all professionals and researchers concerned with the prevention of child abuse and the protection of children. The accessible style will appeal to parents and carers. All books have a policy or practice orientation with referenced information from theory and research.

YOUNG MEN SURVIVING CHILD SEXUAL ABUSE

Research Stories and Lessons for Therapeutic Practice

Andrew Durham

WILEY

Other Wiley Editorial Offices

John Wiley & Sons Inc., 111 River Street, Hoboken, NJ 07030, USA

Jossey-Bass, 989 Market Street, San Francisco, CA 94103-1741, USA

Wiley-VCH Verlag GmbH, Boschstr. 12, D-69469 Weinheim, Germany

John Wiley & Sons Australia Ltd, 33 Park Road, Milton, Queensland 4064, Australia

John Wiley & Sons (Asia) Pte Ltd, 2 Clementi Loop #02-01, Jin Xing Distripark, Singapore 129809

John Wiley & Sons Canada Ltd, 22 Worcester Road, Etobicoke, Ontario, Canada M9W 1L1

Wiley also publishes its books in a variety of electronic formats. Some content that appears in print may
not be available in electronic books.

Library of Congress Cataloging-in-Publication Data

Durham, Andrew,
Young men surviving child sexual abuse : research stories and
lessons for therapeutic practice / Andrew Durham.
    p. cm. – (Wiley child protection & policy series)
    Includes bibliographical references (p.) and index.
    ISBN 0-470-84459-0 (hbk) – ISBN 0-470-84460-4 (pbk)
    1. Adult child abuse victims.   I. Title.   II. Series.
    RC569.5 .C55 D87 2003
    616.85'82239 – dc21

                                                        2002156191

British Library Cataloguing in Publication Data

A catalogue record for this book is available from the British Library

ISBN 0-470-84459-0 (hbk)
ISBN 0-470-84460-4 (pbk)

Project management by Originator, Gt Yarmouth, Norfolk (typeset in 10/12pt Palatino)
Printed and bound in Great Britain by TJ International, Padstow, Cornwall
This book is printed on acid-free paper responsibly manufactured from sustainable forestry
in which at least two trees are planted for each one used for paper production.

CONTENTS

About the Author   vii

Acknowledgements   viii

Foreword by Christine Harrison   ix

Introduction   xi

Part I   The Theoretical Context   1
1   The Social Context of Child Sexual Abuse   3
2   Male-Child Sexual Abuse—Facts and Mythology   16
3   Developing a Sensitive Approach to Researching Child Sexual
      Abuse   32

Part II   The Young Men's Stories   41
4   Seven Lives   43
5   Being Abused   54
6   Trying to Tell   68
7   Sexuality, Friendships, and Peer Relations   83
8   Still Living with the Consequences of Abuse   97
9   Being a Participant   106

Part III   Implications for Practice   111
10   A Framework for Therapeutic Practice   113
11   Assistance in Recovery   125
12   Conclusions   146

Bibliography   151

Appendix A   Thoughts and Feelings Sort Cards   169

Appendix B   Abuser–Victim Flow Chart   171

Appendix C   Feeling Safe and Being Safe   172

Appendix D   Information about Child Sexual Abuse   176

Index   179

ABOUT THE AUTHOR

Andrew Durham has a PhD in Applied Social Studies from the University of Warwick that researched into the impact of child sexual abuse. He also has the Advanced Award in Social Work (AASW). He has over 20 years' experience of providing therapeutic services to children and young people and is a specialist in post-abuse counselling and interventions for children and young people with sexual behaviour difficulties.

He is currently the Consultant Practitioner for the Sexualised Inappropriate Behaviours Service (SIBS) in Warwickshire and a visiting lecturer at the University of Warwick.

He also occasionally works as an independent childcare consultant, undertaking therapeutic work with children and young people, consultancy, lecturing, and training. He is registered with the Law Society as an expert witness and has been an advisor to the BBC. He has previously published papers and chapters on the subject of child sexual abuse.

ACKNOWLEDGEMENTS

I would like to thank my wife Rachel and stepson Sam for all their patience, support and understanding throughout the lengthy time I have been involved with this research.

I would also like to thank Christine Harrison at the University of Warwick and Robin Hill at Warwickshire Social Services Department for their sustained support and encouragement.

This book is dedicated to the courage and survival of the seven young men who shared their stories with me. The royalties from this book will, as far as possible, be shared with them.

FOREWORD

The enforcement of silence has been and remains the most potent weapon of abusers, both individually and collectively. Breaking the silence has likewise been seen as the most vital step towards bringing about change and a safer environment. (Nelson, 2000, p. 394)

The sexual offences against children that this book is about are not only among the most serious and potentially harmful experiences that children can have but the most hidden as well. They are surrounded by a wall of enforced secrecy and silence that generates shame for victims and compounds the abuse they have experienced. To be abused is bad enough; to feel unable safely to reveal this, or to try to do so and not be believed, causes unimaginable damage. This also leaves innumerable children and young people to find their own strategies for survival, without access to any help and support and with lifelong implications for them.

Despite incontrovertible knowledge about the scale and impact of child sexual abuse and its relationship with other forms of violence and abuse against women and children, it has proved difficult to breach the wall of silence. Recent evidence about Internet pornography reveals staggering levels of child sexual abuse, where very few victims are able to report offences and even fewer men who offend are successfully prosecuted.

Two interrelated dimensions are significant in maintaining the hidden nature of child sexual abuse. The first is that this is a major objective of men who perpetrate child sexual abuse and an inherent aspect of the ways in which they target and groom potential victims. High levels of planning and organisation are involved to abuse, and bribes, threats and coercion are used to ensure both compliance and secrecy from children, who are likely already to be socially disadvantaged. When they are apprehended, a characteristic aspect of the accounts of perpetrators is denial and minimisation in terms of the extent and the effects of their offending. The pressure on potential child witnesses is immense, and the evidential demands of the criminal justice system frequently leave them feeling even more disempowered.

The second, and inextricably connected to the first, is a broader social context that mirrors and reinforces the denial and minimisation of offences that challenge so much that is taken for granted about the nature of relationships between men, women, and children. Time and again the extent and scale of sexual offences, together with the apparent ordinariness of the men who perpetrate them, reveals how all the social institutions that are supposed to protect children (the family, schools, hospitals, residential care, etc.) can be used by offenders to abuse them. It is an examination of this social context, rather than concentrating solely on the characteristics of individual perpetrators, that will enable us to account for why sexual offences against children, and for that matter against women, are not taken more seriously and why, despite legal and policy changes, it is still so unsafe for children.

The accounts of young men that lie at the heart of this book are important from a theoretical perspective. They build on what we know already and, while recognising from the outset the scale of abuse of girls and young women, they contribute to critical understandings of how the relationship between power, sexuality, masculinity and abuse is experienced by young male victims. Of equal importance, they contribute to eroding the silence and secrecy on which the power of offenders relies. No claim is made that these accounts are representative, and indeed they reflect great diversity of experiences and views, of strengths and the struggles involved in overcoming the impact of abuse. They may, however, be considered as given on behalf of all the thousands of young people who are the subject of sexual abuse and who are never able to find someone they trust sufficiently to talk about what has happened to them. Indeed, many of the participants were explicit about their hopes that their involvement would benefit other young people.

For those who work with young people, the accounts are also related to practice issues and the ways in which youth-centred therapeutic interventions can be promoted. Hearing the accounts of young men presented here will be painful, but critical if we are fully to understand not just the experiences they have had and their impact but what is helpful in the struggle for survival and recovery in the aftermath of abuse as well.

Christine Harrison
School of Health and Social Studies
University of Warwick

INTRODUCTION

This book analyses the experiences of seven young men, ranging from the age of 15 to 23, who have as children been sexually abused. A life-story method of data collection is used in order to capture as fully as possible a representation and analysis of the personal experience of each young man, exploring common and diverse factors and the unique integration of the impact of child sexual abuse into each individual life. There is little available knowledge of male-child sexual abuse of this detailed nature, particularly from a sample close to or during adolescence.

As a therapeutic practitioner, wanting to take an interest in some of the wider theoretical issues, I became aware that broader social brush strokes were having a particular impact on the manner in which children and young people survived and lived through experiences of child sexual abuse. Child sexual abuse has a long social and political history of discovery–burial–rediscovery–disbelief–burial–rediscovery–denial–rediscovery, in an almost wave-like motion (Herman, 1992; Gilligan, 1997; Oakley, 1997). These public experiences are paralleled by the experiences of the individual child trying to tell and escape from child sexual abuse, an experience where private personal experiences and social constructions collide, leaving the child in an invidious position. Denial and burial by adults who abuse, by other family members and children, can become functional to the preservation of current circumstances. This may be the preservation of a family, an avoidance of further violence and other feared consequences, or the preservation of an individual child's identity, where the abused child fears the negative perceptions of others, through being instilled with an intense feeling of responsibility, every attempt having been made by the person who abused to ensure that others are held to feel responsible. If there is an open social acceptance of the widespread existence of child sexual abuse in a manner that holds the people who abuse accountable for their actions, then it is more likely that children will feel that their experiences will be believed when they tell. If there is a social denial, individual children will be more likely to keep their experiences to themselves.

Theories of child sexual abuse often focus on 'how' child sexual abuse takes place, avoiding the crucial question of 'why' we have child sexual abuse in our society (Macleod and Saraga, 1991). Such theories often ignore social and cultural contexts and concentrate on the psychology of individual behaviour (Kelly, 1996). With the best intentions, professional responses to children who have been sexually abused become defined in terms of 'treatment' or 'therapy'. Such clinical and potentially pathologising responses may unwittingly compound a child's instilled sense of responsibility. A more adequate theory of why child sexual abuse takes place has first to account for the fact that over 90% of child sexual abuse is committed by males (Morrison et al., 1994; Home Office, 1997). Second, why does the abuse have to be sexual? Third, why are burial and denial so prominent in its history? Fourth, why for many years have complacent professional responses been dominated by an individualising medical framework that fails to address wider social factors and therefore potentially colludes with the abuser's denial of responsibility? More recently, social work achievements in challenging the dominance of the medical framework have been confounded by a restrictive and highly procedural legal framework, based on a distrust of children's testimonies (Spencer and Flin, 1990; Durham, 1997a). Such testimonies are only finally believed within the legal system after the child has been subjected to a range of difficult and frightening procedures and, quite often, a highly traumatic court appearance.

Asymmetrical power relationships are shown to be characteristic of child sexual abuse. This study identifies the importance of understanding the diverse and changeable experiences involved in the impact and aftermath of child sexual abuse with elements that are both unique and common. The study identifies some of the survival strategies employed by the young men in attempting to resist and subsequently survive the abuse.

The study identifies and confirms previous findings relating to the particular experiences of males who have been sexually abused. However, the study emphasises the significance of these experiences taking place in a social context of patriarchal relations. This context creates circumstances that allow sexual abuse to happen and hinders the recovery of its survivors. The study shows how a context of patriarchal relations, characterised by compulsory heterosexism and homophobia, has shaped and exacerbated the young men's experiences. This is through internalised oppression and power relationships, which have caused them to respond in a manner that affirms and perpetuates social constructions of hegemonic masculinities. The study recognises that sexuality is a particularly significant constituent of personal identity during adolescence, particularly in a society where heterosexuality is oppressively policed as a vehicle of social control. The study shows processes of patriarchal gender construction, particularly in relation to contested masculinities. These have become more threatening as a result of the young men seeing themselves as being placed on the margin in terms of their masculinities and as a result of their experiences of child sexual abuse.

This book in no way weakens feminist arguments or detracts from the fact that the majority of sexual abuse is committed by males against females (Finkelhor et al., 1986; Morrison et al., 1994; Home Office, 1997). There have been fewer studies of male-child sexual abuse than female-child sexual abuse. The study will attempt to contribute to feminist (and pro-feminist) research and practice by showing how an analysis of gender, power and sexuality can be applied to the experiences of young men. The study advances an analytical practice framework that allows the experiences of children and young people who have been sexually abused to be considered in a context of continuing widespread social oppression and suggests fresh non-pathologising approaches to therapeutic practice.

From my own practice experience, and prior and current knowledge of the literature, there is an assumption that the experience of child sexual abuse is traumatic and has potentially harmful short- and long-term consequences. Also that children and young people who have been sexually abused may require help and support in coming to terms with the experience. Additionally, the extent and success of the recovery is dependent not only on that help and support but also on how a child or young person's other experiences and circumstances, including oppression(s), may interact with the experience of child sexual abuse to produce differing impacts. This means that there may be both common and diverse consequences between different children and young people.

Child sexual abuse is often characterised by secrecy, isolation and the silencing of its victims. This in itself has implications for how such a phenomenon should be researched, particularly when young people, close in years to the experience, are involved. A fear of the consequences of telling may still be present; the messages that may have been implanted by the abuser, in order to maintain the child's silence, may still be influencing the child or young person's ability to tell or discuss the experience in any detail, beyond revealing the fact that it happened. Approaching the study with practice knowledge, and theoretical assumptions that this may be the case, leads to an awareness that the methodology has to take these factors into account not only in order to have access to the information but also to be aware of the potential trauma the participant may have in sharing that information and to be aware that it may not be possible to share such information in a formal manner, nor to be able to verbalise the extent or nature of the experience.

This book will show that it is an absolute prerequisite for a researcher to be mindful of these factors and to be aware that the experience of being a research participant may in itself potentially become an experience of oppression. It will be shown that approaching the research in this sensitive manner has captured and represented the young men's experiences, exploring personal identities, ways of being and their relationships as friends, partners, and fathers. The young men have shared their hopes and fears about their past, current and future lives. The study has closely involved itself with these experiences and has provided important information to a knowledge base for more appropriate and non-pathologising ways of helping young men and others who have been sexually abused.

STRUCTURE OF THE BOOK

The book is divided into three parts: Part I (Chapters 1–3), The Theoretical Context; Part II (Chapters 4–9), The Young Men's Stories; and Part III (Chapters 10–12), Implications for Practice.

Chapter 1 analyses patriarchal relations, hegemony, and contested masculinities, which underpin the dominance of men and the subordination of women and children through historically constructed power relationships. It is argued that political structures of domination are maintained through the preservation of patriarchal power relationships that are represented in both public and private spheres: individual and institutional relationships of hierarchy, domination, subordination, oppression, and control. Power and control in this context are often eroticised through being associated with hegemonic masculinities that are characterised by compulsory heterosexuality and homophobia. It is argued that these processes create, support, encourage, and hide the sexual abuse of women and children, and other forms of violence. Additionally, they exacerbate and deepen the impact of child sexual abuse on its survivors.

Chapter 2 critically reviews the existing literature on male-child sexual abuse, beginning with a discussion of prevalence and definitions, and the methodological problems involved, recognising that there is likely to be a significant degree of under-reporting. Major theories relating to the impact of child sexual abuse are critically discussed. The interacting impact of child sexual abuse and social oppression, most notably racism and disability, is examined. The specific impact of child sexual abuse on boys and young men is explored. This includes research that examines the link between the experience of sexual abuse and the subsequent sexual abuse of others, and research that examines the impact on sexual identity. Drawing on issues identified in the previous chapter, an interacting mythology based on homophobic fears and fears of abusing others is identified as significantly contributing to the harmful impact of the sexual abuse. The chapter raises epistemological questions about the dominance of particular forms of knowledge. It concludes that in explaining causation or impact of sexual abuse, much of the literature focuses on psychological factors in a potentially pathologising manner and fails to adequately centralise the influence of sociocultural factors.

Chapter 3 outlines the methodology of the study. A theoretical relationship is established between ethnography (particularly a life-story approach), feminist praxis, anti-oppressive research, and practitioner research. Researching experiences of child sexual abuse is stressful for all concerned and requires a methodology that establishes a safe environment, facilitates an expression and discussion of painful and fearful feelings and experiences, and provides appropriate ongoing support. In setting up this environment and providing support before, during, and after the data collection phase, the value and importance of practitioner research was established. The potential influence of this on the nature of data collected is acknowledged both as a potential cost, in terms of objectivity, and as a benefit in creating a climate for the production of sensitive knowledge. It concludes that a life-story practitioner research approach, incorporating the principles of anti-oppressive research practice, is an appropriate methodology for the study of the experience and impact of child sexual abuse.

Chapter 4 analyses the research contact and the interviewing of the seven young men who took part in the study and presents vignettes. Their pseudonyms and ages are as follows: Justin (22), Paul (23), Colin (18), Liam (22), Sean (21), David (15), and Ryan (15).

Chapter 5 analyses the circumstances of the young men before they were abused and identifies how the men who abused them took advantage of their circumstances in constructing abusive relationships. It explores the power relationships involved during the sexual abuse, examines the young men's strategies of resistance and considers their feelings and memories of the experience.

Chapter 6 explores the difficult, fearful and complicated circumstances the young men had to face in deciding to tell about their abuse and is critical of the socio-legal framework that has been constructed as a professional response to manage the telling in the sanitised context of a single 'disclosure' event.

Chapter 7 analyses the young men's comments about peer relations. Processes of internalised oppression, in the context of compulsory heterosexism and homophobia, are identified. Some of the young men revealed substantial fears of feeling and being perceived by their peers as being gay. Additionally, there were fears of abusing others, again primarily based on the perceptions of others.

Chapter 8 considers the individual private trauma faced by the young men in terms of memories, nightmares, and flashbacks. Some of the young men turned to the use of alcohol, drugs, gas, and solvents to try and manage their feelings. The research identifies the depth and turmoil of the sadness some of the young men experienced, which was sometimes represented by their behaviour and at other times was expressed in private.

Chapter 9 considers the young men's feelings about taking part in the research, concluding that they were very positive and welcoming of the support they received, and that they may have benefited. However, it is important to be cautious about using terms like empowerment, as the young men's lives continue in some ways to be difficult and disadvantaged, and not helped by experiences of child sexual abuse. The research may have helped the young men reframe and come to terms with some of their thoughts and feelings about being abused, allowing them to reflect on how they have managed so far, but it will not have significantly changed the material circumstances of their lives and it will not have taken their memories away.

Chapter 10 discusses the implications of the research for therapeutic practice and presents a new analytical practice framework. It criticises the current legalism of the childcare system and argues that young people would benefit from services that are more flexible and less bureaucratic. It also argues that it is important to take an approach to helping that emphasises the impact of social factors and the potency of ongoing social oppression, in a manner that externalises many of the factors contributing to the impact of sexual abuse. By centralising the voice of the young person in the context of everyday experience, paying careful attention to the language used and the experiences explained, assistance can be provided in a non-pathologising manner.

Chapter 11 presents a plan for therapeutic work with children and young people who have been sexually abused. The plan places a strong emphasis on flexibility, transparency, and the importance of allowing the child or young person to maintain control. The chapter finally presents a range of practice materials and suggestions of techniques to be used within the therapeutic plan.

Chapter 12 draws together final conclusive comments from the study, in terms of what has been established and achieved, and its overall implications for future practice.

INTRODUCING THE PARTICIPANTS

Justin (22) went to a special-needs boarding school at the age of 14, following difficulties at home and mainstream school. Between the ages of 14 and 16 he was physically and sexually abused many times by the headmaster. He was aware that many other boys were also being abused by the same man and other older boys at the school. He reported the abuse and attended two court trials, alongside many other boys. His abuser was convicted and given 14 years' imprisonment.

Paul (23) lived with his mother and stepfather. His stepfather emotionally and physically abused him severely. From around the age of six or seven, Paul was sexually abused by a man who lived in his neighbourhood. Both the sexual and physical abuse continued until Paul was nine, when he moved into foster care. Prior to this research, he has never talked about the sexual abuse.

Colin (18) lived in foster care from the age of 4, until he left care at 18. At the age of 13, he absconded from foster care and was sexually abused by a man previously unknown to him. The abuse took place over a four-day period; within days of returning to foster care he formally disclosed the abuse, but there was insufficient evidence for a prosecution.

Liam (22) went to a boarding school at the age of 14, following difficulties at home and school. He developed a closeness to a young male teacher at the school, who subsequently sexually abused him at the age of 16. Liam was confused about this 'relationship', as he believes he fully consented. He volunteered to take part in the research, disclosing his experiences for the first time. Following this, he reported his experiences to the police. There was insufficient evidence for a prosecution.

Sean (21) was in public care from the age of 9. At the age of 12 he went to a special-needs boarding school. Around the ages of 14 and 15, he was sexually abused on many occasions by the head of care at the school. He was not aware that other boys were also being sexually abused by the same man. When one of the other boys reported being abused, Sean was questioned by the police and reported his abuse. The abuser absconded the country during the investigation and did not face trial.

David (15) lived at home with his parents. When David was nine, his family was approached by a man named Harry, who had set up a local computer club for boys in the area. David attended the club and was 'befriended' by Harry, who further approached David's parents offering weekend respites at his home. Subsequently, in the confines of his own home, Harry sexually abused David on a regular basis, over a two-year period. David was not aware that other boys were also being sexually abused by Harry. At the age of 12, David was questioned about his time with Harry and reported being sexually abused. He attended a court trial, alongside other boys, and Harry was convicted and sentenced to 18 months' imprisonment.

Ryan (15) lived with his mother and was invited to attend a local computer club run by a man named Harry. This was the same club that David attended. A few weeks later he was playing in a local park where he was approached by Harry, who drove him to his house and sexually abused him. Ryan has little recall of these events, but remembers going to Harry's house on two occasions, where on both occasions he was sexually abused by him. Although Ryan reported his abuse to the police, he did not attend the court trial. He is aware that Harry was convicted for sexually abusing other boys and served a prison sentence.

Part I

THE THEORETICAL CONTEXT

1

THE SOCIAL CONTEXT OF
CHILD SEXUAL ABUSE

INTRODUCTION

This chapter considers the nature of patriarchal relations and argues that they constitute a social context that allows sexual abuse to happen. It is further argued that this social context has a subsequent influence on the private and personal experiences of those surviving the impact of sexual abuse. In considering the specific experiences of boys and men, the concept of masculinity is critically analysed. It is recognised that there are hegemonic or dominant forms of masculinity that have a particular influence on the sexually abused male. The first section, 'Patriarchal Relations', examines the history and construction of patriarchal relations, looking at the intertwining of biological sex with gender, oppressive heterosexism and the widespread historical and present-day domination of women and children by men. The next section, 'Hegemony and Resistance', considers the concept of hegemony and examines forms of resistance to patriarchal relations. It is recognised that subordination is never complete and is always characterised by a level of resistance, struggle and challenge, producing alternative discourses. This is followed by a critical examination of the social construction of masculinities, recognising that they are multiple, dynamic, shifting, and changing. There are, however, forms of masculinity that are dominant or hegemonic, influencing, shaping, and subordinating other forms. Subordinated forms of masculinity therefore have to struggle, resist, and adapt in order to survive in an oppressive social context of heterosexism and homophobia. These factors are considered to be particularly significant in adolescent peer groups.

Finally, the chapter explores the relationship between hegemonic masculinities and child sexual abuse. The feminist movement has raised epistemological questions about the control and production of knowledge, and who this benefits. It has played an important role in facilitating social rediscovery of sexual abuse and in asking the question 'why is the majority of sexual abuse committed by males?' The chapter concludes by recognising the importance and relevance of power, gender, and oppression in developing a fuller understanding of male-child sexual abuse and in establishing fresh approaches to the formulation of appropriate child and young person-centred strategies for helping its survivors.

PATRIARCHAL RELATIONS

In definitional terms, patriarchy is the widespread institutional domination of women by men, at all levels of society, both in private and public spheres. Patriarchy is 'a specifically gendered organising framework' (Cooper, 1995, p. 10), the widespread possession of personal and social power by men, which is theirs simply by being men. Patriarchy has 'the power to transcend natural realities with historical, man-made realities' (Kaufman, 1987, p. 7). By being born a male within patriarchy, a child learns that he is endowed, or rather has been embodied, with privileges not afforded to his sister. This occurs through his development of a masculine gender, as defined within patriarchy. There are two important features here. First, patriarchy is an ongoing process that can adapt and change according to circumstances (Daly, 1978; Kaufman, 1987). In this sense, it is more accurate to use the term 'patriarchal relations' as a more dynamic and less rigidly structural concept. This is not to ignore the influence of oppressive structural divisions on interpersonal relationships; it is what people do and say within the context of these wider structural divisions that determines their impact on people's lives. Second, the distinction between sex and gender, which is purposefully conflated by patriarchal construction.

The intertwining of sex and gender has historically been supported by socio-biologism, using concepts relating to hormones and perceived natural attributes (e.g., physical strength, aggressiveness, weakness, and caring) and relating them to current social circumstances. The historical and social construction of these theories is discussed at length by Cornwall and Lindisfarne (1994), and Kaufman (1987). Kaufman makes the important point, in relation to his discussion on men and violence, that some questions will have to remain unanswered, as the men being studied (both now and in the past) do not exist outside societies. Cornwall and Lindisfarne (1994) argue that the male/female dichotomy has no biological or other essential reality. Anthropological analysis has shown how notions of masculinities are often transient and can be situationally and culturally specific, and that definitions of gender can vary with circumstances, to the extent that assumptions about biology and gender can be challenged. Cornwall and Lindisfarne (1994) refer to changing gay identities, whereby gay men have rejected the feminisation of homosexuality and have taken on macho-identities formerly associated with heterosexuality. The possibility of being gay and masculine challenges heterosexist patriarchal constructions of gender.

Historically, patriarchal relations have been responsible for circumstances of extreme violence against women across the world: Indian sutteeism (the custom of women throwing themselves onto their husbands' funeral pyres); Chinese foot-binding; African genital mutilation; European witch-burnings; and American gynaecology (Daly, 1978). The dynamic essence of patriarchy is well captured by Daly, who uses the analogy of noxious gases that are lived, breathed, but not always noticed, and carried by the body, surreptitiously permeating interpersonal relationships. Daly (1978, p. 3) refers to the need to seek out 'the sources of the ghostly gases' and destroy the false perceptions that have permeated into the minds of women. She identifies four methods that she refers to as being essential to the games of the fathers: 'Erasure; reversal; false polarisation and divide and conquer' (p. 8). Daly describes patriarchy as a complex lie, a hidden web of pervasive deception. Particular importance is paid to the role of language and the notion that women's realities and mythologies have been stolen and reconstructed for the benefit of men. She describes her work as an extremist book written in the extreme circumstances of a culture that is killing itself. This connection between patriarchal relations and the destruction of nature has been identified by other writers (Struve, 1990; Cornwall and Lindisfarne, 1994). Kaufman (1987) argues that patriarchy is foundational to worldwide political circumstances of human domination, which allows the coexistence of Western abundance and poverty and starvation in the Third World.

Patriarchal relations often emphasise commodity and possession. People, by virtue of possessing certain attributes, have power over others. The most immediate example is being male, the possession of a male body; another could be the possession of a white skin (not to suggest that patriarchy subsumes racial hierarchies, Wilson [1993] has shown how patriarchy operates in black groups). This could be accompanied by use of a particular dialect, language or phraseology that would carry forward and extend patriarchal discourses, thus influencing, shaping and often determining interpersonal power relationships. The commodity logic is most notably represented in the construction of gender (Cornwall and Lindisfarne, 1994). Gender is defined as a fixed dichotomy: biology and gender are conflated so that 'male', 'men', and 'masculinity' are treated as a single entity and are defined in opposition to 'female', 'women', and 'femininity'. Through patriarchal constructions, the female side of the opposition is defined as the other and is subordinated by definition. Gendered identities are developed within patriarchal relations by the social acquisition of attributes (e.g., active, strong, and self-reliant for men, and passive, weak, and dependent for women). The intertwining of anatomy or biology with gender roles and socially learned behaviours reinforces a view that the 'normal' sexual orientation and identity is heterosexual (Jubber, 1991) (see Figure 1.1). Additionally, the dichotomous definition of gender implies that two opposites make a heterosexual whole (Cornwall and Lindisfarne, 1994).

In this way, gender is embodied literally as an apparently truthful fixed entity and bodies become gendered. This is particularly evident during adolescence, whereby individuals having experienced puberty and physical changes begin to negotiate serious identities of their own and peer group pressure takes on a particular importance (Moore and Rosenthal, 1993). The process is learning through becoming, beginning at birth with blue for a boy and pink for a girl. The result is a view of gender as a fixed natural order. The process of gendering in patriarchal relations amounts to a suppression and denial of similarities and an emphasising of differences between the biological sexes. For each individual this means a repression of behaviours and emotions not considered to be acceptable for a particular gender, a process of personal struggle and fear. Although this means having to constantly negotiate and deny such fears, for the male the consequence of achieving this successfully is privilege, for the female success or failure means being subordinated (Kaufman, 1987; Cornwall and Lindisfarne, 1994; Wolfe et al., 1997).

These arguments are taken further by 'queer theory', which argues that most social theory takes a heterosexist perspective, in which heterosexuality is

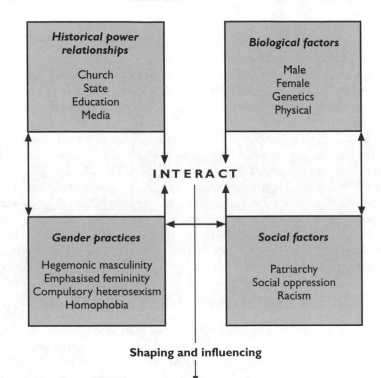

Figure 1.1   The social organisation of sexuality and attraction.

normalised and functional to the social order, never requiring explanation (Sedgwick, 1990; Dollimore, 1991; D'Augelli and Patterson, 1995). Other sexualities are therefore marginalised, problematised, and excluded. Queer theory aims to force a revision of these traditions, arguing that a non-oppressive gender order can only come about through a radical change in the theorising and conceptualising of sexuality, with shifting styles of identity politics and the generation and valuing of new cultures. Warner argues that:

> Because the logic of the sexual order is so deeply embedded by now in an indescribably wide range of social institutions, and is embedded in the most standard accounts of the world, queer struggles aim not just at toleration or equal status but at challenging those institutions and accounts. The dawning realisation that themes of homophobia and heterosexism may be read into almost any document of our culture means that we are only beginning to have an idea of how widespread those institutions and accounts are. (Warner, 1993, p. xiii)

Paradoxically, both Freud (1973) and Foucault (1976) theorise difference from heterosexuality, often oppressively conceptualised as 'sexual perversion' or 'sexual deviation', in a manner that makes it culturally central (Dollimore,

1991). Freud argued that 'perverse' (1973, p. 245) desire remains repressed and becomes transformed into other energies in a manner functional to society. Foucault argued that perversion is not repressed at all, but that our culture actively produces it as a vehicle and product of power that enables social control, defining and producing the margins in order to create and maintain the centre (Foucault, 1976). According to Dollimore (1991):

> In Foucault's scheme deviants come to occupy a revealing, dangerous double relationship to power, at once culturally marginal yet discursively central. Even as the sexual deviant is banished to the margins of society, he or she remains integral to it, not in spite of but because of that marginality. (p. 222)

In Foucauldian terms, homosexuality speaking for itself would be seen as a reverse discourse, demanding validity and legitimisation. Queer theorists argue more simply and directly that queer is and always has been everywhere, in a manner that seeks to unseat the order of sexual difference, 'succinctly expressed in the liberationist slogan "we are your worst fears and your best dreams"' (Dollimore, 1991, p. 227).

Queer theorists argue that power relationships can only be fully understood from the vantage point of 'anti-homophobic inquiry' (Warner, 1993, p. xiv). Marginalisation and stigmatisation of 'the homosexual' are functional to hetero-sexual (particularly masculine) identity (Sedgwick, 1985, 1990). The extent of the social policing of sexuality implied by these arguments underlines the significance and potency of sexuality and sexual identity in interpersonal power relationships. This is borne out by some of the experiences described by the young men in Part II and similarly in the research into masculinities and schooling by Nayak and Kehily (1997). This shows how close proximity and emotional contact between 15- and 16-year-old male pupils in the school setting is seen and experienced very much as a threat to masculine, heterosexual identity. This identity, therefore, needs to be constantly and repeatedly recharged by public repudiation of any form of homoerotic bond. This often takes the form of aggressive behaviours: a public transference of inner tensions and anxieties on to others. Steinberg et al. (1997, p. 11) describe these homophobic performances as 'border patrols' through which the boundaries of heterosexuality are maintained and policed.

Heterosexism is a constituent of patriarchy, an essential characteristic of gender constructions, that is supported through pervasive organisational, institutional, familial and interpersonal relationships. Figure 1.1 summarises some of these arguments to show the social organisation of sexuality and attraction. An oppressive social context of patriarchal relations defines heterosexuality as the only acceptable form of sexuality. In a society where social control is based on a strict organisation of sexual desire and attraction, sexuality becomes a potent force, central to personal identities. Heterosexuality therefore becomes a significant constituent of personal and social power. To deviate from heterosexuality is to have less power in a wide range of social circumstances and interpersonal relationships.

HEGEMONY AND RESISTANCE

Essential to patriarchal relations is that particular forms of masculinity and femininity become dominant and are maintained. In order to examine how this happens, it is necessary to consider the concept of 'hegemony'. This was a term used by Gramsci in his development of work by Lenin (Joll, 1977). In literal terms it means 'ascendancy', 'domination or leadership'. Gramsci (1971) extended the term to use it as an explanation as to how one group in society dominates and subordinates another group. This is not dependent on economic and physical power alone, but has ideological dimensions, whereby large numbers of a subordinate group are led into accepting the values of the dominant group. This is in itself an important addition to Marxist structuralism, in that it develops the dimension of people's interactive relationships and the exercise of power through education, persuasion, and mass appeal (Scraton, 1990). It also adds a dimension of voluntarism and historical specificity, in that people are seen in context and as being able to influence the course of history (Joll, 1977).

Hegemony implies a dynamic equilibrium of opposing forces, a mass consensus or a hegemonic bloc that conceals its conflict within (i.e., until the balance of power changes and internal contradictions become revealed). Thus hegemony implies struggle and resistance, and consensus will always involve contradiction, instability, challenges to, and counter-challenges from the dominant ideology. Hegemony is a balance of force and consensus, with the force appearing to be supported by the majority (Sumner, 1990). It involves a hierarchy of power, characterised by diverse interests, on a continuum of complicity with the dominant ideology. Gramsci (1971) draws attention to the role of institutions and the mass media in supporting and reproducing dominant ideologies.

Hegemony involves passion, an emotional bond between the dominant group and the people. For an idea to appear acceptable and have real meaning, it has to have a personal appeal at an emotional level. It also has to have a feeling of common sense and personal application. The needs, passions, and beliefs of a mass of individuals become aligned with those of the people, institutions and systems that subordinate them.

Dominant discourses have access to, have infiltrated, and are supported by powerful institutions. In relation to sexuality, a social order of power, knowledge, and pleasure has been set up, with sexuality (specifically masculine heterosexuality) being seen as the primary locus of power. Thus, power relations are defined through the body, whereby sexuality has become central as its mode of expression and central to identity (Foucault, 1976; Weedon, 1987). Subordination is never complete and the need to dominate implies resistance by definition, such processes producing reverse discourses. Dominant and subordinate discourses are constructed mutually. Discourses aspire toward social recognition and acceptance and are activated through the agency of individual people. Dominant discourses have access to and support from the dominant institutions of society and the perceived complicity of the majority. Subordinate discourses are resistances to the dominant and as a result are characterised by struggle. Cooper (1995) refers to subordinated groups being able to deploy positive power, arguing that their power should not be solely defined in terms of being resistant to those who subordinate them and that some subordinated groups may have their own access to positive hegemonies, such as citizenship, rights, and so on.

The Women's Liberation Movement and feminism are historically characterised by an ongoing struggle with the opposition of men (Daly, 1978; Herman, 1992). Challenges to patriarchal relations are often nullified, but sometimes accommodated, often through tokenism, so as to reduce their effectiveness. Sometimes this accommodation is short-lived, as situations are through time redefined. Patriarchal relations have the ability to adapt, change and mutate in response to new circumstances. The use of the term 'masculinity' itself in explaining men's behaviours has been criticised for allowing men to abdicate personal responsibility for their actions (Hearn, 1996). A similar example to this is quoted by Carrigan, Connell, and Lee (1987) in relation to their analysis of the work of the 'men's movement:

> It is not, fundamentally, about uprooting sexism or transforming patriarchy, or even understanding masculinity in its various forms. When it comes to the crunch, what it is about is *modernising* hegemonic masculinity. It is concerned with finding ways in which the dominant group—the White, educated, heterosexual, affluent males we know and love so well—can adapt to new circumstances without breaking down the social–structural arrangements that actually give them their power. (Carrigan et al., 1987, p. 164, italics theirs)

Any achievement of resistance or change in patriarchal relations therefore has to be made in the context of anticipating future repression. Discoveries and realisations become buried and therefore have to be rediscovered, the same battles having to be fought over and over again, both on the personal and political level. An important feature of this process, however, is the new information and new strategies of resistance that are produced: a strengthening by struggle, the production of reverse discourses that are more able to resist future counterchallenge, spurred on by the fact that subordination can never be complete and absolute (Cooper, 1995). This is particularly true in relation to the struggle of the feminist movement in establishing a social acceptance of the existence of sexual abuse (Herman, 1992). Part II will show how young men who have been sexually abused had to constantly negotiate their masculine sexualities in a hostile climate of homophobia. They often experienced setbacks and social confrontation in which sometimes the only way out was to adopt language and behaviours that were considered to be socially acceptable. One of the young men described this as 'acting the homophobic'. Another young man described the situation as showing that 'I'm normal'. These were strategies of resistance, with which the young men were personally uncomfortable, but felt had to be regularly adopted in order to detract attention and survive day-to-day peer group interactions. They were outwardly portraying dominant forms of masculinity, while privately wishing to be able to behave differently.

MASCULINITIES

The term 'hegemonic' has been accurately used to describe dominant forms of masculinities (Connell, 1987). By definition, these dominant forms are characterised by an essential control of the self, the environment and others (namely, women, children, and other men). Connell introduced a hierarchy of masculinities among men, 'hegemonic, conservative and subordinated' (1987, p. 110), located within structures of power. This is an important study, as it underlines the importance of examining power relationships between men in order to understand men's relationships with women and children, and particularly men's violences. Taking this forward, it is possible to conceptualise a more dynamic multiplicity of contested masculinites, interacting with other social oppressions. Masculinities are varied, shifting and changing across different historical, situational, cultural, temporal, and spatial contexts (Cornwall and Lindisfarne, 1994). Individual men or boys will present differing masculinities at different times, places, and circumstances (Pringle, 1995; Hearn, 1996). Hearn suggests that the term 'men's practices' (1996, p. 214) more accurately represents an understanding of the diversity of what men do, where, when, how, and why.

There are tensions here. On the one hand, there is an attempt to conceptualise a multiplicity of masculinities that moves toward questioning the term 'masculinity' itself. On the other hand, it is recognised that there are dominant forms of masculinity that render other forms subordinate. When previously discussing hegemony, it was established that where there is subordination, there will be resistance; dominant and subordinated discourses are produced mutually. However, there is no simple question of choice about which 'masculinity' to present where. There are particular forms of masculinity that are deemed to be socially acceptable, and particular forms that are clearly not acceptable in many circumstances. The negotiation of individual masculinities takes place in an oppressive social context of heterosexism and homophobia (Nayak and Kehily, 1997; Wolfe et al., 1997).

In following through some of the arguments put forward by Warner (1993), it could be argued that in many ways the debate is predominantly about heterosexism. Part II will show that, particularly in adolescent peer cultures, notions of acceptable masculinities would appear to be at least a significant vehicle for, if not a fundamental constituent of, homophobia. In this context, heterosexuality would appear to be a defining line in power relationships. In most circumstances, forms of masculinity that are heterosexual are more powerful than others.

Studying masculinities in terms of men's practices (thoughts, feelings, beliefs, actions) is consistent with the life-story approach of the current study (as it was with Connell's later [1995] study), which closely considers the meanings, textures, and dynamics of interpersonal power relationships. The current study follows Hearn's (1996) recommendation for a clearly defined use of the term 'masculinities'. It will specifically relate to received beliefs and understandings of young men (still close in years to their adolescence) about men's practices in Britain in the 1980s and 1990s. Part II shows that sometimes these beliefs and understandings were quite static practical beliefs about how to behave and think in a manner that avoids peer group oppression, criticism, and ridicule. In other societies, or at different stages of the lifespan, in different circumstances, these beliefs and understandings may be very different.

HEGEMONIC MASCULINITIES AND SEXUAL ABUSE

Within patriarchal relations, as we have discussed, dominant or hegemonic masculinities are oppressively defined in terms of a restrictive range of acceptable behaviours. The intertwining or conflation of biological sex and gender potentially creates confusion and doubts for the individual. For the male, masculinities defined in terms of strength, power, and natural domination are not biological realities, and require constant nurturing, affirmation, and repression of unacceptable 'feminine' behaviours (Kaufman, 1987; Connell, 1989; Frosh, 1993). In patriarchal relations power bestows benefits and one way (the prescribed way) to exercise power is to exercise subordination. The greater the need to emphasise or affirm masculinities the greater the need to exercise subordination. Furthermore, the greater the extent to which it is done the greater the power and hence the benefits, but also the greater the lie and the greater the harm done. Often the power is real (e.g., the power of capitalism and politics or the power within an ongoing relationship). At other times, the experience of being powerful is only perceived or felt and soon disappears, as in the case of the sexual abuse of children or the rape of women or other men. The illusion and disappointment at the transitory nature of the experience of feeling powerful through these behaviours is partly the impetus for their repetition. This goes some way to explain the repetition, escalation, and multiplicity of some men's sexually abusive behaviours (Kelly, 1988b).

Masculinities have become inseparably linked to masculine sexualities, often as a set of behaviours separate from emotion (Seidler, 1989). Frosh (1993) not only refers to the phallus as a symbol of masculine authority but as something complicated and unavailable to the individual experience that cannot be lived up to in the manner that the phallus as a symbol represents. It has been argued that masculinities are particularly fragile during adolescence:

> In adolescence the pain and fear involved in repressing 'femininity' and passivity start to become evident. For most of us, the response to this inner pain is to reinforce the bulwarks of masculinity. The emotional pain created by obsessive masculinity is stifled by reinforcing masculinity itself. (Kaufman, 1987, p. 12)

The repression of men's bisexuality is in itself an inadequate means of keeping desires at bay (Kaufman, 1987). Some of this is transformed into other derivative pleasures: muscle-building, hero worship, sports, situations where the enjoyment of other men can be experienced. The fact that homoerotic desires are never completely extinguished is often managed through homophobia (Sedgwick, 1990). Social constructions of gender and their prescriptions of heterosexuality create the inevitability of homophobia as an apparently natural response to repressed 'non-masculine' emotions. Men's violences are therefore not only directed toward women and children, but toward the self and other men as well. Kaufman (1987) traces this back to the acquisition of gender, which he argues is based on the malleability of human desires, the lengthy period of human childhood as a period of prolonged dependency and powerlessness, and sustained subjection to family gender roles. For the boy, he argues, there is the hope of power in the future, by virtue of manhood, and a process of repressing passivity and accentuating activity that amounts to surplus aggression. Violence against women, children, and other men as an extremity of subordination serves to confirm masculinities.

Post-structural analysis recognises the centrality of sexuality as a locus of power in interpersonal relationships, particularly in a society where sexuality is a significant factor of heterosexist social control (Foucault, 1976; Bell, 1993; Warner, 1993; Steinberg et al., 1997). Weedon argues that Foucault's analysis centralises the body and that '... The centrality of sexuality as a locus of power in the modern age has meant that sex has become a focal point in subjective identity' (1987, p. 119). Similar themes have been developed by Struve, who argues that power and control have become eroticised within our culture, referring to 'the norms of sexual abuse' (1990, p. 9) that provide a social framework for the sexual abuse of children. A social context of patriarchal relations creates a high-risk situation for the sexual abuse of children. Power is legitimised by the general association of authority with masculinities and subordination with femininities (Connell, 1987). Additionally, the denial of emotional expression leaves the use of sexual behaviour as a threatening, but available channel for emotional expression. However, this potentially poses a threat to dominant masculinities, as it involves vulnerability, emotion, and dependency. This may, as Frosh (1993) argues, lead some men to see children as the least threatening and most controllable objects.

These factors help us understand why the majority of sexual abuse is committed by males and that the scale and prevalence of child sexual abuse cuts across all boundaries: class, gender, age, 'race', disability (Kelly, 1988b; Herman, 1990; Macleod and Saraga, 1991).[1] The feminist movement has played a significant role in the social rediscovery of child sexual abuse. There has been an ongoing struggle for social acceptance of the existence of sexual abuse and for a better

---

[1] It is important to acknowledge that there are incidences of children and young people being sexually abused by girls and women. It has been argued that there is widespread social and professional denial of female child sexual abuse, which has contributed to its under-reporting (Elliot, 1993; Saradjian, 1998). This is a denial of the act of abuse taking place or a denial of the responsibility of the female committing such an act. Sexual abuse committed by males or females is likely to entail an abuse of power and responsibility, and leave a child feeling hurt and guilty for what has happened. Saradjian (1998) found that there was a greater sense of anger toward females who abuse, on the part of victims. This may be related to social constructions of gender, but possibly additionally to the loss of a primary caregiver and attachment figure, and therefore an enhanced sense of betrayal. However, to enter into such comparison potentially reinforces an oppressive gender construction. It is more helpful to draw a simple conclusion that a child is likely to experience sexual abuse as harmful *per se*, whether the abuser is male or female.

understanding of the pain and suffering of its survivors. In this respect, sexual abuse has parallels with other fields, such as the plight of concentration camp victims and Vietnam war veterans. The social 'discoveries' of these psychological traumas have historically flourished in affiliation with political movements (Herman, 1992). The need for these movements suggests political and social resistance to acknowledging psychological trauma. Patriarchal forces that obfuscate child sexual abuse have been identified in recent research by Taylor-Browne (1997a, b). In 1896 the social unacceptability of Freud's lecture 'The Aetiology of Hysteria', which referred to child sexual abuse as a cause of psychological disturbance in some of his adult women patients, led to its reformulation into a theory relating to fantasies of unfulfilled sexual desire directed toward their fathers (Masson, 1988; Etherington, 1995). This was a denial of the reality of his patients' experiences of child sexual abuse. Referring to this, Herman states:

> Out of the ruins of the traumatic theory of hysteria, Freud created psychoanalysis. The dominant psychological theory of the next century was founded in the denial of women's reality. Sexuality remained the central focus of inquiry. But the exploitative social context in which sexual relations actually occur became utterly invisible. Psychoanalysis became a study of the internal vicissitudes of fantasy and desire, dissociated from the reality of experience. (Herman, 1992, p. 14)

The consequence of this course of events over time has been the growth and dominance of theories of psychoanalysis and other therapies, and a constant redefining and silencing of the true nature of women and children's experiences. Masson (1988), after years of working in psychoanalysis himself, has written extensively about the abuse of power in therapy and its dominance at the cost of more appropriate helping processes that recognise the struggle of personal experiences in their social context. The dominance of psychoanalysis has led to a perpetuation of theoretical perspectives that construct child sexual abuse as a diagnostic category, with professional responses being defined in terms of treatment as opposed to assistance and recovery. Women's and children's experiences are defined in terms of medical pathology, ignoring their political and social context, failing to directly confront the causes of sexual abuse, and avoiding direct confrontation of the abuser; for example, the family dysfunction model that questions responses of non-abusing parents, mostly mothers (Macleod and Saraga, 1988). The male domination of the child sexual abuse industry (Hudson, 1992) provides a further example of women's experiences being taken by men and used for their own theoretical purposes in male-dominated medical and academic institutions.

For present purposes, this analysis brings the concept of gender and power into the experience of the sexually abused male child. It helps us understand the manner in which he may subsequently interpret and analyse his experience and relate it to his received beliefs about appropriate men's practices. Being a victim may not be compatible with these beliefs; such beliefs are likely to contribute to a boy or a man's decision to remain silent or to deny or reframe the experience of being sexually abused.

CONCLUSIONS

This chapter has examined dynamic post-structural understandings of diverse masculinities that shift and change across cultural, spatial, and temporal locations. However, it was established that these masculinities are established and contested in a context of patriarchal relations, characterised by oppressive heterosexism and homophobia. Consequently, particular forms of masculinity dominate, and gain acceptance and support in a wide range of social circumstances. Other forms of masculinity are subordinated and oppressively policed. Alongside recognising difference and diversity, it is identified that social oppression restricts expressions of difference and shapes social choices. In living with the theoretical tensions of allowing these potentially opposing conceptualisations to sit alongside each other, it becomes possible to hold on to and utilise their complexity. It will be shown that this anti-reductionist approach is central to the methodology and analytical framework advanced by the current study.

An understanding of the social construction of masculinities in a context of patriarchal relations gives perhaps the greatest clue toward an explanation of why men commit acts of sexual violence toward women and children. Dominant men's practices are defined in relational terms to the subordination of women, children, and other men. Sex, violence, power, and gender are combined to construct dominant forms of masculinities that are invested in and expressed through the body, and are central to self-esteem and identity. For many men, the everyday experience of patriarchal relations is sufficient to provide the necessary benefits and nurture for being male, although this is not to deny the need for constant masculinising affirmations, and access to 'legitimate and acceptable' closeness to other males. For other men, these benefits are not felt, and other circumstances and negative experiences accentuate self-doubts and repressed emotions, and call into play the need for affirmation through the use of a more overt force. Sometimes physical violence may suffice, but for some the doubt is so great that affirmation has to be experienced through the body, as physical and/or sexual violence and domination. As we have already said, there is an illusion and disappointment of power in these circumstances, which after a short passage of time thwarts the affirmation. This goes some way to explain the repetition and escalation of men's sexual violences (Kelly, 1988b).

Kaufman's reference to Humphrey Bogart's description of Captain Renault, in the film *Casablanca*, as being 'Just like any other man, only more so' (1987, p. 1) has particular salience here. The distinguishing factor between the many men and some men is more a question of degree or attitude, rather than any clinical psychological or psychiatric difference (Pringle, 1995). This view is consistent with Kelly's 'continuum of sexual violence' (1988b, p. 27) and is supported by MacLeod and Saraga, who have argued that a recognition of the importance of gender, power, and 'ideologies of childhood' (1991, p. 8) is helpful to those attempting to help those in need of recovery.

Social constructions of masculinities have a potentially significant, detrimental impact on the manner in which sexual abuse is experienced and on subsequent behaviour that may hinder recovery. Boys and men who have been sexually abused have themselves been influenced by patriarchal relations. The experience of being sexually abused may cause them to feel marginalised, subordinated, or inadequate, in terms of their beliefs about men's practices, and awaken repressed fears and feelings about their sexuality (similar oppressive processes are likely to occur for girls and women, in terms of their received beliefs about 'femininity'). Furthermore, these fears and feelings are likely to be attributed to the abuse, as opposed to any understanding of their patriarchal construction. Sometimes, quite desperate compensatory efforts are made in attempting to regain acceptable, perceived masculinities. These young men can be significantly helped if they receive support and intervention that allows them to establish a fuller understanding of how they have developed these fears and anxieties. Consequently, they will be provided with more resolved, effective, and peaceful strategies for survival that will allow them to move forward in their lives as individuals, friends, partners, fathers, and so on.

2

MALE-CHILD SEXUAL ABUSE—FACTS AND MYTHOLOGY

INTRODUCTION

This chapter reviews the existing literature on child sexual abuse, initially considering how methodological errors and conflicting definitions of child sexual abuse produce contradictory outcomes in prevalence studies. These studies are further confounded by problems of sexual abuse being under-reported. The concept of 'organised abuse' is examined, acknowledging that all sexual abuse is organised, whether or not it is committed against an individual or in a context that involves large numbers of people (e.g., in a neighbourhood network, in child-care institutions, or on an international scale). The following section considers the impact of sexual abuse, establishing that it is harmful and can have long-lasting consequences. Taking this further, the exacerbating interaction of the impact of sexual abuse and social oppression, particularly racism and disablism, is examined. It is argued that the extent of the impact of sexual abuse can be mediated by the assistance of supportive, non-abusing adults, mainly as members of the child's family but also as assistance provided from outside the family. The next section looks at the specific impact of male-child sexual abuse and considers the issue of young men who have been sexually abused having concerns about their sexuality and fears about abusing others. It is argued that these two areas have interacted and developed into a social mythology, a systematic misunderstanding of the impact of male-child sexual abuse, leading to a set of false beliefs. These beliefs compound the fears, feelings, and sense of responsibility of the child or young person, which are further compounded by the false beliefs and perceptions of others.

DEFINITIONS AND PREVALENCE

Definitions of child sexual abuse arise out of particular theoretical commitments and research is then centred on that definition, creating a prevalence that in turn consolidates the theoretical commitment. For example, theoretical understandings about family dynamics (Furniss, 1991) are likely to focus on families and exclude a range of other experiences that constitute child sexual abuse. They also run the risk of placing responsibility with non-abusing family members, rather than placing it unequivocally with the person who committed the abuse (Macleod and Saraga, 1988). Wider definitions based on Kelly's (1998b) continuum of men's violence are likely to lead to higher prevalence rates. These differences represent the contested knowledge base in child sexual abuse research and make comparison difficult (Pilkington and Kremer, 1995a, b). Additionally, prevalence studies are confounded by factors that contribute to the extent of under-reporting, which is believed by many to be considerable (Finkelhor et al., 1986; Urquiza and Keating, 1990; Watkins and Bentovim, 1992b).

A less acknowledged problem is that difficulties may arise due to the sensitive nature of child sexual abuse and the questions researchers may ask of sometimes unsuspecting members of the population. Finkelhor et al. (1986) examined the impact on prevalence rates of methods of data collection, ranging from self-completed questionnaires and telephone interviews to face-to-face contacts. While they quote varying opinions, they conclude that there is a relationship between prevalence rate and method of data collection, and that face-to-face contacts yielded a higher prevalence rate. Gorey and Leslie (1997) in reviewing 16 North American cross-sectional prevalence studies identified an inverse relationship between response rate and prevalence outcome. They argue that adults who have been sexually abused and take an anonymous opportunity to tell their story are more likely to respond to such studies than their non-abused counterparts. Other problems may also skew outcomes, such as sampling techniques that target a specific social grouping such as college students or patients of a psychiatric hospital. This may lead to reverse correlations, drawing conclusions about strong relationships between psychiatric illness and child sexual abuse. It is known that many adults who sexually abuse report childhood experiences of being sexually abused (Fisher, 1994). The reverse correlations that may result from understandings of child sexual abuse, based on samples of adults who have abused, are particularly dangerous. They create fearful, popular misunderstandings about subsequent abusing being an outcome of being abused, misunderstandings not least as this study will show by children and young people.

It is difficult to reach a final concluding definition of child sexual abuse that is able to encompass and accurately reflect such a vast range of unique individual experiences. Some prevalence studies ask participants about a range of personal experiences, collect the results, and then apply differing definitions to obtain different outcomes. Such a study would then lend itself to comparison with a range of other studies. The study by Kelly et al. (1991) is an example of such an approach and demonstrates the variation in outcomes that result. They quote a prevalence rate for contact sexual abuse of 1 in 5 (21%) for females and 1 in 14 (7%) for males. These rates increase to 1 in 2 (50%) for females and 1 in 4 (27%) for males when additional categories of unwanted sexual experiences are included, such as peer experiences and more distant or less direct forms of non-contact abuse and attempts/escapes. A similar and more recent approach was taken by Cawson et al. (2000), who carried out a UK national survey of the prevalence of child maltreatment. From a sample of 2869 young people aged 18–24 years, using random postcode-sampling and 'computer assisted personal interviewing' (Cawson et al., 2000, p. 8), they quoted a prevalence rate of child sexual abuse of 16%. When this is broken down into gender, the rate is 21% for girls and 11%

for boys. These rates applied to all categories of sexual abuse in the questionnaire and where the respondent was aged 12 or less or where the act was committed against his or her wishes. Influenced by these approaches and the work of Finkelhor et al. (1986) and Morrison and Print (1995), a wide and lengthy definition of child sexual abuse, presenting a range of options and defined behaviours, was used in an exploratory study conducted by myself and colleagues:

> Forced or coerced sexual behaviour that is imposed on a child (person under 18 years old). AND/OR Sexual behaviour between a child and a much older person (5 years or more age discrepancy), or a person in a care taking role, or a sibling. AND/OR Sexual behaviour where the recipient is defined as being unable to give informed consent by virtue of age, understanding or ability. *Contact Behaviours* may involve: Touching; rubbing; disrobing; sucking; and/ or penetrating. It may include rape. Penetration may be oral, anal or vaginal and digital, penile or objectile. *Non-Contact Behaviours* may involve: exhibitionism; peeping or voyeurism; frottage (rubbing up against others), fetishism (such as stealing underwear or masturbating into another's clothes), and obscene communication (such as obscene phone calls, and verbal and written sexual harassment or defamation). (Durham et al., 1995, capitals and italics theirs)

Several prevalence studies relating to males have been presented and discussed in the following three reviews to which the reader is referred: Urquiza and Keating (1990), Watkins and Bentovim (1992b), and Mendel (1995). Watkins and Bentovim (1992b), cite North American studies with a range-of-prevalence rate from 6% to 62% for girls and 3% to 31% for males. Mendel quotes a similar range for males of 2.5% or 3% to 33%. Both studies cite methodological considerations as the accounting factor. Urquiza and Keating present seven studies with prevalence rates ranging from 2.5% to 17.3%. These studies span the time period of 1978 to 1989. A factor that may limit the accuracy of a prevalence study is the possibility that a person may consciously *choose* not to report an experience of child sexual abuse, and indeed making sure the victim does not tell is part of the abuse. This underlines the need for research to develop sensitive methodologies that account for the factors that may prevent an oppressed research participant from feeling able to speak out about traumatic experiences.

Under-reporting

The impact of child sexual abuse has the potential to make reporting the experience difficult for anybody. In order for something to be reported it has to be received, if giving information involves stigma or disbelief then it is less likely to be shared. In considering the extent of secrecy and denial set up and maintained by those who abuse (Finkelhor, 1984; Bibby, 1996), it is easy to see how a wider social denial would prevent a child from telling. It is for these reasons that Herman has noted and advocated the powerful role of political and social movements in helping to break the silence of individual circumstances (Herman, 1992).

Reporting sexual abuse would be particularly difficult if the person concerned had already experienced other forms of social oppression or lived in circumstances where he or she had already experienced being silenced, such as an oppressive institution. Thanki (1994) and Gill (1996) refer to abuse in Black communities remaining undetected due to racist assumptions of White practitioners that fail to define circumstances as abusive. Gill refers to 'negative racism' (1996, p. 80), the fear of being labelled racist through being seen as pathologising Black communities. Thanki refers to White practitioners pursuing a 'rule of optimism' through a process of 'cultural relativism' (1994, p. 239), the net result being the undetected abuse of Black children.

Abusers will sometimes use idiosyncratic and secret behavioural cues to communicate to a child that abuse is about to take place. This forms an entrance ritual. For example, turning to a particular television channel or programme may signify to a child that he or she has to go upstairs. The cue may be something more subtle, like putting a pen into a top pocket. These cues, once established, tell the child that abuse is about to happen, that it is secret, and cannot be communicated openly. Once the abuse has been committed, another simple behavioural cue or comment, such as 'time to put your pyjamas on and clean your teeth or time to do your homework now', may communicate to the child that the abuse is over and that there is a return to the previous relationship: father and daughter, stepfather and son, brother and sister or perhaps teacher and pupil. These entrance-and-exit rituals used by abusers are instrumental in denying the external reality of the sexually abusive incident (Furniss, 1991).

Fears and threats of violence to the child or young person, or to others, are also significant (Porter, 1986; Bolton et al., 1989; Grubman-Black, 1990). Threats can involve threats of physical violence, threats that a child will be removed from home, threats that telling will result in the loss of a caregiver, or that telling will result in the boy no longer receiving treats and special attention. This happened in the Castle Hill case (Brannan et al., 1991), where abuse committed by the headmaster of the school gave access to special privileges and protection from a violent pecking order among the other pupils in the school. The social context in which these fears are created gives them credibility and ensures silence.

The particular under-reporting of child sexual abuse by males has been noted by many researchers (Porter, 1986; Lew, 1988; Vander Mey, 1988; Bolton et al., 1989; Hunter, 1990a–c; Urquiza and Keating, 1990; Watkins and Bentovim, 1992b; Black and DeBlassie, 1993; Etherington, 1995; Mendel, 1995). The literature cites many reasons for the particular under-reporting of male-child sexual abuse. Urquiza and Keating (1990) identify the possibility that researchers and clinicians who have little experience of working with males who have been sexually abused may be unlikely to recognise boys and men as a population in need of investigation. Mendel (1995) refers to a similar process taking place in relation to a lack of recognition of abuse committed by females and the difficulties males have in identifying childhood sexual experiences with female adults or older adolescents as abuse. Additionally, a culture of male self-reliance potentially leads to less supervision. It is acknowledged in the literature that males are more likely than females to be abused by someone outside their family (Finkelhor et al., 1986; Watkins and Bentovim, 1992b). Part II of this book will show how and why being sexually abused in the social context of patriarchal relations may prevent males from feeling comfortable in expressing feelings or fears, and being dependent on others, leading to the development of repression as a coping strategy. Part III will show how important it is for these understandings to be central to the knowledge base that informs practitioners in helping young people recover from child sexual abuse.

ORGANISED OR MULTIPLE ABUSE

While a level of organisation and planning characterises all sexual abuse (Finkelhor, 1984),[1] the term 'organised abuse' has been widely and differentially used in the research literature. The DOH (1998) *Working Together to Safeguard Children* proposed the following definition:

> Organised or multiple abuse may be defined as abuse involving one or more abuser and a number of related or non-related abused children and young people. The abusers concerned may be acting in concert to abuse children, sometimes acting in isolation, or may be using an institutional framework or position of authority to recruit children for abuse. (DOH, 1998, p. 67)

Institutions by definition are organised establishments, and when abuse takes place within them adults may have an exclusive power base through which these processes of organisation are utilised for the purpose of creating opportunities to abuse (Doran and Brannen, 1996). Children with disabilities may be particularly vulnerable to sexual abuse, particularly if abilities and opportunities to communicate or resist are limited (Kelly, 1992). The extent of 'organisation' sometimes has an international dimension (Kelly et al., 1995). In circumstances of war, rape and sexual abuse have become a deliberate strategy of male violence between nations (Pringle, 1995). Connections have been made between

---

[1] When people commit sexual abuse it is likely that there will be a pattern or cycle of behaviour that indicates the extent to which child sexual abuse is often highly organised and planned (Salter, 1988; Kahn, 1990; O'Callaghan and Print, 1994; Morrison and Print, 1995; Cunningham and MacFarlane, 1996; Araji, 1997). In basic terms, the cycle goes through the following stages: circumstances and thoughts—fantasy—planning—setting up—abuse—guilt/fear—rationalisation (cycle repeats). Often, the child is made to feel that they have either co-operated or given consent, or even initiated the sexual behaviour. The implication of not having resisted enough or the post-abuse rationalisations by the child of what he or she could have done to prevent the abuse would be enough to set such beliefs in motion. Bibby uses the term 'hooking' children into a 'closed abusing system' (1996, p. 6) and uses the analogy of an angler playing with a fish. Approximately 23% of sexual offences are committed by young people under the age of 18 (Home Office, 1997). In some of these circumstances, given the age of the person abusing, there may not be an extensively developed cycle, although some of the behaviour may indicate that there is evidence of a developing cycle or pattern. Nevertheless, even though circumstances may be more opportunist, the victim is still likely to be left with a sense of responsibility or may have been threatened, or both.

child sexual abuse, child sexual exploitation, and the role of adult and child pornography, indicating a high level of organised and sometimes international communication between the adults involved (Itzin, 1997).

Ritual abuse has been a controversial issue. This has been defined as:

> Ritual abuse is the involvement of children in physical, psychological or sexual abuse associated with repeated activities ('ritual') which purport to relate the abuse to contexts of a religious, magical or supernatural kind. (McFadyen et al., 1993, p. 37)

Alternatively, particularly in America, the term 'satanic ritual abuse' (De Young, 1997) is used. De Young discusses the controversy involved, arguing that the professional community remains confused and divided about the whole issue, which has attracted a great deal of media attention. This illustrates the operation of backlash against feminist perspectives of child sexual abuse (Gilligan, 1997; Oakley, 1997). The public controversy has affected the reliability of research into the issue. La Fontaine's study (1993) concluded that there was little evidence to support its existence. Kelly (1994) argues that a more stringent methodology was used for this study than for other areas of child sexual abuse. This is an indication of the readiness to disbelieve, and this has been added to by allegations against practitioners of overzealousness. De Young refers to 'satanic conspiracy' or 'cultural connivance' (1997, p. 91) and expresses the concern that the cultural and media controversy may result in some more 'ordinary' type of sexual abuse being overlooked in the attempt to prove satanic ritual abuse.

Another example of backlash that leads to the disbelief of children and young people is the notion of the deserving victim. Taylor-Browne refers to moral panics and the 'Issue-Attention Cycle' (1997a, p. 6, 1997b) as processes that 'obfuscate' child sexual abuse. The need for blame to be attributed to a small group of people was taken up by Kelly in relation to the use of the term 'paedophile', which takes attention away from the recognition of abusers as 'ordinary men' (1996, p. 45). Another related issue is the alleged 'false memory syndrome'. It has been shown that the prevalence claims of the False Memory Syndrome Foundation are wildly inaccurate and in no way substantiated by credible and reliable research evidence (Dallam, 1997). Taylor-Browne (1997a, b) points out that this issue has received large-scale coverage in the newspapers, which discusses the ordeals of parents and blames the therapists involved. She makes the point that very little media attention is paid to those who require help because of the abuse that they have never forgotten.

THE IMPACT OF CHILD SEXUAL ABUSE

This section considers theoretical understandings of the impact of child sexual abuse and argues that many of them fail to adequately acknowledge the influence of social and cultural factors on children and young people's experiences. One model that has been widely used in research is Finkelhor and Browne's (1986) Four Traumagenic Dynamics Model, which conceptualises four categories of impact: traumatic sexualisation, stigmatisation, betrayal, powerlessness. These categories are considered in terms of dynamics, psychological impact and behavioural manifestation. They draw together previous research into a useful lens through which to view the experience of the individual. Ranges of conditions and reactions are presented as possibilities for the individual experience. Although the model mentions social problems and the negative perceptions of others, it remains in many ways overly structured and diagnostic. As a consequence, the impact of sexual abuse is largely explained in psychological or behavioural terms.

For a fuller understanding, social and cultural factors require greater consideration. Stigmatisation and the negative perceptions of others could be largely generated by a young person's internalised oppression and received social misunderstandings about gender and sexuality. Patriarchal gender constructions could lead a young person who has been sexually abused into beliefs about not being 'appropriately male' or not 'appropriately female'. Having these feelings could lead to a range of compensatory behaviours and feelings, such as a boy behaving aggressively in order to appear 'masculine' among his peers or a girl feeling afraid to resist inappropriate sexual advances in order to appear 'feminine'. These behaviours can lead young people into considerable difficulties, inviting negative attention and possibly behavioural labels or diagnosis that create further feelings of powerlessness, betrayal, and distrust of adults. The model has been referred to or used by other writers and researchers (Porter, 1986; Bolton et al., 1989; Watkins and Bentovim, 1992b; Mendel, 1995; Feiring et al., 1996) as a tool for analysis of research data or in the development of further theoretical understandings. Hall and Lloyd add an additional category, 'Enforced Silence' (1989, p. 45), which refers to the specific processes a person who abuses may use to ensure the silence of sexually abused children.

Another theoretical and diagnostic categorisation that has been used in attempting to understand the impact of child sexual abuse is Post Traumatic Stress Disorder (PTSD) (Mendel, 1995). This involves characteristic 'symptoms' following significantly fearful and stressful events, which include flashbacks, where the event is re-experienced, sometimes numbing, other times increased arousal, and avoidance of stimuli associated with the event. A further adaptation of PTSD is PSAT, Post Sexual Abuse Trauma (Briere and Runtz, 1988), which specifically refers to childhood adaptations to sexually abusive experiences manifesting into adult symptoms. This attempts to identify a separate set of diagnostic categories specific to sexual abuse. Closely associated to PTSD and PSAT is the process of dissociation. This has been associated with the impact of child sexual abuse by many authors (Steele and Colrain, 1990; Watkins and Bentovim, 1992b; Friedrich et al., 1997). They refer to dissociation as a physiological and psychological process that involves a separation of mental processes that are usually integrated. Thoughts, memories, feelings, and emotions are split off from the current stream of consciousness. A dissociative response to child sexual abuse is a functional adaptation, an amnesic barrier repressing the impact of the experience. Again, a greater acknowledgement of social factors may lead to a greater understanding of what some of the dissociative processes actually involve and how they are triggered by day-to-day social experiences.

The personal circumstances of the opposing experience of blocking memories and feelings and the uncontrolled flooding and re-experiencing of those memories and feelings in PTSD has been paralleled with the social experience by Herman (1992). The oscillation of social belief followed by a reaction of reframing and disbelief supports and mirrors the private experience. A hostile social context, characterised by hegemonic masculinities, potentially compounds the impact of the individual experience of child sexual abuse, creating a sense of responsibility and failure in the child. Such a process could drive a child into further secrecy and ultimately result in behaviour that would confirm or invite psychological diagnosis, which would label and fail to assist the child. While diagnostic categories provide a lens and useful summaries that may assist understanding, each individual circumstance is different and must not be compromised by categorisation and diagnosis (Bolton et al., 1989).

A psychological or psychiatric diagnosis that largely excludes the voice of the young person and fails to adequately acknowledge the role of the social and cultural experiences and processes that have been lived through is pathologising and will inevitably compound the impact of the social oppression. This section has highlighted this in relation to the patriarchal gender constructions. It has particular salience in relation to the impact of racism, an issue that receives little consideration in the child sexual abuse literature.

THE INTERACTING IMPACT OF CHILD SEXUAL ABUSE AND RACISM

When the experience of child sexual abuse is paralleled by social oppression, the impact of the abuse may serve to compound some of the experiences the oppression may already have presented. This can apply to many situations where the individual for whatever reason has been socially oppressed, whether by virtue of age, simply being a child in an environment not sensitive to the needs of children, or having a disability and being constantly excluded from aspects of social living, creating feelings of isolation and powerlessness.

Although the issue of racism is neglected in a great deal of the child sexual abuse literature, some authors have recently considered the issue (Wilson, 1993; Thanki, 1994; Cowburn, 1996; Gill, 1996; Jackson, 1996). In order to consider the particular interaction of the impact of child sexual abuse and racism it is necessary to clarify a definition of racism as an oppressive process as distinct from descriptions of culture and identity. A social and political definition of racism has been adopted (Fryer, 1988). This definition takes into account and assumes a social and political context of a racist, White-dominated power structure that supports and encourages individual actions. Thus racism is defined as 'White people misusing or abusing power to oppress Black people'.

Definitions have the problem that, over time and with a changing context, their applicability or relevance may also change or that there may be examples of experiences occurring outside its strict confines. This is an anti-oppressive definition, in that it assumes an active and automatic historically and socially embedded process of racism taking place (James, 1980; Fryer, 1988; Cowburn, 1996; Jackson, 1996). This is both in terms of individual actions and the operation of wider oppressive power structures. Additional problems may involve people defining themselves differently, but still experiencing racism on account of how they are perceived by others. There is often a confusion between definitions of racism and prejudice. Both involve people holding preconceived ideas and assumptions about people or groups that influence their subsequent opinions, attitudes, and actions. However, racism, as defined here, refers to people actively using the advantages of being White in a White-dominated power structure.

The experience of racism can have a range of effects (Angelou, 1969; Hooks, 1984; Ahmad, 1990; Jackson, 1996) and may cause a child to feel hurt, confused, angry, sad, shocked, upset, isolated, different, resentful, and bitter. It may cause them to deny what is happening or change personal characteristics so as to fit in with expectations. They may begin to hate themselves and feel responsible for their experiences. They may become aggressive or alternatively become with-drawn. They may question themselves and reject positive aspects of their own culture. They may reject their own family.

An experience of child sexual abuse may cause a child to experience a range of feelings, some of which are not dissimilar to the above experiences of racism: guilt, anger, loss, frustration, blame, betrayal, confusion, helplessness, isolation, respon-sibility, sadness, bitterness. Behaviourally, they may become withdrawn, aggres-sive, moody, untrusting, sexually active, and self-harming. The concurrent experience of child sexual abuse and racism can be particularly difficult as the impact of one may in many ways reinforce and confirm the impact of the other. Additionally, a Black child wishing to report sexual abuse may be afraid to approach a White-dominated agency and will have to consider the potential per-sonal and family consequences (Wilson, 1993).

Interacting processes of abuse and oppression are also applicable to disabled children who have been sexually abused (Kennedy, 1992; Briggs, 1995b). The increased risk and vulnerability of children with disabilities highlights the need for personal safety programmes. As Briggs has observed, 'Abuse exaggerates children's emotional problems which relate to their disabilities' (1995b, p. 26).

MEDIATING FACTORS

As some people are more severely affected by child sexual abuse than others, it is important to establish which factors prompt resilience (Chandy et al., 1996; Anderson, 1997). The impact of child sexual abuse may depend on a number of characteristics and the individual's reaction to them. These include: the nature and closeness of the relationship between the survivor and the abuser; the frequency of the abuse and the nature, duration, and extent of the abuse; the use of force, aggression, and threats; the gender of the person committing the abuse; and the age of the person being abused. Research suggests the younger the age the greater the impact (Urquiza and Capra, 1990; Watkins and Bentovim, 1992b; Hunter, 1995).

The experience of sexual abuse is harmful, but the degree of harm is unique to the child concerned. Generalisations from research are potentially harmful and may cause professionals to consider certain experiences as being less harmful. Conte and Schuerman's (1987) study of factors associated with an increased impact of child sexual abuse suggests that effects vary between children. They identify the importance of individual experiences and resistance strategies and conclude that a very powerful mediating factor on the impact of child sexual abuse is the presence of an effective support system, provided by supportive, non-abusing adults.

These findings are supported by Hunter (1995) and Chandy et al. (1996). Also, Feiring et al. (1998) note that adolescents rely less on adults and more on their peers for approval and advice and that this may not always be supportive (as Part II will confirm). Gilgun (1990) conducted a life history study of 34 men, 23 of whom were survivors of child sexual abuse. The study identified the presence of confidants and other supportive persons in the child's life as significant mediating factors. This included both family and non-family members, sometimes persons in authority. The supportive persons were primarily men, but included same-age female friends, partners, and older women. In the absence of such support, there were reports of negative behaviours being developed, such as sexualised behaviour and its use, mainly masturbation, as a coping mechanism to deal with stress. Lack of social support and a sexualised environment were associated with the subsequent abuse of other children. The additional presence of physical abuse was sometimes associated with subsequent rape by the victim of sexual abuse as an outcome.

The young men who participated in this study were sexually abused by adults who were not members of their family. For some of the young men, being estranged from their families placed them in a position whereby they became more vulnerable to abuse. It is important to remember that both boys and girls are sometimes sexually abused by members of their own families (Cawson, 2002). Some are sexually abused by other young people. Approximately one-third of sexual offences are committed by young people under the age of 21, and just over one-fifth by young people under the age of 18 (Morrison and Print, 1995; Home Office, 1997). These varying circumstances will have an effect on whom and how the child or young person feels able to tell about being abused, or indeed, whether or not to tell anyone.

These studies highlight the importance and significance of personal and social support in helping young people recover from child sexual abuse. In circumstances where this would not be immediately available from within the young person's family, it would have to somehow be built in to a helping strategy, providing reasonably easy access to ongoing assistance and support (Gilgun, 1990). Ongoing personal and social support would help the child talk through and come to terms with the trauma experienced. It would help ensure that responsibility is placed and remains with the person who committed the abuse. It should also help the child to develop insight into some of the social and cultural processes that may become problematic as a result of the abusive experience.

THE IMPACT OF CHILD SEXUAL ABUSE ON MALES

There have now been a number of reviews of the literature in relation to the child sexual abuse of males (Vander Mey, 1988; Bolton et al., 1989; Watkins and Bentovim, 1992b; Black and DeBlassie, 1993; Mendel, 1995) and many other studies treating males as a distinct group to study in relation to child sexual abuse (Nasjleti, 1980; Porter, 1986; Lew, 1988; Grubman-Black, 1990; Hunter, 1990a; Mezey and King, 1992; Durham, 1993; Gonsiorek et al., 1994; Etherington, 1995; Bagley and Thurston, 1996a).

Urquiza and Capra (1990) in their review of the literature, which rests its clinical findings primarily on empirical research, look at initial and long-term effects. The initial effects (many of which are identified as becoming long-term) include emotional, behavioural, and sexual disturbances, such as delinquency, shame, depression, non-compliance, relationship difficulties, sexualised behaviours, and aggression. They refer to the 'strong' finding in the psychological literature that shows that males tend to respond to stressful and difficult situations in a behavioural or externalising manner. Behavioural disturbances are identified as a common finding, supported by a wide range of literature and research. They also identify that such behavioural responses may have the negative effect of deterring potentially helpful and supportive responses from others. They indicate that not all boys respond to abuse in this externalising manner, recognising the importance of individual experiences interacting with family and environmental factors, and make the point that few studies of child sexual abuse have attempted to address these types of factors.

Two recent studies have attempted to address individual factors by using life-story methods. Mendel (1995) conducted a study by means of postal questionnaires (using standardised measures), of a sample of 124 men, with a subset of 9 men who were interviewed face-to-face. A range of short- and long-term psychological and behavioural consequences were identified. These categories relate well to Finkelhor and Browne's (1986) Four Traumagenic Dynamics, but have been applied with specificity to the experience of males.

Etherington (1995) conducted in-depth interviews of a sample of 25 men. The study identified a range of problems experienced, including difficulties in defining the abuse, either due to repressing memories of the abuse, or confusion in relation to pleasure or arousal experienced during the abuse, or feelings of responsibility. The men had difficulties in reporting their abuse, in addition to disbelief, fear of judgement, shame, and guilt. Most of the men reported sexual problems, difficulties with intimate relationships, and severe depressive feelings. Five of the men had been convicted for sexual offences. Etherington's study recognises the influence of male socialisation and has gone some way to consider the impact of social and patriarchal factors.

Both Mendel's (1995) study and Etherington's (1995) study have relevance to the current research, because they are recent and use face-to-face interviews, particularly the latter. However, both these studies refer to an older adult population (mainly aged over 35 and often much older) and, in *attempting to draw generalisations*, may be skewed through reverse correlations and by the extent of counselling or psychotherapy they had received.

Many authors make reference to the problematic aspects for the sexually abused male of social and cultural expectations and definitions of 'masculinity' (albeit often in a rather limited and static sense) and the manner in which males are socialised to respond to stress and emotional feelings (Nasjleti, 1980; Rogers and Terry, 1984; Sebold, 1987; Lew, 1988; Vander Mey, 1988; Gilgun and Reiser,

1990; Grubman-Black, 1990; Hunter, 1990a; Watkins and Bentovim, 1992b; Black and DeBlassie, 1993; Etherington, 1995; Mendel, 1995).

The experience of victimisation and a clear expression of emotional distress are not consistent with hegemonic masculinities that encourage denials of emotional feelings and definitions of the self in terms of activity, achievement, control, and personal power, often expressed as dominating others. Two specific problematic areas for *some* males who have been sexually abused that stem directly from these considerations are, first, the sexual abuse of others and, second, fears and confusion relating to sexuality, sexual functioning and sexual identity.

SEXUALLY ABUSING OTHERS

The issue of males who have been sexually abused subsequently sexually abusing others has been identified by several authors. One study by Conte and Schuerman (1987) quotes this occurring at a rate of 2%, although the study is not broken down by gender on its symptom checklist. Other studies, relating to boys alone, ranged from a rate of 13% (Friedrich et al., 1988a) to a rate of 50% (Sansonnett-Hayden et al., 1987). A pooled prevalence of several studies was 22% (Watkins and Bentovim, 1992b). The conflicting outcomes of these studies suggest methodological problems and reverse correlations, which inflate and distort statistical relationships. An exploratory study conducted by myself and colleagues (Durham et al., 1995) identified this problem. Some boys only reported being sexually abused during the process of social work intervention in response to their inappropriate sexual behaviours, the implication being that without the sexualised behaviours their own abuse would not have been reported. This suggests an undetected population of boys who have been sexually abused and do not develop inappropriate sexual behaviours. This is not to deny that many inappropriate sexual behaviours also remain undetected. It may also conceal substantial cultural acceptance of male-on-male aggression that in many situations may have a sexually degrading element.

For some boys, there clearly is a problem of inappropriate sexual behaviours, which may result in the abuse of others. As with theories relating to the impact of child sexual abuse, theories that explain sexually abusive behaviour (Ryan, 1989; Kahn, 1990; Morrison and Print, 1995; Cunningham and MacFarlane, 1996) often take a predominantly psychological perspective and sometimes as a consequence inadequately acknowledge the interaction of social factors. Theorising from 'clinical' experiences, Ryan (1989) describes the path of 'victim to victimiser' as a circular and self-reinforcing process, based on internalised negative rationalisations of the person who abused them. Secrecy and isolation prohibit the child from validating feelings or correcting distorted assumptions, for example, about feelings of responsibility and experiencing pleasure and arousal during the abuse. This leads a child into irrational thinking, a declining self-esteem, guilt, confusion, powerlessness, and anger. Ryan (1989) refers to such a child developing fantasies of retaliation in order to regain control. This in turn leads to planning negative behaviour and sexually abusing others. A fuller theoretical understanding of sexually abusive behaviours would explain why they are mainly committed by males.

Rogers and Terry (1984) in their research using a 'clinical' sample of six males refer to young men who have been sexually abused being confused about their sexual identity and attempting to regain or reassert their 'masculinity' through identifying with their abuser and recapitulating the victim experience through engaging in sexually abusive behaviours. Again the term 'masculinity' is used in a static and structured sense, and the study therefore fails to recognise that a more subtle and complex range of factors may be influencing the young man's behaviour. An internalisation of wider social and cultural factors relating to patri-archal constructions of masculinities may play a significant part in some of the psychological processes that lead some males toward sexual aggression. Many young men who sexually abuse others have not been sexually abused themselves (Durham et al., 1995; Durham, 1997b).

These studies imply a direct link between abuse and abusing, which this review has challenged. A prior experience of sexual abuse is neither necessary nor suffi-cient as an explanation of sexually abusive behaviour (Grubin, 1998). It is impor-tant for research to establish the factors that account for why the majority of males who have been sexually abused do not sexually abuse others. This returns us to the resiliency perspective. The presence of supportive adults is a significant factor in preventing negative outcomes (Conte and Schuerman, 1987; Gilgun, 1990). A large study by Hunter (1995) supports this viewpoint and explains other factors that contribute to sexually abusive behaviours in male victims of sexual abuse. The findings indicate that personality (depression, low self-esteem, low self-confidence, and an inability to be assertive) is an independent predictive factor of sexual aggression and that sexual victimisation experiences do not predict personality. It would appear that the child who has the opportunity to discuss his fears, distortions, and rationalisations involved in experiences of child sexual abuse, alongside receiving support and insight into the basis of his fears about masculinities, would be more likely to recover from the experience, be less likely to develop the negative sequelae discussed in this chapter, and not have to live with the fear of inevitably abusing others.

SEXUAL IDENTITY AND SEXUAL CONFUSION

Males who have been sexually abused may express significant concern about their sexuality and sexual identity, based on a variety of factors relating to the circum-stances of the abuse (Gilgun and Reiser, 1990; Urquiza and Capra, 1990; Gill and Tutty, 1997). The person committing the abuse is likely to have been male. Along-side concerns about sexual arousal and possibly the experience of pleasure during the abuse, this may cause additional concerns (Porter, 1986). Gill and Tutty (1997) conducted an exploratory qualitative study of 10 adult men who had been sexu-ally abused, recruited from counselling agencies. They argue that it is important to make a distinction between four aspects of sexual identity: biological; gender; social sex role; and sexual orientation. The men in the study were clear about their biological identity and their sexual orientation. However, they indicated a degree of confusion about gender and social sex role. This confusion was related to societal perceptions of 'masculinity'.

Adolescence has been identified as a significant period when the development of identity is related to sexuality (Moore and Rosenthal, 1993). It is also a time when young people may become unsure of their sexual orientation (Gilgun and Reiser, 1990). Jubber (1991) identifies that there is often a limited education between generations about sexual function and sexual behaviour. As a result, the cognitive dimension develops slowly and socialisation is haphazard. He also argues that adolescence is a critical period for the development of sexuality and that, although their sexual needs are neglected, adolescents receive a clear message that heterosexuality is 'the socially designated and privileged goal of sexual development' (Jubber, 1991, p. 38). Jubber goes on to suggest that:

> In the absence of a formalised process of sexual socialisation and in the face of much social ambivalence and moralising, many groups and individuals are left to their own devices regarding sexual socialisation. It is thus hardly surprising then that there are almost as many routes to adult sexuality as there are adolescents and that the outcome is a great variety of forms of sexuality and sexual pathologies. (Jubber, 1991, p. 39)

Many myths and falsehoods about gender stereotypes and sexuality can be circulated among peers, the main forum for learning about and experimenting with sexuality and sexual behaviour in the light of impoverished and confusing adult information. The acceptance or rejection by a peer group in confirming sexual identity becomes all-important. This is one of the reasons why peer groupwork is advocated as a means of support for males who have been sexually abused (Leith and Handforth, 1988; Kweller and Ray, 1992; Scott, 1992; Watkins and Bentovim, 1992b; Durham, 1993, 1997b).

The important factor is that many adolescents experience confusion and anxiety about the development of their sexual identity, and their behaviour will be influenced by social expectations. Moore and Rosenthal (1994) refer to the fact that adolescents overestimate the sexual experiences and competencies of their peers. An adolescent who has been sexually abused may attribute this confusion and anxiety to the experience of abuse, and develop fears about sexuality. If the person who abused was male, the male adolescent may as a result confuse the experience with gay sexuality (Porter, 1986; Gilgun and Reiser, 1990; Myers, 1989). In referring to studies that report correlations between gay sexuality and child sexual abuse within gay male populations, Bartholow et al. (1994) identify significant methodological problems and conclude that there is no evidence of a cause-and-effect relationship between child sexual abuse and adult gay sexuality.

In a patriarchal context, the identities of gay young men become marginalised and oppressed. This is likely to have an impact on the self-esteem and confidence of gay young men, which could in turn increase their vulnerability to child sexual abuse. Again, the impact of an experience of sexual abuse is likely to interact with the impact of social oppression and may have an impact on sexual identity development (Bartholow et al., 1994). It has been established that compulsory heterosexism and homophobia creates many problems for all adolescents and in particular compounds the trauma of the sexually abused male. The conflicting and contradictory messages create a potential for all boys to experience sexual confusion in one form or another. For the sexually abused boy, a belief in the socially perpetuated myth that, for everybody else, the development of sexuality is a straightforward and enjoyable process is perhaps the one that does the most damage.

CONCLUSIONS

This chapter has critically reviewed a wide range of factors from the existing literature on child sexual abuse that are relevant to the current study. Many prevalence studies are confounded by methodological problems alongside a significant problem of under-reporting. The term 'organised abuse' is misleading, as all sexual abuse is organised. In analysing the controversy over 'satanic ritual abuse' and the alleged 'false memory syndrome', it is identified that perhaps the greatest problem is that these debates contribute to a backlash that ultimately serves to obscure and break down an understanding of the widespread, socially embedded nature of child sexual abuse. Existing research indicates very strongly that child sexual abuse has a harmful impact. Family and/or social support is a significant mediating factor to this harm.

Influential models and theories relating to impact of child sexual abuse are predominantly psychological and fail to adequately acknowledge social and cultural factors that reinforce and in many cases explain some of the psychological processes. This raises epistemological questions about how and why particular types of knowledge are created in particular ways and why they readily gain acceptance. Psychology and science are underpinned by a masculine discourse that often excludes the voices of women, children, and other oppressed groups (Burman, 1994; Gilligan, 1997). The voice of the child is often absent or abstracted from the child sexual abuse research and literature. Including and accounting for these voices, and seeing child sexual abuse in its social and cultural context, would more accurately demonstrate how its impact is further compounded by its interaction with experiences of oppression, such as racism or disabilism.

Finally, in considering the specific impact of male-child sexual abuse, an interacting dual social mythology has been identified. There is a systematic misunderstanding of the impact of male-child sexual abuse, leading to a set of false beliefs. These beliefs compound the fears, feelings, and sense of responsibility of the child or young person, which are further reinforced by the false beliefs and perceptions of others: first, that boys who have been sexually abused will sexually abuse others and, second, that boys who have been sexually abused are or will become gay. This may be compounded by the child's experience of sexual arousal and physical pleasure during the abuse if the person abusing was male, or lack of arousal and pleasure if the person abusing was female. To be abused is to be gay and to be gay is to be an abuser. These factors are not supported by the research and more often arise through methodological error, reverse correlations, and misunderstandings.

Furthermore, it is important to note that research does not remain purely in the

MALE-CHILD SEXUAL ABUSE—FACTS AND MYTHOLOGY

realms of academia. Dominant discourses lead to research, which in turn reinforces popular views. This material feeds into social constructions that create caricatures and stereotypes, further creating and maintaining popular views. These perspectives may influence the thinking of the sexually abused child and can cause considerable harm and anxiety. It is therefore important for research to more fully represent the voice of the child or young person, accounting for diversities of experience and the impact of social oppression. It is also important for research to recognise and explore the positive potential for being made strong through survival. This would avoid inadvertently reinforcing an expectation of failure (Sanford, 1990). Research and other professional practices have the responsibility to treat this subject in a manner that is anti-homophobic and rejects the patriarchal model of sexuality and sexual deviance. Not to do so is to replicate social oppression.

3

DEVELOPING A SENSITIVE APPROACH TO RESEARCHING CHILD SEXUAL ABUSE

LIAM: *If I talk about it it's in the tape machine, on the paper, and not stuck in here, in me anymore.*

INTRODUCTION

I approached this study as a specialist social work practitioner, with considerable experience of therapeutic work with children and young people. I was aware that it was necessary to develop an approach that would allow the young participants to share sensitive information about themselves and their lives, while at the same time providing a supportive therapeutic response. I considered it a priority to allow the young men as far as possible to feel and be in control of the process. The study therefore took the form of lengthy, unstructured interviews, with the pace and format largely being determined by the participants. The study recognised strongly that the young men have had traumatic experiences and may well be in the midst of struggling with a range of ongoing problems and difficulties. In setting out the methodology, a theoretical relationship is established between ethnography (particularly a life-story approach), feminist praxis, anti-oppressive research, and practitioner research.

THE LIFE-STORY METHOD

For most of us it is very difficult to be constantly aware of the limitations and of the relativity of conceptual knowledge. Because our representation of reality is so much easier to grasp than reality itself, we tend to confuse the two and take our concepts and symbols for reality. (Capra, 1975)

One of the issues identified in ethnography is that positivism (abstracted empiricism) and scientific rationalities have been unable to capture the quality of people's lives (Garfinkel, 1967). Ethnography has therefore favoured qualitative approaches and questions the sharp distinction between social science and its object (Hammersley and Atkinson, 1983). An important principle in ethnography is reflexivity, which emphasizes the interactive process between the researcher and the researched. Such interaction influences the nature and direction of the research, which is in itself identified as being social action. Implementing research may transform the direction of research, and social events may stimulate further research. Formal theory may generate substantive theory and vice versa. The emphasis is more on the discovery of theory, rather than testing an already formulated theory (Glaser and Strauss, 1967). The interactive process may involve self-disclosure and lead to a nearer equality in the relationship between the researcher and the researched.

One approach that seeks greater equality and closeness and gives primacy to human action and lived experiences is the life-story method. Plummer (1983) traces the origins of its recognition to Thomas and Znaniecki's (1958) study of *The Polish Peasant in Europe and America*. He describes life stories as being like 'snowflakes' (Plummer, 1983, p. 7), unique and never of the same design. The individual's actions as a human agent participating in social life are revealed. Researchers who study life stories get close to people and pick up their understandings, taking in the ambiguities and confusions of everyday experiences.

A life-story method is appropriate for the study of sensitive topics, where the research has the potential to become a difficult and possibly traumatic experience for participants. It brings the researcher closer to the lives and needs of its participants and is therefore compatible with an anti-oppressive methodology (Clifford, 1994). In saying this, it has to be acknowledged that some people may find it easier, for a variety of reasons, to respond to the anonymity of a questionnaire or a telephone line (Finkelhor et al., 1986). Qualitative and quantitative methods have their place alongside each other and produce different, but complementary data (Hammersley and Atkinson, 1983).

Life-story research will inevitably deal with small samples and may to some extent be idiosyncratic and characterised by particularities and circumstances that may make the experience less representative or less generalisable to wider populations. The research may also be biased and skewed by the particularity of the relationship between the researcher and participant and may therefore not be replicable. This study used unstructured interviews, to allow a high level of freedom, flexibility, and participant control, as a conscious attempt to limit this potential bias.

Approaching this research with existing knowledge about child sexual abuse highlights the importance of telling the two stories in the research report (i.e., the experience of the participant and the experience of the researcher in collecting the information, giving a full account of the research relationship, the background of the researcher, and its potential influence on the data collected). Such a report may also comment that the study is not intended for generalisation, but is a specific account of the processes of particular experiences that may or may not have elements in common with the experiences of others, but which nevertheless

contributes to an overall understanding of a particular area of study. It is important to acknowledge that the final research outcome is still only a representation of
its participants' experiences, and that collecting, analysing, and reporting the
information itself creates new meanings and understandings (Denzin, 1997).
Feminists have taken these arguments further and argued that research should
be sensitive to its social and political context and should take action to influence
that context as part of its process.

FEMINIST RESEARCH PRACTICE

Feminists (Oakley, 1981; Harding, 1987) have argued that orthodox research has
been male-dominated, has taken a formal (positivist) approach in both its method
and its reporting, and has excluded women's experiences. Feminist research has
sought to include all aspects of life as being relevant to research, valuing individual experiences as an important theoretical resource.

The principle of reflexivity is a central concept within a feminist research
paradigm (Roberts, 1981; Cain, 1990). Feminist researchers attempt to locate themselves in their research on an equal basis to its participants; the process is as shared
and democratic as possible. Any threat to this process would result in a reformulation of the research design, so as to protect and maintain the goal of working
toward a democratic equality between the researcher and the researched. Feminist
research is usually characterised by respect and empathy and attempts to directly
address the power differentials between the researcher and the researched. It often
has a focus on oppression and the plight of disadvantaged groups, influencing
change. Issues of methodology are not just about obtaining data but much more
about how data is generated by a contextual interactive research process, the
impact of that process on its participants, and the relevance of the standpoint of
the researcher. Gender and power have been central concepts in feminist research,
and this research directly implicates women as the knowers and seeks to make
women's voices heard (Reinharz, 1992). Notions of relationship and friendship
between the researcher and the researched are common in feminist research; the
researched are respected and never viewed as subjects, data collection is often
described as sensitive, and unstructured conversation interviews are valued. The
research participant often has a significant level of control or consultation over
the direction of the research.

It has been argued that feminist research has ignored the cross-cultural perspective, by homogenising the gender category of women (Harding, 1987; Rice,
1990). This position is well stated by Hooks, who acknowledges the primary
importance of sex discrimination as being the basis of all oppression, through
being the practice of domination that most people experience. In challenging all
hierarchy in our society, Hooks argues that the overall social status of Black
women is particularly low (1984).

The current study identifies hierarchy within the masculine gender category
and argues that sexually abused males could be described as being subordinate to

dominant cultures of hegemonic masculinities. The research shows that some of the young men felt different from the dominant group of males and lived in fear of that difference being discovered. In this respect, they participated in the complexities of their own hidden, private lifeworld, but driven by their fears made efforts to significantly participate in the lifeworld of the dominant male group.

The process of producing a life-story document may have a therapeutic benefit for those who take part, particularly when sensitive issues are being discussed and emotions and feelings can be shared or let go of (Bowen, 1993; Clifford, 1994). Feminist research also seeks to identify and clarify issues of power; a demystification for and with the powerless can create potential for change, because a paucity of information and knowledge about certain groups can accentuate and perpetuate their powerlessness (Reinharz, 1992). In undertaking this research, it was hoped that the generation of knowledge and information about male-child sexual abuse could help break down some of the fears and feelings of isolation and powerlessness of others.

ANTI-OPPRESSIVE RESEARCH PRACTICE

Feminist research practice has clearly identified the need to research issues of power and social disadvantage. Further development of this has led to the identification of a specifically anti-oppressive research practice (Humphries and Truman, 1994). As more and more research is conducted, improvements are made and a greater understanding is achieved. In order to contribute to social change, it is necessary to challenge social divisions and assumptions that perpetuate the status quo. Respect for diversity and difference and responding in the here and now to actual and potential processes of oppression is central to the methodology and method of anti-oppressive research practice. Wide-ranging aspects of social divisions, based on class, age, 'race', gender, sexuality, and ability are specifically acknowledged.

In seeking to understand lived-out oppression, instead of focusing on the characteristics and idiosyncrasies of an oppressed group, research questions are formulated around the social processes and experiences of oppression. This involves a deliberate focus on strengths and coping, as opposed to looking at deficits and weaknesses. An understanding of the context of social disadvantage enables a perspective of people surviving in the midst of adversity, as opposed to a pathologising focus on the characteristics of failure. Sanford (1990) refers to this as being *Strong at the Broken Places*, the title of her book, which argues there should be a greater emphasis on hope and recovery and a celebration of being strengthened through survival and being able to move forward.

A progression of anti-oppressive research practice would be for research to begin to focus on the social processes of being powerful. For example, how men benefit from patriarchal relations or how the social processes of heterosexuality work to create advantage. This was particularly relevant to my own research, with its focus being on the working of patriarchal forces in influencing the lives of sexually abused males. It identified how easy it is for males to consciously co-operate with the social pressures created by hegemonic masculinities and homophobia, to work toward their own advantage (of perceived recovery), and evade uncomfortable or painful feelings. The research showed how a sensitive methodology can create a safe environment for an acknowledgement and exploration of those feelings and processes. This would be a safe haven away from the normal workings or replication of these social processes; an environment based on sensitivity, trust and caring, with an open motivation to work toward improvement and healing. The overriding aspiration of this research study was that its participants will benefit and that the generation of new information about the experience of child sexual abuse will help others with their recovery.

In conducting the research interviews, I was conscious of the dynamics of an older person, with a professional status, interviewing young people and children. The role of trust has been a crucial feature of the research, crucial to my satisfaction that the participants were willing and were likely to benefit, and crucial to the participant's ability and desire to impart sensitive information and be reasonably confident about the response such information would create. A supportive and caring response created an environment of safety and facilitated safe discussion. The features and context of the research environment had to be clearly explained and tested out by myself and the participants, before the research proceeded.

Child sexual abuse as an area of research enquiry has specific difficulties in that silencing, not telling, and secrecy are features of the experience and may have an impact on the participants' ability to recount their experience. It is therefore important for the researcher not to rely exclusively on verbal accounts and to remain open to accepting and valuing alternative methods of participant communication that may otherwise become marginalised or remain unheard. An anti-oppressive life-story method should make it possible to bring disabled children into research; for example, the use of communication boards that encompass the language of child sexual abuse for children with learning difficulties (Kennedy, 1992). Two of the young men who participated in my study utilised poetry, cartoon graphics, and artwork to supplement their stories.

Empowerment is a central concept for anti-oppressive research practice, but it can mean different things to different people and is open to misuse. It can be used by researchers to make themselves 'feel good' about their actions, or it can truly be a conscious relinquishment and handing over of power, on a permanent basis from the advantaged to the disadvantaged. Unfortunately, the former is often the easier to achieve. About empowerment, Humphries states:

> the notion is so ill defined as to accommodate any and all theoretical positions, and consequently to serve as a justification for oppressive practices. (Humphries, 1994, p. 185)

Empowerment in anti-oppressive research is a process of involving people in partnership toward the meeting of mutually defined needs. Being empowered is potentially a significant experience in itself, which may then generate new research data. However, caution is required in the use of the term 'empowerment' It must take account of the ongoing lives and living standards of research participants and the structural and social disadvantage that they may continue to endure.

PRACTITIONER RESEARCH

There is a clear connection between social work practitioner research and feminist praxis, which emphasises the importance, when researching sensitive topics involving marginalised groups, of having an appropriate methodology. The greater the extent of a person's social marginalisation the greater the likely risk of further exploitation through research. Social work practitioner research is therefore poised in a position of wanting to represent the stories of some of these marginalised groups, with awareness of the extent of the power differentials (Parton, 1999). Social work practice involves itself with some of the most vulnerable and possibly the most under-researched groups in society. The ethics and values of social work are compatible with those of anti-oppressive research practice (Mullender and Ward, 1991; Everitt et al., 1992; Thompson, N., 1993; Pringle, 1995; Brown, 1998).

In approaching the research as a childcare specialist social work practitioner, I had a prior experience and understanding of working with and alongside children and young people, and an understanding of the nature and impact of child sexual abuse. This significantly influenced my approach to the research and was pivotal to its methodology and method: first, by giving me an understanding of how taking part in research about the experience of sexual abuse could have a detrimental impact on participants; second, by giving me the skills and experience to feel able to conduct the research appropriately, in a manner that actively seeks to counteract and limit the potential for such impact. This was both in terms of how the data collection interviews were conducted and the ability to provide ongoing support before, during, and afterward. The responsibility toward participant welfare was a priority over and above data collection.

It may be possible to argue that such an approach is inconsistent with the traditional or conventional roles and boundaries of the researcher, and that it should be for outsiders to provide such help and support. However, it is maintained that it is the process of providing the help and support as an integral part of the research practice that is not only ethically appropriate but is a research method in itself as well, entirely appropriate for the collection of sensitive data. *Such data may only become accessible in the event of such help and support being provided*, otherwise it may remain hidden and unexpressed (Cain, 1990). The knowledge produced by the research was the outcome of transitory research relationships. These relationships were purposely supportive, being informed by social work experience that was knowledgeable about the impact of sexual abuse. The ethics, values, and knowledge of the researcher around issues of child sexual abuse were made known to participants at the outset. Participants knew that they had a choice about what they would say, and they were aware that the aspiration of the researcher, about them taking part, was that they would benefit. They were aware that the researcher had the experience and skill to respond appropriately to their experiences, in a manner that was likely to help them. The research showed that hidden fears were expressed by participants, who were safe in the knowledge that they would receive sensitive, informed, anti-hegemonic[1] responses.

My previous social work involvement with the young men who participated in this study had established a level of trust. This was central to their decision to take part and enabled them to feel safe in discussing personal and sensitive issues. While some of the trust with the participants who took part in the research had been built up over a number of years, it was still necessary to spend time with them in discussing and explaining how my role had changed. Taking part in the research would mean a change in the relationship and the nature of the work that was planned to take place. Many of these issues were carefully discussed with potential participants during the sampling stage of the research. The young men who chose to take part did so with a full understanding of what to expect, knowing that they would be offered open choices and support throughout and for some time after their participation.

Listening to further and new accounts of child sexual abuse is in itself a further, unique, new, stressful experience for the researcher. Anybody undertaking such a task will need to have ongoing support and supervision. The provision of ongoing informed and effective support through supervision is a necessary and important component of a sensitive and anti-oppressive research methodology.

In completing the data collection phase and either through winding down and closing the contact with the young men or in providing follow-up support, there were less intensive forms of contact. These contacts occurred through either telephone conversations or further face-to-face meetings that were more informal, lighter, and not necessarily focused on issues of child sexual abuse. They served to place the research interviews back into a wider perspective of day-to-day living, in a manner that was in a longer term sense a debriefing process. This was both for the young men and for myself. This was a deliberately intended outcome. It was again informed by my prior practice knowledge and experience of how to appropriately close down professional therapeutic or counselling relationships.

I approached this research from the open and clearly acknowledged standpoint of a social work practitioner, with an awareness of the potential impact and bias this may have on the data collected. This made an essential contribution to the research design and methodology that attempted to minimise the potential for negative consequences. It made me aware of the importance of providing support before, during, and after the research process. The nature of this research and its methodology are such that it is reasonable to argue that it is best carried out by a researcher with therapeutic practice experience and skills. This becomes more pertinent in that the research involved me in the writing of criminal injuries' compensation reports, advocacy and attendance at criminal injuries' compensa-

---

[1] Some consideration was given to the use of the term 'counter-hegemonic', which involves challenging existing hegemonies through their substitution with alternative hegemonies. Positive counter-hegemony could include concepts such as citizenship, children's rights, and so on. An 'anti-hegemonic' approach more directly focuses on the production of power through challenging the apparatus and technologies of hegemony itself. These issues are discussed at length by Cooper (1995), who conceptualises mutually pluralist and diversified strategies of resistance that can be both counter- and anti-hegemonic.

tion appeal hearings, attending child protection planning meetings, assisting the making of further statements to the police, and extensive follow-up support, both face to face and by telephone.

The provision of participant support during all stages of the research was set as a priority above and beyond data collection. If necessary, the research data collection would have been abandoned. Throughout the research every effort was made not to compromise the well-being of participants for the purposes of the research. The research itself showed that the interviews of the young men were first and foremost opportunities for them to talk about their experiences and receive informed and supportive responses. Through talking and through the manner of the responses received, there was a level of resolve to *some* of the misconceptions and harmful beliefs the young men had held on to for substantial periods of time. In this respect, the interviews were in some ways dual occasions of social work practice and research.

Taking this further, the conversion to a research relationship of what was previously a singularly social work relationship has changed the nature of those relationships. From the outset, the participants were aware that my involvement with them was additional to any previous social work involvement, and that they had consciously opted in to this involvement with an expectation that they would in some way benefit and make a contribution to the plight of others. This created for the young men a special situation in which they had increased control and had expertise about the information they were giving. Additionally, their experience of me had changed, in that our conversations were being recorded and extra attention was being paid to detail, in a rigorous manner, as a necessity of the research process. They were aware that the research was being conducted for a PhD and that in this respect they were helping me. Chapter 9 will discuss in detail how the young men felt about taking part in the study. The information shared became valued and in the public domain, rather than remaining problematised and in the private domain.

CONCLUSIONS

The nature of this study takes the researcher close to the lives of its participants, in order to gain a socially contextualised representation of their experiences and understanding. The research method was informed and shaped by the related methodological fields of ethnography, feminist praxis, anti-oppressive practice, and practitioner research. It was a qualitative study that, by using a life-story approach, engaged seven young men in lengthy, unstructured discussions about their experiences of child sexual abuse. Feminist approaches provided an understanding of the patriarchal construction of knowledge and the importance of gender and its relationship to power. They emphasise the political dimension of research, which is about social change, before, during, and after the research. Feminist approaches emphasise the importance and value of centralising marginalised voices, allowing people's stories to be told and heard.

Through being conducted by a specialist childcare practitioner, the research was approached with an awareness of the sensitive nature of child sexual abuse as a research topic and of the potential harm to the participants. Through knowledge developed from the field of practitioner research, the methodology allowed the existing therapeutic skills of the researcher to provide support and appropriate responses to emotional distress. Anti-oppressive practice provided an awareness and understanding of the power differentials in research. Attempts were made to minimise these differentials, while at the same time acknowledging that they cannot be eradicated. From the outset, the participants were informed, both verbally and through a formal written agreement, about the purpose of the research and how the knowledge gained would be used. They were made aware, as fully as possible, of what would be required of them and how long it was likely to take and were given clear unequivocal opportunities *not* to take part. They were allowed a maximum level of control over the length, nature, and duration of the interviews and were offered support and counselling before, during, and after the research.

In asking the question, 'What perceptions do young men have of the experience of child sexual abuse and how do they perceive and understand its impact on their lives?', the study entered the world of the young person, which took the form of dialogue, poetry, metaphorical language, drawing and painting, through which they conveyed their understandings of their experiences. The research emphasised understanding and meaning and tried to represent the complexity of the young men's experiences. The research therefore concentrated on a small sample and maintained the integrity of the accounts the young men gave. This made the research complex, but brought it closer to being a more accurate representation of reality, making full use of the young men's own words and expression of meaning.

LIAM: *It's hard for me to remember this because basically I've blocked it out for many years. I don't talk about it or anything. You know, it's only just now that it's coming back. I trust you, this is basically the reason why I came today, trust somebody and talk about it, openly, like I think I've told somebody, you're not the only person that's going to read this, if it gets published or anything, you know, so I mean what the hell, you know, if I talk about it it's in the tape machine, on the chapter, and not stuck in here, in me anymore.*

Part II

THE YOUNG MEN'S STORIES

4

SEVEN LIVES

INTRODUCTION

This chapter describes how the seven young men who took part in the study were selected from a wider sample selection of potential participants. It considers the process of the interviews that subsequently took place and discusses the post-interview phase, where some of the participants received optional follow-up support and counselling. The chapter concludes with vignettes for each of the seven participants (all names are pseudonyms).

SELECTING PARTICIPANTS

The sample for this study was selected from my professional social work contacts with young people. A pool of 24 potential participants was identified, this included 11 boys who had been abused through a community network. I had worked with these young men in two groups separated by age for a period of 18 months (Durham, 1993, 1997a). Ten had not requested any individual work, and therefore I decided it was not appropriate to approach any of them to become an individual participant. From the remaining sample of 14, 3 had moved to other towns and cities and were therefore less available in practical terms, although one had been approached prior to moving on, but for other personal reasons had decided that the time was not right for him to take part. He has continued to remain in periodic contact and has expressed interest in the outcome of the research. The other two simply lived too far away and were therefore not approached at the initial stage. Of the remainder, three were currently receiving a service from myself, in relation to sexual abuse they themselves had committed, and I made the decision that at that particular time it was not appropriate to change the focus of my involvement with them.

One young man was 17 years old, of mixed parentage (African Caribbean/European), living in a White adoptive family. He had received a service from myself over several months; this was initially requested in relation to family conflict issues. His two sisters had recently reported early childhood sexual abuse. During the process of expressing opinion and feelings about his family situation, this young man gave an indication that he had similar experiences, but was not wishing to be any more specific. In responding to this situation, I had allowed this young man to receive reassurance, without having to speak about anything he did not wish to. Most of my work with this young man had focused on issues of racism and peer group struggles; he also had anxieties about his sexuality. My decision not to approach him about taking part in the research was based on my knowledge of his reluctance to *specifically* discuss experiences of sexual abuse and the potential risks to his fragile family circumstances.

Another young man, who was 19, had been sexually abused over a number of years at his residential school. I had provided some support for him in the past, but he had left the area. When he returned to the area, he heard of my work from one of the other participants, and contacted me, expressing an interest. However, his circumstances were turbulent and he eventually received a prison sentence. At his request, I visited him in prison. Following this, there was some written communication, but, unfortunately, there were further complications in his circumstances. He had to move several times, and, having other priorities, he stopped writing.

In approaching potential participants, particularly anybody whom I had been engaged with in an in-depth working relationship, I was aware of some potential difficulties. First, creating a sense of obligation, and, second, creating a sense that future services were dependent on taking part in the research. To avoid these problems these issues were openly discussed, and it was made clear that I had to be satisfied, first, that they would benefit and, second, that their decision to become involved was as much a voluntary one as it possibly could be. Chapter 2 considered the potential for some people to respond better to more anonymous opportunities to discuss issues of child sexual abuse. This may have been the case for some of the potential participants in this study. Those who were selected were those who made a conscious decision to discuss their experiences with me. The young men made their decisions in the light of clear and extensive information about what the nature of their participation would be. This would sometimes involve allowing a young person to make his decision after several discussions, with some passage of time. It was also made clear that if a young man did not wish to take part, he could still receive the ongoing support that was being offered to other participants. This applied to the young man discussed above, who had left the area, but subsequently remained in touch and expressed interest in my progress.

These accounts of initial approaches and sample selection demonstrate the sensitivity required and the need to directly address the potentially oppressive consequences of asking a young person to take part in research that explores personal experiences and sensitive issues. Six young men were selected from the initial pool population, and one was selected additionally. This method of sampling has been described as 'focused or judgmental' (Arber, 1993, p. 71). The final sample was selected by the following criteria:

- being male, under the age of 25, and having experienced childhood sexual abuse (contact sexual abuse);
- expression of a positive wish to take part in the research, in the light of full knowledge and information;

- a judgement by me that the potential participant has understood the potential impact of the research and was likely to benefit;
- availability for a series of lengthy interviews.

The seven young men who agreed to take part in this study were all previously known to me, through my professional contact with them as a social worker employed by their local authority. I had known Liam, Justin, Paul, Colin, and Sean for several years. With the exception of Ryan and David, my formal involvement with the young men had ceased, and they had themselves chosen to maintain sporadic contact with me. Sometimes this would take the form of utilising the 'drop in' services of my work base, other times it would be in the form of telephone contact or leaving messages. Having little or no family contact, they would occasionally contact me for advice or support, job references, or to report positive progress in their lives. Through these contacts, the prospect of taking part in a research project was discussed at length with each young man, over a period of four months. This created opportunities and time for the young men to fully consider the implications of taking part and to ask questions and listen to my explanations of what the nature of their participation would be. The young men were made aware that I was conducting the research as part of a higher degree and that my aspiration was to get it published as a book. It was made clear that discussing the details of their experiences of child sexual abuse would be potentially stressful and that every effort would be made to provide support and understanding.

THE INTERVIEWS

The interview stage of the research took place over an 18-month period, which spanned the years 1994 to 1996. The interviews took place in a variety of settings in accordance, as far as possible, with the wishes of each young person. This included in their own homes, at a social services day centre, or at a public venue such as a cafe, or on one occasion a pub. Where possible, each young man was given a choice of venue. When a public venue was selected, the session was made lighter and less formal. Given the nature of the research topic, it was important to consider safety issues, both for the participants and me. This is not to undervalue the trust that had developed and that had enabled the young men to feel safe about their participation, but to ensure that each participant understood that these issues had been considered and that openness and accountability were maintained without compromising confidentiality.

In conducting the interviews, apart from a mutual awareness of the topic of research, there was no specifically imposed structure, and each participant was afforded the maximum possible control over the interview process. The interviews took the form of conversations, often with myself taking a listening role, occasionally asking a relevant question or a gentle comment to maintain the focus. In most cases, once a participant began to feel comfortable, he would engage in lengthy descriptions of his experiences. While I would listen and not interrupt, I took care not to create any uncomfortable silences. This was a question of judgement; the nature and process of each interview varied between individual participants. My previous knowledge and experience of providing therapeutic counselling was crucial and allowed me to feel confident that I was making appropriate responses across these differing circumstances by maintaining an awareness and acknowledgement of each young man's vulnerability and stress, while at the same time providing positive encouragement and support that were sensitive and appropriate to their age and understanding.

As the stories unfolded, each young man's struggle for meaning became evident. Sometimes the process would generate additional information, as past understandings were revisited and reinterpreted. This was particularly true of Colin's story, where a personal relationship with an older female was redefined by Colin as having aspects that were abusive. A sense of struggle is evident in all the stories. Justin, Paul, Colin, and Liam were more verbal and able to speak at length without interruption. Sean preferred to discuss the more difficult and distressing aspects of his experiences in brief sentences. Both Ryan and David were 15 and still very close in time to their experiences of sexual abuse (in comparison with many other studies, *all* the young men in this study were close in time to their experience of child sexual abuse). Ryan expressed his feelings in poetry and David used painting and drawing; David also required more therapeutic help and reassurance during the interview. At his suggestion, following my use of the expression 'on the road to recovery', a large roll of wall paper was used to draw out the road and map out his memories and feelings, showing the past and his aspirations for the future, vividly representing his advances and progressions, alongside contradictions and setbacks. Some of these techniques are discussed more fully in Part III.

To summarise, the young men who took part were engaged in a sensitive interview process, the pace and format of which was in the main of their own choosing. As a result, a safe and anti-hegemonic environment was created, which enabled them to feel safe to discuss distressing experiences of child sexual abuse. The young men were able to go to the heart of their experiences and say how they felt and how their lives had been affected. The research methodology allowed a freedom to explore perceptions in ways that opened up new meanings and understandings. The research will show that this allowed feelings of self-blame and responsibility to be shifted on to the abuser. The young men were able to discuss experiences and personal fears that they had held on to for a long time and felt they could not openly share with their peers or close friends, for fear of ridicule and embarrassment. Some of the comments made had never been said before. They were secure in their belief that the research environment was a safe situation in which to explore some of the more difficult aspects of having been sexually abused. The offer of support and understanding allowed each young man to test out and explore his feelings and beliefs. The environment was created with the knowledge and understanding that it was likely that the young men would wish to express such feelings, given the appropriate and sensitive opportunity.

POST-INTERVIEW PHASE

After the interview phase, each participant was given the option of receiving ongoing support. This was taken up substantially by Justin, Colin, and Liam and to a lesser extent by Sean and David. The post-interview contact involved face-to-face work and telephone contact. As time progressed, the face-to-face contact faded into telephone contact. Often the contact would relate directly to the research, other times it widened out to more general support work. Some of the participants still maintain an occasional telephone contact. None of them has pursued other forms of more formal support or therapeutic help. Whenever this had been discussed, the response was in the main a combination of not needing further help in a formal sense and a reluctance to speak to a stranger.

The post-interview contact sometimes involved a more formal response and drew upon my social work expertise. A reporting of additional past abuse by one participant involved my attendance at a child protection planning meeting. Following his interviews, Liam, who had never reported his abuse, chose to report his experiences to the police. At his request, this involved my attendance with him at one of the police interviews. The research generated information from David that led to the writing of a further report to the Criminal Injuries Compensation Authority and resulted in an additional award. The research information was also used to secure compensation for Justin and Ryan. In Justin's case I attended a criminal compensation appeal hearing, and later at his request took him to revisit the boarding school where he was abused.

SEVEN LIVES—VIGNETTES

(all names—child and adult—are pseudonyms)

Justin

Justin was 22 years old and for the past 6 months living with his partner Ruth and their two children David and Leo. At the age of 14 Justin had 'special educational needs' (as defined by the Education Act 1981) in relation to emotional and behavioural disturbance, following the divorce of his parents. He was placed at a residential school when he was 14. He was physically and sexually abused on numerous occasions between the age of 14 and 16 by the headmaster of the school John Austin. He attended two court trials as a witness to this abuse. The headmaster was convicted and sentenced to 14 years' imprisonment. Many other pupils from the school testified against the physical and sexual abuse they had suffered.

After leaving school, Justin describes himself as losing control. His story describes a great deal of emotional pain, anxiety, and private fears, especially around this period. Justin also talks about the court appearances and the stress he suffered during a lengthy waiting period. During this period, Justin committed some criminal offences. At the age of 17 he was privately fostered by a neighbourhood friend. He began drinking alcohol and inhaling excessive amounts of butane gas in an attempt to block out his memories. This has had a serious impact on his health, leaving him with sustained liver damage.

After this period, Justin met his current partner and has fathered two children. Justin has continued difficulties in maintaining this relationship, finding it very difficult to extend trust. He continues to have flashbacks and private anxieties about his sexuality. He has re-established contact with his father and is beginning to address some of the difficulties he has with his mother, mainly as a result of her disbelief and sending him back to school when he first reported his abuse.

In applying for criminal injuries compensation, Justin feels he had unfair treatment at the appeal hearing and felt that he was the person on trial. He was relieved to have the award, but felt that the money was tainted and spent it quickly. The award presented him with difficulties in relation to his state benefits, which he considers to be unfair.

Justin was very positive about taking part in this research project and feels that he has benefited from the support and the opportunity to explore his feelings in detail.

Paul

Paul was 23 years old and living with his oldest sister, after having broken up with his partner Claire after a period of intensive conflict. He continues to have some contact with Claire and his two-year-old daughter. Paul had welcomed the opportunity to talk about his life as he felt that things had come to a head and that he would benefit from talking through past events that had troubled him for many years.

Paul's earliest memories reach back to around the age of five, when he, his two older sisters Gail and Sally, and younger brother Peter lived with their mother and stepfather. At this time his two half-brothers Kevin and Martin also lived with him, prior to their adoption when Paul was around seven years old. For many years Paul carried a deep sense of responsibility for the fact that he was unable to protect Kevin and Martin from his violent stepfather Raith, who also lived in the family home. Paul describes his sense of guilt as having an overwhelming negative influence on his life.

Paul's story relates a great deal of emotional and physical abuse being inflicted on all the children in the family by Raith. Paul was particularly singled out and has described a whole catalogue of extreme physical abuse and emotional torment. At the same time Paul was sexually abused by a man whose name he does not know. He lived in the next street, where he used to play outside with his friends. Again Paul has given a vivid account of these memories.

When Paul was nine, he, his brother, and two sisters became subjects of care orders and moved into foster care. Within two years of this move, Paul's mother died and his stepfather disappeared. Paul remained in the same foster home until he was 19, when he moved into housing association accommodation.

Paul has explained how his experiences of physical and sexual abuse have damaged and disabled his life. Throughout his adolescence he had deep fears about his sexuality and was worried that his abuse meant that he was gay. Paul describes how he has had to manage his life to maintain an image of heterosexuality. He felt isolated and had to keep his feelings to himself. He lived in fear of discovery, as he felt a deep sense of responsibility for his own abuse. He was ashamed and believed that any discovery of his abuse would invite ridicule. His story relates the many contradictions and struggles he has experienced as a result of being physically, emotionally and sexually abused. Paul has been very specific about how his private fears have seriously affected his relationships with adults, with peers, and with intimate partners. Paul feels he has benefited from taking part in this research project.

Colin

Colin was 18 years old and living alone in rented accommodation, after having broken up with his partner and mother of his two children. Colin had welcomed the opportunity to talk about his life in terms of his sexual abuse and the difficulties he was now able to recognise he had been having with his relationships and in general.

He had spent 14 years in local authority care and was now living independently. He became the subject of a care order at the age of four, following a period of physical abuse and neglect. For nine years he had lived in one stable foster care placement with his younger sister Alice. Colin's placement broke down when he was 13. Alice remained in the placement.

Colin was moved to a short-term emergency placement and had to change school. This was the beginning of a very uncertain period for Colin; for four years he was unable to settle down. Within a month of moving to the emergency placement Colin explains how he had absconded following an argument and was picked up by a stranger, who lured him with the prospect of alcohol and drugs. Colin was driven several miles away to a house, where he was sexually abused several times over a four-day period. He refers to the abuse as 'the four days'. Colin reported the abuse within days of his return to the emergency placement. Although the police were able to track down the abuser, it was considered that there was insufficient evidence to take the case to court.

Colin's story explains how within a month of reporting his abuse, at the age of 13, he became embroiled in a turbulent relationship with an 18-year-old woman named Penny. This relationship lasted for nearly four years and produced two children, both of whom are now adopted. There were many failed attempts by Colin to separate from Penny. He also resisted professionals' attempts to separate them. Upon reflection, partly as a result of these research interviews, he has now redefined this relationship as involving aspects of sexual abuse. During this period, Colin drank heavily and smoked cannabis. He also went through a period of sniffing butane gas. There was evidence that he had been drinking large amounts of alcohol from around the age of 12.

Colin's story describes his feelings about his initial sexual abuse by a male and explains the impact of this abuse, both privately and in the manner in which he relates to other people. He explains his attempts to accommodate the experience and describes his intense fears of being gay and deep suspicions about how he is viewed by his peers as a result of his abuse. He has also described his fears of abusing others. Colin feels that being sexually abused by a male has left him with sexual problems and sexual confusion, to the extent that he often finds it difficult to enjoy sexual relationships.

Liam

Liam was 22 years old, homeless and living with friends, following the break-down of a two-year relationship with a female of a similar age, named Tanya. This breakdown had precipitated many issues and feelings for Liam in relation to past events, including the death of his father and sexual activity that had taken place between Liam and a teacher Carl at a boarding school, when Liam was between 15 and 16. During the initial stages of the research, Liam did not fully define the experience as sexual abuse and referred to it as a relationship. As the research contact progressed, Liam redefined the experience as involving aspects of sexual abuse and asked for my assistance in reporting it to the police. As the incidents had occurred six years ago, the investigation did not result in prosecution, but it contributed to previous concerns and another similar investigation in relation to other boys.

When Liam was eight, his father died suddenly at work. He was an ambulance driver and had been suffering from stress. Liam was the youngest of three. He had a sister four years older and a brother two years older. His mother found the situation increasingly difficult to cope with and had enlisted the help and support of the social services department. By the time Liam was 13, he was beginning to get into difficulties. His school attendance was sporadic, and he was drinking and smoking cannabis. He was often late home and sometimes away overnight. On one occasion he was picked up when hitch-hiking and narrowly escaped being sexually abused, as his story will describe. This resulted in a police investigation, in which Liam feels he was blamed and made to feel responsible for what had happened. To this day, he carries strong feelings and bad memories about this course of events.

When Liam was 14, with the help of a charity Liam's mother paid for him to go to a mixed boarding school, as she felt it was imperative that he moved away from the area. Liam regards this as a life-saving decision, even though at the time and since his relationship with his mother has been very strained. Liam was very happy with the time he spent at boarding school. However, while at the school he developed a closeness to a member of the teaching staff Carl, which at the age of 16 became what he described initially as a fully consenting sexual relationship.

Liam's story describes these events and highlights the struggle he has had in coming to terms with his sexual feelings, the impact of being picked up at the age of 14, coming very close to being sexually abused, and the ambivalence he feels about a sexual 'relationship' with his teacher that he strongly feels he consented to, but is also aware that it was sexually abusive. Liam describes the impact of these events on his sexuality and his subsequent relationships with women.

Sean

Sean was 21 years old and homeless, having recently moved out from living in temporary accommodation with a friend. Since leaving care at the age of 18, Sean had not lived in his own accommodation, but had constantly survived on the hospitality of friends. Since the age of 17 he had been unemployed. He was in the process of setting himself up in a joint tenancy with a friend of his mother.

Sean had been the subject of a care order since the age of nine. He was the second youngest of four children. During his time in care, he lived in eight different foster homes, four of which had been disrupted. In between these place-ment moves, Sean had on three occasions attempted rehabilitation with his mother. Each attempt had been unsuccessful, largely due to financial circum-stances and health problems experienced by Sean's mother. These pressures made it very difficult for Sean's mother to exercise care and control over him, his brother and two sisters, (Karl, Mary, and Louise) who were also the subjects of care orders. Sean has never known his father.

At the age of 12, Sean's life was very disrupted. He was unhappy and was getting involved in delinquency and drug-taking, which had resulted in court appearances. He was excluded from school and became the subject of a statement of special educational needs (Education Act 1981). It was recommended that he attend a residential school on a termly basis. Sean was placed at an all-male boarding school 40 miles away from his home.

At the age of 15, Sean was showing sexualised behaviour toward male adults. This concern, alongside reports from another boy, led to an investigation. Sean reported that he had been repeatedly subjected to sexual abuse by Mr Lister, the head of care at the school. As head of care, Mr Lister was in a central and powerful position in the school. This included making decisions about behaviour grades that would result in the provision or restriction of privileges. He also made decisions about permission to return home at weekends. He lived on the school premises in a cottage, to which he invited pupils and sexually abused them. In Sean's case, the sexual abuse had taken place over a period of six to nine months. Sean was not aware that there were other boys being sexually victimised at the school by the same person. Mr Lister disappeared during the course of the in-vestigation and was believed to have left the country.

Sean's story explains the details of these events and describes the impact that sexual abuse has had on his life, both at the school and since leaving school. Sean explains how he now feels that he has recovered from the experience. He now has a stable relationship, fixed accommodation and a full-time job. He has always maintained that he wanted to be left to 'get on with it', that he never welcomed the involvement of the police, and wouldn't have wished to go to court.

David

David was 15 years old and still attending school. He was living at home with his mother, father, four brothers and two sisters. Eighteen months previously, David had attended a court trial, along with twelve other boys, to give evidence against a man named Harry, who was a computer studies lecturer. He had sexually abused several boys who had been temporarily in his care. David was abused from the age of nine to twelve. Previous studies (Durham, 1993, 1997a, 2000) have exam-ined the professional response to this situation, which had involved the setting up of support groups.

Following an initial approach to David's school for names of boys who would benefit from attending his computer club, Harry approached David's mother and father and offered to provide weekend respite for David. Subsequently, in the confines of his own home, Harry sexually abused David on a regular basis. The abuse took place in the context of the provision of care and positive attention. The material standard of comfort that Harry could provide was far greater than that which he had experienced at home and was therefore welcomed and enjoyed.

David was confused and unsure about whether or not he could or should tell his mother about the abuse. David felt that often she was too busy either working or looking after a large family for there to be opportunities in which he felt he could talk to his mother about what was happening. In addition, in material terms David found the weekends away comfortable. He had considerable ambivalence about his relationship with Harry, who was the provider of considerable material comfort and favour, but who also sexually abused him, which he found difficult to understand and was embarrassed about.

At school David was isolated and found it difficult to make friends. He was often victimised by some of the other pupils at school. On such occasions he used to run out of lessons or run home. His problems increased when some pupils discovered that he had been sexually abused. He was accused of being gay. This fed into David's personal anxieties and added to his feelings of being responsible for what happened. Additionally, he had been accused of lying by the defence barrister during the court case.

Eighteen months after the closure of the support groups, David asked his mother to contact me, as he was having nightmares and problems with his peers at school and wished to receive further help. On hearing about the research project, David expressed a wish to take part. During the course of discussing his feelings, David reported that the sexual abuse had taken place to a much greater extent than had been indicated by either his first statement or the court trial. David was clear about the fact that, beyond my informing the police, he did not wish to pursue the legal aspects of the matter any further. This wish was respected.

Ryan

Ryan was 15 years old and living with his mother. His 19-year-old sister lived away, but often returned home to stay for two or three weeks at a time. His father left when Ryan was three years old, after a series of violent incidents toward Ryan and his mother. Ryan does not wish to find his father or have contact with him and feels anger toward him.

At around the age of 10 or 11, Ryan had attended computer club activities set up by a man named Harry (the same man who abused David). Just after the period when he had attended the club, Ryan was playing in a local park and 'by chance' met Harry. As Ryan's story explains, he cannot recall exactly how, but he ended up in Harry's car and travelled to a house, the location of which he has never been able to recall. When he was at this house, he was sexually abused by Harry and eventually driven back to near his home. Ryan recalls two incidents of this nature.

During this period, Ryan was very unhappy and spent large periods of time away from home, often absconding. There was a period of intense conflict between Ryan and his mother, often relating to problems Ryan was experiencing in relation to his sexual abuse. Ryan did not express anger toward Harry, but his mother did. Ryan, sometimes ambivalent and passive about the abuse, was reluctant to go to court, but his mother felt strongly that he should go. As a result, Ryan was often reluctant to discuss anything relating to the abuse with his mother.

Further tensions were caused by Ryan absconding from school and returning home late, being very moody and difficult to manage. Ryan also became involved in petty law-breaking incidents, which resulted in police involvements. There were occasions when Ryan very clearly put himself at risk. Staying out very late, sometimes all night in dark, cold places with insufficient clothing. It was after one such incident that Ryan initially reported his abuse to his uncle. During this period, as a result of baiting and name-calling from his peers Ryan changed school. There are large periods of time he cannot remember, particularly situations of stress. At times he still feels that he is not believed about what he refers to as his 'memory blocks'. He felt that he was pressurised by the police at the time of the investigation, when he was driven to several locations in an attempt to find the houses he was taken to by Harry. There is much that Ryan feels he has now forgotten, but he is clear that he knows it was a very bad time for him.

Recently, Ryan has been offered a sum of money from the Criminal Injuries Compensation Authority for the sexual abuse he has suffered. A report based on information gained by the research process was submitted by me in support of his claim.

5

BEING ABUSED

JUSTIN: *Me, I just came in the category for just screaming and shouting at and beating up and being sexually abused.*

INTRODUCTION

The experience of sexual abuse often involves a child or a young person being coerced into abuse through processes constructed by the abuser, to allow sexual abuse to be committed without detection and to instil a sense of fear and responsibility in the child or young person, so as to prevent them from feeling able to tell. This coercion may involve sexual, physical, and emotional acts that may or may not be understood, but by virtue of age and/or circumstances cannot be consented to. Such an event is likely to be experienced as a trauma. The circumstances and combinations of these processes are as many as there are children who have been abused. The beliefs and circumstances are tailor-made by the abuser for the individual child, maintaining their silence and compliance (Finkelhor, 1984). When the sexual abuse actually commences, the child is likely to experience this as a starting point or a change in a relationship, but for the person who commits the abuse this is likely to be the culmination of a whole series of thoughts, events and planning, all of which the child is unaware.

This chapter analyses the power relationships between the young men and the adults who sexually abused them. It shows how the adults set up circumstances that would make it possible for them to sexually abuse the young men (boys). The particular circumstances of Justin and Paul before they were sexually abused are contrasted. Justin was abused alongside other boys at a residential school, Paul was abused on his own by a man who lived in his neighbourhood. The chapter moves on to consider the experiences of the young men during the period when they were being abused, again considering the situational power relationships involved, how combinations of threats and persuasion were used, and how the young men tried to resist. A common feature was that the young men were unaware of the prior intentions of the adults involved and how they were instilled with a sense of responsibility for what had happened to them. The analysis is continued by considering the relationships that were purposefully constructed by the abusers. Some of the young men were offered treats of money, others were threatened severely. Sometimes, extreme threats would be combined with kindness or positive attention. This meant that for some of the young men, there were positive aspects to this relationship that created a sense of voluntarism or co-operation and responsibility.

BEFORE ABUSE

Justin was abused by his headmaster, who was in the position of highest authority at a residential school for boys with behavioural and emotional disturbance. The alliance he made with parents was a crucial aspect to his being able to maintain the secrecy of his abusing and contain it within the school. This began with the initial school admission interview—a very different face was presented to Justin in a brief moment when he was away from his mother.

> **JUSTIN:** ... *he interviewed everyone. ... Well he took me outside, we'd gone for the interview on the Wednesday and he said I was going to the school on the Saturday and I said, 'well, I don't want to go to it', to my mum. He said, 'well, we'll go outside and have a word'. He took us outside and then pinned us up against the car and says, he starts pointing and says: 'I can be two things to you, I can be your father or a bastard' ... and then went back inside and my mum says 'well, you're coming to the school ...'*

It is clear that even at this initial stage, Justin was aware that this man was abusing his personal and situational power. To his mother, he presented as a powerful person in a professional position. His power was derived from his masculinity, and its representation of control, and his authority of being the headmaster of a formally recognised educational establishment. However, in the context of Justin being on his own, his power was differentially used. His immediate power was expressed in the form of physical force, conveying the message to Justin at the outset that his power could be misused and that with Justin there was no need for the pretence of respectability. Justin was aware of the incongruity of the situation, but was resigned to the fact that he would have to go to the school. The headmaster used circumstances of 'normal' power relationships as a springboard for committing sexual abuse. He had set up an abuse regime that employed a pecking order, whereby older boys who had been physically and sexually abused by him in the past were given a parallel and sometimes elevated status to members of staff and were used in the process of abusing other children. They themselves were encouraged to abuse other boys.

> **JUSTIN:** *They came and picked me up on the Saturday afternoon ... when I get there this kid Henry, the hardest kid in the school, puts these rubber gloves on to search me ... he's the hardest kid in the school and like he was*

like a member of staff ... the headmaster used to let him have the run of the school ... He was his right-hand man.

Many of the boys were engaging in violent and aggressive behaviours (which may sit alongside compulsory heterosexism and homophobia), while during the same period of time they were being sexually abused by the headmaster and in many cases being forced to engage in sexual activities with each other. The fact that sexual abuse was taking place between pupils would have likely compounded feelings of responsibility and prevented boys from being able to tell. This was alongside the fear of the hierarchy and the need to assert aggressive forms of masculinity in order to survive and maintain a level of status. The exercise of personal power through physical force served to confirm a pupil's status in terms of 'hardness and toughness', which in association to being a strategy for resistance and survival may have, in a very personal sense, served to counteract some of the impact of the sexual abuse, particularly in terms of allowing the boys to reassert their masculinities.

Paul was sexually abused by an adult male neighbour who lived near to his home, where he used to play football in the street. He was abused on his own, in isolation from other children, but sometimes in the presence of another adult, a female. The abuser may have gained knowledge by observing Paul in the neighbourhood and recognised from his disposition that he was an unhappy child who was likely to have restricted opportunity or ability to report being abused.

Before Paul was sexually abused, he had experienced considerable physical and emotional abuse at home at the hands of his stepfather Raith. Paul experienced the circumstances of his sexual abuse by the neighbour as being less painful and in some ways a relief and escape from the extreme physical violence that was being inflicted on him at home. He provides a vivid recall of what happened at home, where for him being on the receiving end of violence, aggression, and cruelty was the norm. He makes the point that he still carries the scars in his memory and on his body and that he has never talked about it before now.

PAUL: ... *I can only remember violence, shouting, aggression, and hatred. They're the only things I can remember from being a kid. ... He would try and tell us that our mum didn't want us, our mum didn't love us and we were making a mess of her life. He used to tell us that she'd told him that she wished she'd killed us at birth. ... He used to fill the bath with cold water and chuck me in it and held me under the water. He did that a few times. ... One night I went to the bathroom, Raith jumped out of his doorway and there was a coat hanger hanging on the banister and he picked it up and he hit me with it, the hooked end of it and it went into my side and I've got a scar there now. He just pulled it out and tore the skin away. ... He made me sleep on the stairs because I'd wet the bed ... he would never change the mattress or change the bedding, so it always used to stink ... He*

> *tied me in a sheet once; rolled me up in a sheet and tied the two ends and said*
> *he was never going to let me out. Once he banged my head against the wall*
> *that much that I passed out. . . . I've never talked to anybody in this detail.*

Being anywhere else, other than at home, was for Paul a release. Being sexually abused didn't hurt in the same way and involved receiving treats and some positive attention. From what Paul says it would appear that he was selected from a group of boys. It is likely that the man would have identified his withdrawn disposition, his suffering, and depression and made a judgement that he would be able to abuse him and prevent him from telling.

> **PAUL:** *We used to play up the other side of the street against some*
> *garages. We used to play with an old, beat-up can of coke, and this guy*
> *came out once and he was asking what the noise was and we said, 'Oh,*
> *we're playing football', and he says, 'Oh, haven't you got a ball?' and we*
> *said, 'No,' and he said, 'Do you want to come and find one?' and we said,*
> *'Yeah, all right.' He said, 'Who wants to come and help me find one,' and a*
> *couple of them went, 'Yeah, I'll go,' and I just stayed in the background 'cos*
> *I was pretty quiet and he said, 'What about you?' pointing to me and I said,*
> *'Yeah, all right.'*

Paul soon became ensnared into an abusive situation, that continued for over two years. He estimated that he was sexually abused well over a hundred times and subjected to a wide range of abusive acts. The sexual abuse stopped when his family left the area, shortly before he was taken into care by the local authority.

> **PAUL:** *Then we go into his house, go upstairs and he would like lift me up*
> *to have a look on the top of wardrobes and on the tops of shelves, things like*
> *that and then he would put me back on the floor and obviously my clothes*
> *would have come un-tucked and he would say, 'Oh, tuck you back in', and*
> *he would pull the rest of my clothes out and undo my trousers . . . we used to*
> *go up there and play football maybe two or three times a week and every*
> *time we went up there it would happen . . . The next step was the same thing*
> *would happen again, but then he would lay me down and he took photo-*
> *graphs. That scares me now, you know, the photographs, because I don't*
> *know where they are and you know, you hear of things, child porn rings and*
> *they print magazines. When I was older, I'm talking about probably 16, I*
> *used to think is my picture ever going to appear in one of those.*

The contrasting circumstances of Justin and Paul draw attention to how their powerlessness was used to the abuser's advantage. For Justin, Mr Austin had established control over almost every aspect of his day-to-day living environment including most of the people who were part of it. He made no attempt to hide from Justin the fact that he could present himself differently in different circumstances, using his personal power in contrasting manners, ranging from a presentation of respectable authority to the blatant use of physical violence. For Paul, his stepfather completely controlled his home environment. Within this environment, Raith's abuse of power was exercised in the form of physical force and verbal threats behind the closed doors of a family home, beyond the detection of those outside, with the possible exception of the man who sexually abused him. Paul's anxieties and defeated powerlessness seemed to stand out among the peer group, from which he was selected to enter a man's house to look for a ball. He returned to the house many times and was repeatedly sexually abused.

BEING ABUSED

This section considers the young men's recollections of being sexually abused and how they remember thinking and feeling at the time. Continuing initially with Justin's experiences at his boarding school, explaining that eventually Mr Austin took him to the 'sleeping-in room' and sexually abused him. Sometimes one or two of the powerful older pupils would be present and take part in setting up the abuse. Justin was in a situation where he knew, because he was going to be sexually abused again and again, that by co-operating the experience was over; the uncertainty of waiting was over, for a short period of time at least. This was a coping strategy for Justin that at the time marginally reduced the anxieties of his situation. Upon reflection this could and has been rationalised by him, and by others, as giving consent and wanting the abuse to happen. For Justin, these fears are compounded by his being eventually manipulated into a situation where he had to report to his headmaster to be abused.

JUSTIN: *Yeah, it was like my fault, I was actually there. No, I've thought of that loads of times, you know, why did I walk down to the room, because I knew what was going to happen when I got in the room, from being told by all the other people, but it's just fear that takes over. It's like you're not actually in control of your body. It's like the fear's there in control. . . . You know it was always on your mind like, when's he going to come and get you again. It was just like constantly waiting for it to happen to you. You just do it to just get it out the way. . . . Or you'll be sitting on the toilet and all of a sudden you come out and that's it, down in the sleeping-in room. . . . He'd have Henry and that lot with him. . . . Henry had the run of the school . . . like Austin's servant. . . . Scary thoughts. . . . It's the fear of having somebody* *like three times your age, it's a bit terrifying. You just freeze and it just happens.*

Justin was aware that many other boys were being sexually abused. He witnessed or heard about sexual and physical violence on an almost daily basis. He had an awareness of the status and categorisation of the other boys in the school and the relationship they had with Mr Austin, in terms of how they were being abused and the privileges they may or may not have received, and concludes he 'just' came into every 'category' of abuse—emotional, physical, and sexual.

JUSTIN: *Some kids were only getting beat up, not sexually abused, 'cos Austin would have some for beating on, some for shagging, some for scream-ing and shouting, calling them all the names under the sun and things like that. He'd have ones for particular ones. Me, I just came in the category for just screaming and shouting at and beating up and being sexually abused. I just came in every category starting from the day I said, 'well, you can just start being a bastard', so he was a bastard to me.*

At Sean's school, the man who abused him was the head of care, and so similarly, but not to the same extent as Mr Austin, commanded authority and was therefore in a powerful position of control over many aspects of Sean's daily life. For certain pupils he set up a different relationship, treats were given for not breaking rules. Several pupils were abused in parallel, but each pupil was not aware and believed himself to be alone in his experience, until rumours and suspicions began to establish themselves. In a similar manner to Mr Austin, Mr Lester, the head of care, used his position to command the respect of parents, but his methods of controlling the pupils he abused were tied up with their isolation and the secrecy of what was taking place. Sean only received elevated status when he was in Lester's house. When he was back in the school, there were no special favours or privileges and the reality of the abuse was denied by Mr Lester in his dealings with him.

SEAN: *Kids used to live there with him, but they were never there. I think he used to invite people over there to get away from the school and stuff, to sit down and watch telly and have a fag and stuff. Basically to relax and get away from everything ... you know it's all right here and all the rest of it ... He would tell me to do things, he had a few pornographic videos, there would be the two of us watching this video, that would turn me on. He used to talk about it and take it from there. I knew why he would tell me to go to his bed. He was like the head of the household sort of thing, he would just tell the other members of staff whatever and that was it.*

There are parallels with Justin's experience, in that Sean knew that Mr Lester had substantial control over his day-to-day life, and he lived with the thought that he could be sexually abused again at any time. Mr Lester had the authority to interrupt lessons, change sleeping arrangements, cancel weekends home, and so on. Whenever possible, Sean would resist being abused by hiding, after being told to go to the house.

> **SEAN:** *He used to just ask if I wanted to go over, or tell me that I was going over. I used to get nervous and try to get out of it somehow, but that didn't always used to work. I think most of the time I used to go and hide somewhere and hopefully he would forget about it and that was it ... I just wanted to keep it to myself. A really bad memory that I wanted to keep to myself, I was just pleased when it was all over. ... I didn't know when it was going to happen next. I was nervous all the time.*

Liam was abused by a young teacher, who was very popular and able to relate to some of the older pupils 'on their level'. Liam explained that every year there was a pupil who became the teacher's favourite, a 'golden boy'. Through this he was afforded an unofficial 'head boy' status, which appeared to have some recognition among other pupils.

> **LIAM:** *He used to help me with my maths and anything else really. He'd just be there for me if I needed him. ... There was a lot of us used to go up to his flat at night. Have a beer and have a laugh sort of thing. One night everybody else had gone and he was going on about a massage or something, and I thought, yeah, cool, go for it, massage, you know, sounds good to me and of course one thing led to another you know, and I was a bit confused about it all really. Er, it felt good sort of thing. ... It was comfortable. ... It's the sort of something that you don't want to get out, 'cos then you get labelled as being a queer.*

Again this shows contrasting circumstances of abuse. With Justin it was based on fear, which created a strong sense that the man abusing was beyond any form of reproach from anybody, having almost complete control over the boys' living environment. With Liam it was a situation of abuse where friendship and co-operation were betrayed through a process of creating a strong sense of mutuality, the experience of sexual pleasure, and a high level of reward and special attention. Both circumstances illustrate the extent to which child sexual abuse is highly organised by those who abuse.

Colin's circumstances were similar to Paul's, in that his home circumstances were extremely difficult, he had just left a long-term foster home, and had moved to a short-term placement, which he hated and had run away from. He was 13, lost, isolated, lonely, and depressed, and suddenly found himself in the company of a man who was being very friendly and buying him drinks and who had quickly learned that Colin could be tempted with an offer of cannabis. Like Paul, he was sexually abused on his first contact with the man, who had likely perceived Paul's isolation and depression as an opportunity for exploitation and abuse.

The man's power and attractiveness was exercised through his presentation as a streetwise adult. He was prepared to defy the law, both by buying him alcoholic drinks and by the pretence of being able to supply illegal drugs. Colin believed that he had found a man he could trust and tell his story to.

COLIN: *He was saying he had some draw and he could get some drugs and stuff. I think it was the whole situation really. He just stripped you of all the power over what was going on. It was a very fine-tuned form of manipulation. Just like getting into somebody else's head and saying that's what you want to do, you want to come back to my place and have a smoke, and then you know, you just don't see anything wrong with him. . . . Looking back at it, I was that manipulated that I don't think I could have walked out. For a start I didn't know where I was. I didn't know where he was or how far he'd gone. I didn't know what would happen if he saw me leaving the house. I didn't want to risk getting done over or anything. It just seemed that the only option was to stay put.*

Once Colin was at the man's home and beginning to be aware that he was in danger, his immediate situational resistance was weakened by his being given alcohol. From that point onward he had to cope with being in a state of shock over what had happened to him. His resistance was finally broken down by a show of physical force.

COLIN: *I was sitting on the sofa, I'd had Bacardi and Coke. I was pretty gone by that time and then I don't know, my instincts said there's something wrong here, and then I got pounced on. Literally like, he just came over and started trying to take my jeans off. The fact that he could out-power me so easily, that was pretty terrifying in itself really . . . he could just move me round like a rag doll . . . my life was at risk . . . I would grab him, he would just move my hand, push me off, crush my hand or whatever. . . . Before I knew what was going on, my jeans were half off . . . it was like being trapped, I didn't have any way of getting out . . . I didn't know whether I was going to get out of it alive or not, didn't know what was going to happen.*

After Colin had told about his abuse, some of his peers became aware of what had happened to him and began to use the information against him. This was particularly true of a young adult female who Colin met within a month of his being abused. In trying to come to terms with his experience of being sexually abused by a male and being afraid of rumours that had circulated about his sexuality, Colin thought that the best solution was to have a sexual experience with a female and let everybody know this was happening.

> **COLIN:** ... *I had something to prove, I just wanted to prove to myself that I was normal, and I just wanted to prove that I was straight. ... She did quite a bit of flirting. ... She just showed a general interest in me, I suppose, she made hints. ... Well, at the time it felt pretty good, you know, it was like I'm okay, I'm normal, fine, that's really good. Initially, my fears disappeared for a couple of days, and then they started coming back again and I wasn't sure why. I think it was to do with the fact that she would go with anyone, it wasn't really an accomplishment. ... It was just like I didn't understand sex at all. I didn't understand anything about it. I knew what to do, but I didn't understand any of the emotional side of it, and why people do it basically. So to me it was just a meaningless act ... it was another situation where I was being completely controlled, I didn't have any say in whatever. I suppose initially I had some control, 'cos like I was in it for my own gains. So at the time I thought it was a good idea. I'm in it for what I can get out of it. That's where it ends. But she took it further than that, she just turned the tables and pinned me.*

Looking back Colin sees the relationship as 'another form' of sexual abuse. At the time it was more difficult to see. At the initial stages, he was happy to have and be seen to have a relationship with a female. Thinking now about the violence he experienced leads Colin into seeing this relationship as being abusive.

> **COLIN:** ... *I mean like being pinned down and doing exactly the same things I told her I didn't like. That was just blatant abuse. Sleeping with somebody the age of 13, that was pretty sick, when you're 18 anyway, that's another form of sexual abuse. Emotional abuse, big time, 'cos like she was always after reactions, always going out to hurt people. It was just a completely abusive relationship.*

These accounts highlight the level of fear, shame and confusion the young men experienced, as they were manipulated and forced into being sexually abused. They illustrate the extent to which the young men took on a level of responsibility for what had happened, despite the impossibility of escape or avoidance and the level of threats and violence, entwined with treats, rewards, and special attention.

RELATIONSHIPS PURPOSEFULLY CONSTRUCTED BY THE ABUSER

The nature of the relationship that had been purposefully constructed by the abusers with the young men (as children) was central to the abuse and had a significant bearing on telling. Several of the young men explained that they were made to feel as if there was some form of trade-off or transaction associated with the abuse. This in itself would create a sense of equality and fairness in the exchange. In reality it was a further manipulation and abuse of adult power and a further means of silencing the young men. Something would either be given or happen that would make their immediate circumstances better. This usually involved distorting and abusing the dependency of the young men, most of whom, as we have discussed, had very difficult life circumstances. Justin, Sean, and Liam were away from home at boarding school. Justin's parents had divorced. Liam's father had died. Paul had been severely physically abused at home. Colin's long-term foster placement had broken down and he had run away from his new placement, in a very distressed and depressed state.

Justin had the hope of improved privileges and status within the school and protection from some very violent older pupils. Liam received emotional support and counselling. He was coming to terms with the death of his father. He also had the privilege of staying up late in a teacher's flat, evading the normal school curfew rules. The same was true for Sean, who also received free cigarettes. Paul had the privilege of short periods of time away from a very violent stepfather and the opportunity of spending time with an adult who wasn't going to physically beat him.

Notions of having taken part in a trade-off fed into some of the young men's concerns that they had responsibility for what had happened and that they had co-operated with the sexual abuse and enjoyed the benefits of the exchange. Colin was handed £20, which caused him to believe that he 'prostituted' himself. Justin constantly questions himself about why he walked down the corridors to the sleeping-in room seemingly of his own volition. It was only several years later that Liam was able to see his experience as involving aspects of sexual abuse and report what had happened to the police. His discussion shows evidence of the struggle he had in seeing that he was exploited. Ryan and David remain confused about their relationship with Harry, although they are both clear that they believe they have been sexually abused and that they do not wish to meet him again. The relationship with the abuser for Paul, Colin, and Justin alternated between friendliness and severe threats of physical violence. This would set the limits, as if to say whatever happens at the end of the day there is no way out for you. The accounts reveal how skilfully the adults used their intimate knowledge of the young men and how skilfully they deployed power in ways to make the young men feel they had co-operated, even alongside extreme threats of harm.

> **DAVID:** *I enjoyed the hugs and every thing. They were all right and the trips. I didn't want those to stop, but I didn't want anyone to know. I've still got memories of the abuse in my head.*

> **JUSTIN:** *Sometimes he was the nicest guy you could ever know. Seriously like, it's a horrible thing for me to actually say like, but sometimes he was really nice, but that's just a cover to get his own way ... that really hurts to say that, but you can't help but say that, 'cos sometimes he was really nice. I mean you used to go out to the mad swimming pools. You know, you used to get the best of everything. ... Sometimes his discipline would be out the kindness of his own heart.*

In spite of all the harm and suffering Mr Austin inflicted on Justin throughout his years at the boarding school, Justin, although very clear about how he feels about being abused, has managed to maintain a level of compassion toward him. He also remains generally positive about his other experiences at the school.

> **JUSTIN:** *I don't know what to think of the geezer. I hate him now, but you just don't know what to think. What was going through his mind, why was he doing it. I mean I always thought he was a sick, perverted bastard, which he was, but there's times when I think well he might have just had something wrong with him or he might have been doing it for just to show us that's the only way he can show how he feels. ... I'd like to go back and see the school, I mean most people wouldn't want to go back to a place where those shit things happened to them, but I've had a lot of really good things happen to me there as well. It gave me my education and everything. The only thing I didn't like was being abused there. I hate him, but in another way I've got some respect for him. ... It's hard to say he was a right, right bastard really, because he wasn't always a right, right bastard.*

Liam had difficulty in disentangling strands of neediness, help, exploitation, and abuse. As he mused over the course of events, he began to doubt the complete voluntarism of his involvement in what he often referred to as a relationship. There are many contradictions in the way in which Liam rationalises his experiences. These statements were made before he made his decision to report the experiences to the police as incidents of child sexual abuse. His comments embrace a wide range of considerations, including comments about the teacher's young age and similarities of interest. He describes a strong sense of having enjoyed the experience and of having gained considerably. Gradually, Liam reached the viewpoint that he had been sexually abused and that this had happened to other boys previously.

> **LIAM:** *I'd talk to him about this and have a few tears, you know, and like he'd just cuddle me and not try anything on. If he was truly exploiting me he'd be only after the one thing. But he'd give me a cuddle and that was it. We were very, very close and that was really comfortable. . . . I've tried to put myself in his shoes, and from his shoes it would be exploitation really, you know, there's not another word for it, but the way he went about it, it just didn't feel like I was exploited at all. . . . I needed someone to talk to, I needed someone to be there for me, you know, and I needed someone to be close to. . . . I mean maybe he exploited me for his own reasons, but on the same level he was so understanding and cool about everything that it didn't enter into my mind about being exploited.*

For Paul, the relationship set up by the man who abused him, although charac-terised by threats and fear, was experienced as positive by comparison with the relationship he had with his violent stepfather Raith. There was almost a sense of loyalty toward the man who sexually abused him, simply because of the fact that, unlike Raith, he never actually hit him. This highlights the extremities of Paul's childhood and how abusers use and exploit children's perceived vulnerability and neediness.

> **PAUL:** *. . . sometimes he wasn't gentle, sometimes he was, you know. It almost sounds as if I like him, but sometimes he was quite aggressive and sometimes he hurt. . . . I liked him for his friendliness because other than the times when he turned nasty, which he did when he threatened me with a knife, which he did a few times. . . . After he'd finished his sessions of abuse he used to be kind. I would probably say, it makes me feel sick to say it, I would probably say, yeah, at times I would say that I did like him, because he would, besides what he was doing, he was being nice. You knew what he was doing was wrong. I knew that in the back of my mind, and in the back of my mind I always wanted to tell somebody.*

Ryan, in describing his feelings about Harry, the man who sexually abused him, seems to have a view that there is a certain way in which he should feel about him: very angry. He had a view that he hadn't taken 'an active part' in the abuse and was therefore not responsible. He was 12 at the time he was sexually abused. There is an incongruity between the experiences being described and the feelings associated with them. There were large parts of Ryan's experiences that he couldn't remember. This may indicate a level of dissociation (see Chapter 2) that may have become functional to Ryan's survival. Ryan described that there were times in his present life where he exercised what he described as 'memory blocks', when he felt distressed or under some form of threat. Chapter 11 will show how Ryan was able to get in touch with some of his powerful feelings through poetry. The contradictions in the following statement indicate a level of confusion, alongside an understanding that what happened was, in retrospect, clearly manipulation and an abuse of power.

> **RYAN:** I don't really feel anything, I don't know why. I don't feel like angry or anything like that. I don't feel all right that it happened. If Harry sat down by me on the bus, I'd probably ram his head through the window. I'm not angry, I'd just think if he sat next to me he's just being cheeky. . . . I can play down what happened with Harry because it weren't really my fault, he was taking advantage of the situation and his power. I wasn't really an active part in it. If I had been an active part in it I probably wouldn't have said anything about it to anybody. It would have been partly my choice, and if it had been partly my choice, I wouldn't have felt I needed to say anything about it to anybody.

Sean identifies contradictions and confusion about the relationship that had been constructed by Mr Lester, a man who he initially experienced as supportive and helpful. His silence was maintained by being instilled with a sense of normality about what was happening. His belief in normality was linked to his sense of survival.

> **SEAN:** I got on with him at first, until I found what he was like. . . . I think it was all us used to think of him as Big Dad. If anybody had a problem, they'd go to him and he would sort it out sort of thing. . . . Basically, it was the very first time anything sexual happened to me and I thought this was it. This is what was to happen. . . . It felt the right sort of thing to do, it was all right. It was supposed to happen sort of thing. At the time I thought it was all right, I was only young and I thought it was the right sort of thing to do. Now I think oh, it was horrible.

With hindsight, Colin is clear about the process he went through. He is now clear that in most of what happened he was being trapped and manipulated. Even with this hindsight, he continues to have concerns as he still feels he could have walked out of the situation.

COLIN: ... *looking back at it now, it was just another way of trapping me really, manipulating me. 'Cos like he'd already shown me the physical strength. He'd already got inside my head, so he already had the power and control over me physically and mentally. So discussion was probably to put me at ease a bit more, a bit like saying, 'stay, yeah, I can talk to you a bit, don't try anything because I've already shown you what I can do.'*

CONCLUSIONS

This chapter has examined the power relationships between the young men and the adults, how the adults' power was derived, and how it was used to force or manipulate the young men (as boys) to co-operate with being sexually abused and subsequently cause them to feel blame and responsibility.

The study has shown that the subordination and powerlessness of the young men was not always complete or total, in that wherever possible the young men would attempt to employ strategies of resistance, finding circumstances where they could employ a level of personal power. Justin was aware that by co-operating with the sexual abuse, he would get it over with and for a short time be released from the painful uncertainty of not knowing when it was going to happen. He was also aware that it made other aspects of living at the school easier for him, in that he wouldn't be bullied by the older boys. In going into a neighbour's house, Paul was avoiding his stepfather. After Sean had been told to go over to Mr Lester's house, he would hide in the hope that the instructions would be forgotten. At other times the resistance was internal, through the manner in which the young men considered, interpreted, or tried to forget what was happening to them. Ryan was able to put the details and emotions of his experience out of his conscious mind, although he was always aware that he had been sexually abused. He was unsure about the extent to which he could control this blocking, if at all.

A common feature in all these circumstances is that the boys did not know the prior intentions of the adult who abused them and that this was worked to an advantage by the abuser. The adults knew them and used their intimate knowledge of them to their own advantage. Each adult was making contact with them with the express purpose of sexually abusing them, having either set up a situation that would make this possible, without getting caught, or having made a calculated assessment of the likelihood of the child being unable to tell, alongside instilling a sense of voluntarism and issuing or implying a threat that would ensure they would be afraid to tell. This inequality came about not just because of what the young men did not know but also because the adults knew about their lives and knew how to ensnare them into compliance and silence.

6

TRYING TO TELL

> **PAUL:** *I didn't want to tell anybody, because the way I felt about what happened, I thought that's what everybody must think, it's my fault.*

INTRODUCTION

This chapter analyses some of the comments the young men made about trying to tell about their sexual abuse. Telling about their sexual abuse meant that they had to face considerable anxieties. Some of this was about what the young men believed about themselves, and some of it was about people's reactions and being believed. The young men also had to weigh up the potential course of events that would follow their telling, what they would lose, and what they would gain. The use of the term 'disclosure' in socio-legal circumstances is criticised, in that it constructs the complicated process of telling into a single event. The study examines the complications of the circumstances the young men were in and considers the difficulties they had in attempting to tell. There were many factors that prevented the young men from feeling able to tell, not least feeling responsible for the abuse. Some of the young men feared the consequences of telling, both in terms of being blamed and being threatened not to tell. They also feared that telling might potentially lead to a disruption of social and family circumstances. In telling, some of the young men became involved in legal processes that were in most cases experienced as being extremely stressful.

DISCLOSURE

In professional and legal circumstances, when a child makes a statement about being sexually abused it is referred to as 'a disclosure' (DOH, 1991, 1992, 2002). This term is widely used in the literature and needs to be examined. Throughout this study, the use of language has been carefully considered. Language is not a passive conveyer of information, but actively constructs meaning. For example, the term 'abuse victim' essentially has a different meaning to 'person who has been abused'. In the former, the absence of 'person' defines the individual primarily in terms of having been abused and makes this the most significant part of them. The latter clearly states that the individual is a person who has had a particular experience. The use of 'person' leaves the individual open to being considered in a wide range factors and circumstances other than that he has been abused. They are essentially freed from their abuse, as opposed to being inextricably entangled with it. The latter creates a sense of freedom and conveys a belief and understanding of the person's ability to move onward and away from the abuse, developing diverse strategies of coping with and resisting perceived consequences of having been abused.

The use of the term 'disclosure' as a description of the event when a child reveals that he or she has been sexually abused is a simplification and distillation of a very complicated series of events. Disclosure conveys an assumption that telling about child sexual abuse can be a singular event that can be contained and captured in an hour, usually on videotape. This belief has become enshrined in policy, primarily through the *Memorandum of Good Practice* (DOH, 1992), which was recently superseded by *Achieving Best Evidence in Criminal Proceedings* (DOH, 2002). It is a professional and sanitised imposition on a diverse, complex, and painful process of events that have components of guilt, relief, anger, pain, all with related consequences. When a child tells that he or she has been sexually abused, the private is changed to the public and professional attention is drawn to intense personal conflict and turmoil. It is not a singular event, but an intersection of many factors: fear of consequences; fear of others' beliefs about the child as a result of him or her being abused; a sense of responsibility and voluntarism leading on to fears about sexuality; the ending of a period of isolation; embarrassment; shame; guilt; stigma; relief; release. It is potentially an iconoclastic experience with fundamentally far-reaching consequences, because it is bringing everything that is happening into the public gaze and laying it open for scrutiny.

The comments from the young men demonstrate that 'disclosure' has cataclysmic power, often based on a long history of self-doubt and anxiety that begins at the first instance of sexual abuse, and will often involve a series of attempts or considerations to tell and decisions not to tell. Socio-legal processes that construct 'disclosure' as an event, a single interview, potentially intensify the impact of the abusive experience. All seven of the young men found telling about being sexually abused difficult, having absolutely no control over the subsequent course of events.

CIRCUMSTANCES OF TELLING

The reasons for the young men not feeling able to tell, wondering whom to tell, or making the decision not to tell were varied, but interrelated. Some involved the young men having private feelings and fears about themselves and what people would think of them, linked to feelings of voluntarism and beliefs about being responsible for the abuse. Other reasons related to fears of reprisal from the person who had abused them and the potentially disruptive consequences, including involvement of the police, going to court, telling family members, the possibility of friends finding out.

For some of the young men, being sexually abused involved receiving treats and special attention that would be lost as a result of telling. For Sean, Justin, and

Liam, being abused by members of staff at their boarding schools meant that telling would entail a disruption of their education and possibly their removal from the school. Some of the young men had mixed feelings about the person who had abused them. The positive feelings they had toward their abusers fuelled their fears of voluntarism and feelings of sexual confusion and homophobia.

Justin reveals very clearly that the process of telling is complicated and involves many of the considerations that have been discussed. For Justin, telling would mean literally escaping from the school and preventing further abuse, which was ongoing with an increasing intensity. He had learnt that, in order to tell, he had to literally escape from the school. This brings to mind Herman's (1992) parallels of sexual abuse with the trauma experiences of people in concentration camps. Particularly when listening to Justin's stories of how he attempted to organise group escapes and his experiences of being caught and being returned to the school. He explained what happened when a group of them stole a car and managed to get away, and how Mr Austin's good reputation and positive relationships with the parents and his situational power eventually defeated them.

> **JUSTIN:** Oh, as soon as we got caught or got home we was actually going to tell the parents and go to the police ... all the way back all we did was tell them we'd been abused at the school. We had to make statements. Louis went back to the school, Alan went home with his parents. I had to get bailed out by my uncle and that. On the way back my mum and Joe managed to get, persuade me to change my statement and I got sent back to the school. ... Louis didn't get caught until he got home. He was the one that got away and then he didn't want to make a statement. ... Alan ended up coming back to the school. He was forced into retracting his statement by the parents, basically the same reason as me. They don't want all the hassle of the court case and that. Louis was weird anyway, he seemed to want it to happen to him. He tried it with me once. He was terrified of Henry.

Justin often tried to organise escapes, but he finally realised that he had to go on his own. Before he set out, a member of staff had told him to make sure he wore an extra jumper. The incongruity and distortion of the power relationships within the school continued from beginning to end. When he had first arrived at the school, he had been formally searched and threatened by another pupil; when he left, an adult member of staff had advised him about his health and safety before running away. Justin found it difficult to assess the relative power of some members of staff when set against the power of some of the older pupils, which was in reality power by proxy operated through them by Mr Austin.

> **JUSTIN:** ... I was trying to arrange a few of the kids to run off with me, but when it came to the crunch only two of us run off. It started with 20 of

> us. Then my mate backed out and went back to the school. I was in the town
> and I thought no way am I going back to the school. . . . I got a lift, just stuck
> my thumb out. I pleaded with him to take me home. I said, 'look, I've just
> run away from my boarding school, I've been sexually abused, you can take
> me to the police station if you want.' . . . I phoned up the school and spoke to
> K, he knew what was happening. I told him I was going, he gave me jumpers
> and clothes to run off with. He's a good man.

Sean has significantly less recall of the circumstances of his telling, but indicates that this may have been blocked out, rather than simply forgotten. As previously discussed in relation to Ryan, this may indicate a level of dissociation.

> **SEAN:** I only forget certain things. I can't remember anything about what
> happened after the abuse had happened, about the police coming and ques-
> tioning me and all the rest of it. All I can remember is them coming in and
> asking a few of us what happened. And, apart from that, I can't remember
> anything about it. I think that's through choice, that I chose not to remember
> anything about it. At the time it happened, I thought I was the only one it
> was happening to. It was only afterwards when the police had been that I
> was told that it had happened to several of the other boys, but at the time I
> thought I was the only one . . . teacher's pet.

Ryan remembers the day he told about his abuse as a traumatic process and indicates the build-up of events and circumstances before he finally made the decision to tell an adult that he had been sexually abused. He was emotionally and physically ill and had intended to run away. Colin also had similar feelings.

> **RYAN:** I don't know why I didn't tell anyone. I suppose I thought I was
> going to get into trouble, but I can't really remember that far back. It's all
> really, really blurred, but it was definitely a bad time. I remember the day I
> told my uncle, and I remember everything that happened that day and 'cos
> I'd been out all night the night before and I was in bed burning up with like
> kind of hypothermia-type thing. My uncle came up and he was speaking to
> me and I was crying and I told him. And he came down and told my mum
> and I came down and stuff and I had run away the night before and I was
> like suffering from exposure.

FEELINGS ABOUT TELLING

Paul has already explained how he had experienced the adult world as hostile. This was further compounded by his first real attempt to ask for help. From then on he was very cautious about what he told anybody.

> **PAUL:** *You knew that what he was doing was wrong. I knew that in the back of my mind, and in the back of my mind I always wanted to tell somebody. I told somebody once. I told a friend of Gail's mum, 'cos she saw me walking and asked me where I'd been and I said to her something like, 'That man in there he does things that are wrong. He does rude things.' And she looked at me and said, 'Don't be so silly, stop making up stories and go home.' And that was that, the first and last time I tried to tell anybody. ... Even when I was older and I knew adults would understand, at the back of my mind I thought well what happens if I tell the wrong adult. ... I never knew who the right or wrong adult was, so I never let it go ... and I got the impression that anybody I told was going to say, you know, that I was making it up, that I was lying and that I was looking for attention. ... It's been something that I've been carrying around for so long and that has caused me so much grief.*

Feeling responsible and being confused also had a significant bearing on Paul's decision not to tell anybody about being sexually abused.

> **PAUL:** *I've never talked to anybody, not in this detail. ... I didn't want to tell anybody, because the way I felt about what happened, I thought that's what everybody must think, it's my fault. It wasn't until I was about 15 or 16, when a few more of the pieces had been put together that I started to tell people about my past. I think that the thing that most people knew, all they ever really knew was the fact that I'd been beaten up as a kid and my life was rough. They didn't know any details, that's all I wanted them to know.*

Colin had a strong sense of having co-operated with being abused, as he believes he had an opportunity to get away and didn't take it. This was further compounded by the fact that he was confused about some aspects of physical pleasure he had experienced during the sexual abuse. Colin has explained how frightened he was, how he feared for his life, how he was throttled, and constantly physically overpowered by a strong man. This is incongruent with any sense of voluntarism, but does not prevent him from blaming himself.

> **COLIN:** *I can remember thinking I should have done that and I should have done this and I should have done that. Guilt and regret really. I should have tried harder to fight him off and I should have left him. Because it was my first sexual experience, for some unknown reason I automatically assumed that it would make me homosexual. That built up a lot of anxiety and self-questioning. . . . I thought that if anybody found out that it happened, that they'd automatically think that I was queer. So just letting people know was a big risk, but then like saying, 'oh, by the way, there was certain aspects of it that were quite enjoyable,' people would be, they'd build up a wall straight away.*

Colin's feelings of responsibility and shame were reinforced by a carefully timed payment, even though he received one final threat alongside.

> **COLIN:** *Well, he came in with 20 quid and I can't remember whether he gave me 20 quid before or after. But, anyway, he just went out and came back and said there's a taxi booked and you're going home and he stuck 20 quid in my hand. I think that was before he phoned the taxi, but, you know, that's just like the ultimate stab really. I just felt like a male prostitute then. I felt completely used and paid for services rendered, you know, it just made me feel really cheap. I can remember him saying, 'don't open your mouth, don't say anything.' . . . I think it was linked to the money, just another form of making sure I keep my mouth shut. It was just breaking down my confidence even more.*

Colin had intended not to tell anybody about what had happened, but had eventually found the whole situation too much to cope with. He was in a situation of torment, powerfully summed up as 'mental dirt'.

> **COLIN:** *I didn't have any intention of telling anybody really. I didn't want the 20 quid, I just wanted to get it over. I wanted to tell somebody, but I thought it was my fault. So that brought up a lot of anxieties about what people would think. Just basically what people would think of me. I was just paranoid about what I said to people, what they'd think. Just generally being annoyed or victimised ... I was just really overwhelmed and confused. I didn't know what was going on and I needed to tell somebody before I exploded because it was driving me mad and I couldn't think straight and like I was just feeling like shit all the time. I'd get in the bath and I'd scrub myself senseless, but it's more like mental dirt.*

Paul was also subjected to a confusing combination of severe threats against himself and his family, paralleled by what he experienced as expressions of concern and kindness.

> **PAUL:** *He went straight into his kitchen and slammed the door and he came out with a knife with probably about a four-inch blade on it. He walked up to me, pushed me against the wall hard and put the knife on my throat and he said, 'I don't care what you think. If you tell anybody about anything that happens in this house I'll come after you and I will kill you.' He said, 'I know who your family are and I will kill them as well.' ... And it frightened me so much I remember. I remember I was crying and he sat me down in the chair and he liked hugging me, calmed me down, but all the time you know ... you know he turned back to being nice again, but all the time he was trying to calm me down.*

FEAR OF THE CONSEQUENCES OF TELLING

The abuse regime to which Justin was subjected was extremely pervasive, incorporating almost every aspect of his daily life at the school. Telling meant entertaining many possible consequences, ranging from being beaten up by Mr Austin, or by other boys, not being believed, to losing an education and school that were in some ways enjoyed. The senior position of Mr Austin within the totality of the institution was an extreme manifestation of a particular type of power that closed off all avenues of telling. These circumstances show very clearly that telling is a complicated and frightening process, which even some members of staff were unable to break through.

> **JUSTIN:** *... see that he had over you 'cos of him being an ex-boxer like, he did have a few good moves with him like, he was hard to get to with a punch.*

On one occasion he was asked directly by a member of staff whether anything was happening to him. He was in the tantalising situation of having an opportunity to tell, but having to weigh up the relative power of this teacher compared with Mr Austin and some of the older pupils who were 'working' for him. He was aware that many other boys were in the same situation and of many other older boys who had over time become part of the abuse system. Justin was made aware that he would have to face the violence of these boys, should he consider making any attempt to tell or resist being sexually abused. In understanding how difficult it was for him to tell, it is important to remember that his abuse was ongoing and was having a severe impact on him.

> **JUSTIN:** ... *I don't think I was so much frightened as didn't want to go into the hassle of going to court at the time. ... I always did want to tell, but who could you tell that would believe you.*

At the time, Liam's sense of voluntarism was so great that he did not wish his abuse to be discovered. He describes an occasion where he actively covered up what had happened when Carl's brother discovered him and Carl in bed.

> **LIAM:** *I was asleep. Robert [that's his brother] came in, saw there was somebody else in his bed, lifted up the covers. I was pretending to be asleep. We had to blag that one through. 'Cos other people found out, I just said look I just fell asleep up there, sort of thing. We were having a chat and I fell asleep. I don't know how I blagged it. I just said to him, tell him that nothing happened. I just fell asleep in the room and you put me into the bed and nothing happened.*

Sean had made the decision himself that he didn't want to tell about being abused and that he envisaged that he would find talking about it very difficult.

> **SEAN:** *I just didn't want to talk to anyone, I just wanted to be left alone. ... I didn't really want to get involved if anything did happen, like he got caught or somebody told, grassed on him or anything. I didn't want to get involved with it ... all the pressure and hassle and being asked questions. I just wanted to be basically left alone and kept all to myself.*

TELLING FAMILY

Justin reached the point where he was too overwhelmed to think about telling anymore, especially as his previous attempts to tell had been thwarted. In the meantime, the abuse he was suffering continued to escalate beyond his endurance.

> **JUSTIN:** *I wanted to tell my mum. I just wanted to run off straight away. I felt dirty and everything like. I felt like that for ages afterwards, but then it just got worse and worse there.*

Paul's comments about not telling his foster carers highlight the importance of confidentiality. Professional carers need to be very clear with children and young people about how they manage confidentiality issues with family members, friends, and other professionals. This may potentially be in conflict with a particular family's lifestyle, but underlines the professionalism of good foster care. Paul's comments also highlight the importance of appropriate, male role-modelling in foster care and the need for the recruitment process to explore the potential impact of traditional stereotypes and what young people may believe is implied by particular aspects of adult behaviour.

> **PAUL:** *I never told my foster parents because I was afraid what Bill would think and I didn't think that Rita would understand. Also I didn't know who else they would tell, their friends and their family, they're not professional people. . . . I think if I had have told my foster mum I think she would have talked to me nice about it and stuff, but she wouldn't have understood. If I spoke to my foster dad, he would have talked about something else and just say I was stupid or leave the room. He comes from the men don't cry era. I was worried about him finding out I'd been abused because I thought he would have judged me. I was worried that he might maybe think that there was something not quite right about me, that I was unusual or queer. At first I was worried about anybody knowing, but especially someone like my foster dad. I knew he wouldn't understand. I often used to wonder what he would think about it. Sometimes I really wanted to ask him when I saw a story in the news paper, but to be honest I don't really think he used to take much notice of them.*

David found it hard to find an opportunity to talk to his mother about what was happening to him. He was also struggling with the fact that his mother had sent him to spend time with Harry.

> **DAVID:** *I tried to tell my mum, but it was hard. . . . I wanted to tell anyway, because I was getting bored of going. My mum usually had people round and knocks at the door and everything, so I found it difficult to tell her.*

Ryan felt a sense of relief when he told his family or, as he says, when he 'came out about it'. The next chapter will show how readily Ryan and some of the other young men make a link between telling about being sexually abused by a man and their feelings and anxieties about being gay.

> **RYAN:** *. . . I cried when I came out about it to my auntie's boyfriend. I cried to him when he was asking me about it. . . . I had no choice once I told my uncle. I'm glad because I was up and down a lot then. Before I told anyone I was like always locked away in my room and stuff. . . . Once it was all out in the open and stuff I started getting my head sorted out.*

TELLING FRIENDS

Justin kept his feelings to himself for quite some time and did not have any intention of discussing them with his friends. Eventually, he reached a point where his feelings overwhelmed him, and he had to start talking about his experiences.

> **JUSTIN:** *I couldn't stop thinking about it. I was having a nervous break-down. . . . I was just sitting outside a friend's house with my best mate . . . all of a sudden I burst into tears, shaking and trembling and everything just came out and that's when Sally took me under her wing. Paul went and got her. I think I'd only just moved into Sally's, living there a couple of days and that's when Sally knew everything that had happened to me . . . I was just in bits for days and days and days.*

In the context of an established and personal friendship, Paul eventually felt able to talk about being sexually abused in general terms; the experience for Sean was similar.

> **PAUL:** *. . . As I got older I got new friends. I had one friend, Graham, that I would talk to a lot and that used to help. We didn't just use to talk about my life and me, we talked about things in general . . . he was a very good mate. Besides Claire, he was probably the best friend I ever had . . . he was really the first person I told that I was sexually abused. He didn't know the details of my abuse. It just came out in conversation.*

It was several years before Sean began to talk to anybody about his abuse.

> **SEAN:** *I think the only person I talk to was the girlfriend I've just broke up with. I didn't exactly tell her, I just said there was a male member of staff at the school that was messing around with a few of the boys and I was one of them. I didn't exactly say what he did and how he did it. . . . If I have to talk about it, I just say that there was a few of us there that was being abused and that would be it then and leave it alone.*

EXPERIENCES OF POLICE INVOLVEMENT

From the outset, although Justin clearly wished the abuse to stop and for Mr Austin to face the consequences of his actions, he wanted to limit the extent of his involvement and did not wish to talk about everything that had happened. In this way he preserved some of his limited power and prevented further harm, which he fears he may have experienced as reabuse.

> **JUSTIN:** ... I told them I was only going to tell them about two incidents and they said well two incidents will be enough for what they want, so that's all I told them about. I'd have been there for ages if I'd have gone through the lot ... that would have really messed up my brain. 'Cos I don't like to think it happened to me as often as what it did.

Colin anticipated that he would have problems in dealing with the police by virtue of their authority.

> **COLIN:** I can't remember that much detail about the police interview, but I can remember feeling pretty terrified talking to the police, authoritarian figure and that. It was OK, it was a lot better than I thought it would be.

Colin and David both had medical examinations to find evidence of their abuse, the outcomes of which in both cases was inconclusive in terms of finding reliable forensic evidence. Colin has a vivid recall of his medical, which he considered to be another form of sexual abuse, and highlights the importance of legal and professional processes becoming more child-centred and less driven by evidence and legal considerations. Colin wanted his abuser to be caught and so consented to a police medical, in order to produce forensic evidence. He was, however, again in a position where he was subjected to a situation dominated by adult power, having little power and control himself over a high level of intrusion, breaching his bodily integrity. By having to undergo a medical examination, Colin had the subtle message that his words (his telling) were not sufficient, the evidence on his body counted for more that his words.

> **COLIN:** The check-up by the police surgeon—I think that in some ways that's just as bad as the abuse. It's demeaning. Like you have to strip off in front of this stranger, being a bloke as well, and then like you have some examination done. And it's not very pleasant having somebody look up your arse and it's very close to the experience and it just brings quite a few things back. Like while you're lying there it's just another totally helpless situation. I did it because if there was anything that could have nailed him I'd have done it. It wasn't very pleasant. I was pretty angry at the time, over- whelmed by memories about what had happened to me. Almost being back there again. I felt as if I was being abused again. It's just being in a position

where I felt I didn't have any power over what was going on. I just had to do as I was told.

GOING TO COURT AND OTHER LEGAL PROCEEDINGS

Justin and David had the experience of giving their evidence in court. Children's testimonies are extensively policed and distrusted within the legal system, which is often unfriendly toward children and young people (Spencer and Flin, 1990). Previous studies by me (Durham, 1993, 1997a, 2000) highlighted the amount of preparation children and young people require before having to face the ordeal of giving evidence in a criminal trial. In going to court the young men suddenly found themselves in a venue that was formal, male, and authoritative, characterised by a long history and powerful legal discourses. Upon arrival, they had to give a very clear and unambiguous public recount of their experiences of sexual abuse. They had to move from having to deal with the experiences through repression and dissociation to having to present a consistent and rational account. It is self-evident to say that this is likely to be frightening for a child or young person.

JUSTIN: *The first time I went up there like, it shit the life out of me, I was terrified, I didn't want to face him. It was horrible the first time in the first court, but when we went to court the second time, to the same hotel again, it just seemed a lot calmer. ... They made you feel welcome in the hotel. We were playing card games with the coppers. ... They gave us these yellow balls to rip under the thing in the court ... you could take it out on the ball, they did it on purpose. There was a pile of torn pieces from the other boys. Yellow sponge all around my feet. I tore up about six balls while I was giving evidence.*

When David went to court, he was subjected to a harsh cross-examination and accused of lying, which had a devastating impact on him for several years. He required considerable help in understanding the adversarial process in court— why an official or professional person accused him of lying.

DAVID: *Court was difficult, the solicitor said that I might have been lying. I was scared, and I was worried that they wouldn't believe me. ... It was a weight off my shoulders.*

In going to court, there are high costs at stake; for Justin, the stress involved was a price he was prepared to pay to have his experiences validated. For David, once the ordeal was over, he experienced a level of relief. Sean made the judgement that going to court was a price too high to pay.

> **SEAN:** *Well, thinking about it, I don't think I could have done that [gone to court], all those people watching me, talking about it, I couldn't talk about it in a room full of people.*

Justin applied for compensation and had to attend two appeal hearings before receiving his compensation. Some of the material from the research interviews was presented by mye at the second hearing in support of Justin's claim. (Material from the research interviews of Ryan and David was also used to inform their written applications. Both were happy to report to me that they had been awarded sums of money.) The first hearing had been very difficult, the panel members were unable to appreciate the extent to which sexual abuse had disrupted Justin's life and would not accept that there was any connection between some criminal offences he had committed and being abused. Justin felt that he was on trial, that the experience was worse than going to court, and that he was 'punished in questions'. The second panel were entirely understanding and Justin had a very different experience. He has a vivid recall of these events.

> **JUSTIN:** *The first one [Compensation Appeal Hearing] was terrible ... Well, I just steamed out of that 'cos they turned round and said I weren't gonna get it because of my record. I just burst into tears and walked. ... I was really upset and I was sick on the way home ... it's just all blocked out 'cos that was a really bad day. That day really hurt me I think ... I was punished in questions, punishing questions. It felt like I'd just been put through the mill. My nerves and everything, I was just gone, pins and needles from head to toe. ... It's just the way they were, their attitude ... like it was my fault. ... They were different on the second time, they had two different men and the same woman there. ... I thought I handled the second one very well.*

When Justin finally received his payment of compensation, he had very mixed feelings about having the money and the fact that it had not come directly from the man who had abused him. Recently, another young man who had been sexually abused told me that he wasn't sure whether or not he wished to apply for compensation, as he thought it would be like payment for services rendered. Justin's comments echo a similar sentiment. Since his abuse, Justin has been virtually unable to hold down any employment and is therefore receiving state benefit. His receipt of over £12 000 compensation led to his benefit being stopped.

JUSTIN: *I was happy I got that much money . . . but it only made me happy for a little while, not too long. The money started doing my head in after a while of having it. . . . It was good getting that much, but it would have been better if it had come out of his own pocket. . . . If it had been his money, I'd have probably had more pleasure out of spending it . . . the only thing that made me feel good was when they put him down, the day they put him in jail. That's the only time I've ever felt any pleasure out of it.*

CONCLUSIONS

The last section has considered the professional and legal use of the term 'disclosure', which constructs the child's telling as an event. This has been contrasted with the complex reality of the circumstances of the young men. Telling, trying to tell, or deciding not to tell is not an event, but a process that begins alongside the abuse. It is inextricably bound up with the messages the child receives from the adult during the abuse itself. For the child or young person, the decision whether or not to tell involves the weighing up of many considerations and possible consequences. Telling inevitably involves an initial loss of control, which may replicate the abuse. There is no certainty of a desired outcome, and there is often the belief that telling will result in being blamed.

Justin has explained how many of his attempts to tell were thwarted and that there were severe consequences of being caught in the process of trying to tell. For Liam, telling was only a consideration several years later, when he was able to reflect upon his feelings and experiences with a degree of perspective. He was so convinced and persuaded, through a process of manipulation by the abuser, that he was 'comfortable' with what was happening to him. Sean simply did not wish to have to deal with the likely consequences of telling and was simply prepared to wait and persevere with being abused, as he knew he was soon to leave the school. Paul did not speak about being sexually abused until many years later. He had no idea whom to tell. As the years rolled by he became more and more ashamed about himself and deeply believed that telling would have to involve confronting and accepting the shame he felt. Colin felt that he was responsible, partly because he had been given money and partly because he feels he could have escaped, but at the same time he has described how he was threatened and physically throttled. Colin's feelings and anxieties sometimes override his memories of how frightened he was at the time. The young men were not able to see that their fears and anxieties about telling were central to the manipulative relationship that had been set up by the abuser, with the express purpose of silencing them.

The young men's involvement in socio-legal processes has, by disempowering them, in some ways replicated or resonated with the abuse they had initially reported. Colin has discussed vivid memories of his medical examination, which he considers to be in some ways as bad as the abuse. Justin explained that he found the first compensation hearing to have been more stressful than when he gave evidence in court, which he had already described as stressful, although he recognised that measures were taken to help him through the experience. David had bad memories of being accused of lying. These comments show that the young men experienced their involvement in socio-legal processes as being unhelpful, adding to the problems they were already having to cope with and carrying little recognition or acknowledgement of the struggle they were experiencing.

7

SEXUALITY, FRIENDSHIPS, AND PEER RELATIONS

LIAM: *You know, it's acting the homophobic sort of thing. Society dictates that that's the way you should be at my age.*

INTRODUCTION

Before further considering the young men's experiences in relation to their friendships and sexuality, it is necessary to have an understanding of the particular importance of sexuality during adolescence. Figure 1.1 identified sexuality and desire being constructed through the interaction of a variety of factors: social, biological, historical power relations, and gender practices. It was established that gender and sexuality have significant influences on interpersonal relationships, particularly in terms of equality and the balance of power. In this sense, sexuality becomes a significant form of disciplinary power, constructing and impacting on a range of cultural, social, and economic practices and relations. Images of sexuality shape and are shaped by the culture and social context in which they are situated. This study shows that sexuality becomes a particularly potent force in a society where particular types of sexuality are oppressively and extensively policed. This makes sexuality an important site of social interrogation. Foucault in discussing sexuality states that:

> It appears rather as an especially dense transfer point for relations of power: between men and women, young people and old people, parents and offspring, teachers and students, priests and laity, an administration and a population. Sexuality is not the most intractable element in power relations, but rather one of those endowed with the greatest instrumentality; useful for the greatest number of manoeuvres and capable of serving as a point of support, as a linchpin, for the most varied strategies. (Foucault, 1976, p. 103)

Sexuality and sexual identity are particularly important during adolescence, when, following puberty, for most people there is an increase in sexual drives and sexual awareness (Moore and Rosenthal, 1993). The sexual experiences of teenagers are shaped by their social context. For many, peer group experiences are particularly significant and overtake family influences. In reviewing a range of studies, Moore and Rosenthal (1993) argue that teenagers sometimes learn inappropriate values and engage in unwanted sexual behaviours before they are ready. They may acquire many myths about sexual behaviour; for example, overestimating the sexual experiences of their peers. This study shows that young people become acutely aware of the power of the social policing of sexual desires and the drive toward compulsory heterosexism and homophobia (Nayak and Kehily, 1997). Adolescence is a time when patriarchy takes residence in the body.

FEARS ABOUT SEXUALITY

All the young men in this study expressed concerns about their sexuality, with reference to having been sexually abused by a male. Many of these concerns were expressed in terms of being discovered by their peers and being considered to be gay as a result of the experience. These concerns appeared to interact and compound private feelings, fears, and beliefs resulting from the conflation of same-sex child sexual abuse and gay sexual preference and were exacerbated by feelings of responsibility and concerns about the experience of physical pleasure, or of having a relationship with the abuser that was experienced as being to some degree positive.

These concerns appeared to be intensified by 'traditional' heterosexist beliefs about behaviours and experiences deemed not to be masculine and a peer culture of homophobia. It has been established above that there are potentially difficulties and myths to contend with on a large scale for any boy growing up in Western society. The conflicting and contradictory messages create a potential for all boys to experience sexual confusion in one form or another. Chapter 2 concluded that, for the sexually abused boy, the belief in the socially perpetuated myth that for everybody else the development of sexuality is a straightforward process is perhaps the one that does the most damage.

Believing and reacting to myths, wrong information, and misunderstandings can be particularly stressful for any adolescents who are trying to come to terms with and develop understandings of their sexuality. Bremner and Hillin refer extensively to the process of 'internalised oppression' (1993, p. 27). They define oppression as systematic mistreatment and misinformation, and discuss how such information is reinforced by a variety of social interactions. Eventually, it becomes internalised, believed, and acted upon against the self and others in a manner that reinforces and perpetuates the misinformation.

Internalised oppression subordinates the individual to wider dominant beliefs and understandings that eventually become deemed to be the right understandings. This can result in a process of self-discipline and repression. This is consistent with Foucault's use of the 'metaphorical panopticon' and 'confessional'; the belief in the permanent gaze and scrutiny of others and the need to explain oneself in terms of justification, based on the scrutiny of others—in most cases the scrutiny of peers. Beliefs and scrutiny become internalised, and often believed and incorporated into behaviours and attitudes. The particular context of internalised oppression referred to in this study is compulsory heterosexism (the oppressive view that the only or at least the most valid sexuality is heterosexual) and homophobia. Heterosexual behaviour is prescribed and gay or lesbian behaviour (including bisexuality) is proscribed.

Many of the comments below demonstrate the particularly compulsory nature of heterosexism during adolescence and the need to actively demonstrate a perceived heterosexual identity. For the young men in this research study, this is urged on by beliefs that conflate child sexual abuse with gay sexuality. Porter's (1986) work showed that such beliefs can be confirmed by the heterosexual identity of the abuser and can cause a boy to believe that it was his gay sexuality that led to him being sexually abused. For such a boy (and, indeed, as will be seen, for most of the young men in this study), the internalised oppression of compulsory heterosexism and homophobia takes a particularly strong and deep root. This can lead to a range of anxieties that result in such fears not being talked about, rendering the young person unavailable for therapeutic assistance and accurate information. From this research it would appear that compulsory heterosexism and homophobia are central to the discourse of male-child sexual abuse.

Some of these processes can be seen from comments made by Liam, who approaches his concerns with a clear distinction between what he privately believes and feels and how he wishes to be seen by his peers. He also states very clearly how his peer culture dictates how he should be and how he should behave and that there are social costs for non-conformity. While he does not accept the norms privately, publicly he feels he has to openly conform, particularly in view of his experiences of sexual abuse, the discovery of which he believes would constitute proof that he does not conform to the norm. As a survival strategy, Liam explains how he would often resort to 'acting the homophobic', and he is very clear by his description in his understanding of what this means and why it is necessary to behave in such a manner.

LIAM: *I'm surprised I'm not homophobic after this lot, I should be. . . . Well, you know, you'd think like after the experience you'd think: Oh, I don't want that to happen again, it's never going to happen again and like you know he was queer and he tried it on and all that, so I wonder whether or not I should be homophobic. You know, given the norm, most blokes are homophobic. Like you know, say, 'Oh, you're queer, better sit down, or stand against a wall.' . . . I mean being a young bloke and all that, shagging the women and everything, that's what I'm supposed to be doing. I mean I've just had a slander situation, being called gay, and I've just laughed it off. I said, 'Yeah, I'm queer, great you know, I'm shagging a bird, course I'm queer.' You know, it's acting the homophobic sort of thing. Society dictates that that's the way you should be at my age. If you're a bloke, if you're a lad, going out for a beer. . . . Inside I would like people to know the way that*

I really feel, but it's just not acceptable, so I just keep my mouth shut. There's very few people that I've told: you, Tanya and Cindy. ... I don't feel at all that what I want is a bloke. I don't want a sexual relationship with a bloke, I don't want that, I don't see the point in it. I mean I enjoy sex with women. The closeness of a bloke would be an important thing to me, being really close to somebody. Really, really, really close, but without the sexual part. Like there's a fine line I know. I know there's a fine line between it, but, er, if I was really, really close to a bloke, it would be on the verge of like, you know, me being queer, if you know what I mean, getting called queer sort of thing because like I'd like to get so close to a male because I don't know whether it's something to do with my dad subconsciously. I don't know, but on the other hand I only want to go and shag women, I'm afraid that's my only interest you know, with the women. ... If somebody tried to label me as a queer I'd defend myself right to the hilt, even though I've had a relationship with a bloke. I'd still say who do you think you're talking to sort of thing. I mean I've thought about it, am I gay, am I gay? I've sat down and thought to myself am I queer, am I gay, and I thought: No, I'm not queer, I'm not gay, but you know, am I bisexual. I don't feel bisexual, I don't have feelings for blokes. I've experimented with that situation, I mean I denied it for a long time, but I just thought, you know, what's the point of telling people about it, where does that get me. It doesn't get me anywhere talking about it. I've done it, I know I've done it and everything and like, you know.

This lengthy comment from Liam illustrates how he has to engage in processes of repression. He is aware that some of his feelings inside would not be socially acceptable and would damage his perceived heterosexual reputation. Liam believes that, even though he has such feelings, expressing emotional feelings toward males would not be consistent with being seen as masculine and to some extent does not fit in with his own beliefs and definition about what being masculine entails. To express such feelings and beliefs would result in subordination through a damaged reputation among his male peers; indicative of a male hierarchy. Liam is acutely aware that expressing emotional or sexual feelings toward a male would be completely out of the question. Ryan was aware of some of these issues and indicates that he feels he is able to take an open-minded perspective, but when it comes to relationships among peers, he indicates a similar awareness to Liam of the internal and external conflicts involved. His comments demonstrate a considerable level of insight, in being able to rise above the pressures of his peer culture.

RYAN: *Well, no-one's sure, are they? ... I'm definitely not, because I've tried it. I don't regret trying it, I just know that at this particular moment in*

> *time I'm not homosexual. . . . Like the most macho acting male. A lot of the time people who are really acting macho and hard and sleeping with all these girls and that are trying to deny something. Deny being attracted to lads. So I mean no-one's sure about anybody and no-one's sure about themselves until they try it. It's just like drugs and alcohol. No-one's sure about what effects it's going to have on them. No-one's sure if they're gonna like them and that, until they do it.*

Paul had developed a sensitive antenna to how he was perceived by his peers and would often consider situations from conflicting perspectives, in order to be sure that he was seen as 'doing something right', his motivation was a consistent belief that having been sexually abused by a male meant that he was gay. His experiences are almost totally referenced toward his peers and his status among them.

> **PAUL:** *I think females were more important because I thought if I hung around with lads I always thought people would be able to tell what happened and would think: well, you know, he's a bit queer. Whereas if I was with females people would think: hey, Paul gets on with the girls, can't be anything wrong with him . . . you know, Paul gets on with all the girls, he must be doing something right. . . . I would have been so scared of being labelled as being gay and, you know, because other kids and sometimes other adults they don't see the fact that it was forced on you. You know they have such a narrow view they can't see that it's forced on kids. Kids don't go along with it willingly.*

Paul had his private doubts and fears about his sexuality and lived in fear of this being discovered by his peers. From his comments and in the same respect from the comments we have already heard from Liam, some of the normal trials and tribulations of teenage peer group interaction, in the context of learning to express and develop sexuality, are considerably sharpened by the experience of child sexual abuse.

> **PAUL:** *It was an image I felt I had to have, 'cos otherwise people would be able to tell. It's like the fact that after you did games you had to go and have a shower. I would wear my trunks in the shower, because I thought if anybody saw my genitals, they would be able to tell that another man had touched me. . . . You know, all they had to do was just look at me and the way I acted and they would be able to say, you know, he's queer, there's something wrong with him.*

Paul's concerns only related to the masculine culture among his male peers and men. He did not experience the same level of threat from females and felt he could be more true to himself. He was able to find a male peer whom he could talk to and found the research relationship with me to be a safe situation in which to express his feelings. Justin also had considerable fears about how he was perceived by his peers.

> **JUSTIN:** *All of my friends are really wary when they know I've been abused. I don't care, I don't mind. I'll talk about it anywhere. They think you're gay or you're gonna do something to them. . . . I don't mind people knowing, but I'm worried about what they're going to say, what they're going to think afterwards like, when I've left the room. While I'm there, to my face they'll be nice, but it's what they say afterwards to other people and things like that. Oh he's a queer, he's bent, he's this, he's that, he's the other like, just because I've been abused.*

Ryan also had anxieties about peers discovering his abuse and described telling of his abuse as when he 'came out about it'. He sees this as a positive process.

> **RYAN:** *Stuff used to remind me of it, but that was like straight after I told people and came out about it. Just a lot of the time before I came out about it I used to get problems like that but, erm, what triggered it off was silly things, I don't know, stupid things like kids would just be kidding and insulting each other and saying 'bender' and stuff like that. That would make it come back. . . . I used to get anxiety all the time, anxiety attacks. I'd get paranoid about people finding out and stuff like that.*

David also expressed a concern that being called names at school was influencing the way he interpreted what had happened to him and why.

> **DAVID:** *Being called gay, it used to upset me and make me think that I was, because of the abuse. I worried about it for quite a long time. Sometimes I was frightened to go to school.*

Colin was afraid of people's perceptions of his sexuality that were compounded by significant private fears and beliefs. The repressive processes of internalised oppression disrupted one of his closest and most reliable friendships, causing him to become further isolated and estranged from a potential source of support.

COLIN: *Like with Nigel, we were really close at school. Whenever there was any hassle for each other, we'd always be there. We were more like brothers than anything else. During school time it wasn't a problem, we were just very close friends, but after the abuse I got really paranoid emotions and fears that it might just go a bit further than that, so I avoided him. We seem to have drifted away since we left school. It's really weird, 'cos he still gives me a hug when I go to his place, there's still quite a strong bond there. That sometimes gets me a bit paranoid, even now, but not half as much as it did. It still does now and again. . . . I don't see anything wrong with it, I don't see it as homosexual, it's just a paranoia.*

Colin found his peer group particularly threatening and only maintained a small circle of close friends. There were occasions when his anxieties would lead him into difficult situations, because of the assumptions he was making about the people he came across, and he often found the world to be a hostile place. He would often find himself behaving in a homophobic manner in situations that raised fears about his own sexuality, and which he constantly relates back to his experience of being sexually abused. The way Colin believed that others perceived child sexual abuse interacted with his private fears and anxieties. He would often privately scrutinise himself in a desperate search for meaning and understanding.

COLIN: *There's still some thoughts going through my mind about sexuality, especially related to anything sexual. Like do I really like females in a sexual way. That comes into my head, that's a major one. I still think it boils down to the fact that the 'four days' [the period when he was abused] was the first sexual experience I had, and I still carry some anxieties about that money, and even though they are not as strong as they were, you know, when something goes wrong they come back again, and then sort of, well, I don't know, I convince myself that what I was thinking was right and it's back to square one again. Like I'm thinking about what happened and I go through all the old stuff, like I could have done this and I could have done that and I could have left, and then I'll have a few beers to get it away and the next day I think about it and I'll be able to sort it out in my own mind, you know, go through all the 'well, it wasn't my fault because of this, that, and the other.'*

Colin was very concerned about his perceived image and, as has already been explained in Chapter 5, how at the age of 13 he became embroiled in a sexual relationship with an 18-year-old female. Although the relationship was very destructive in many ways, Colin felt it was necessary to continue with the relationship for the sake of his image among his peers. He felt that he was getting persecuted *because* 'word got around'. This was also an attempt to help himself come to terms with his own private concerns of having experienced physical pleasure when he was abused by a male.

> **COLIN:** *One kid found out and was calling me queer. So, yes, I don't know whether word about the abuse had got around or not. So, having a female by your side, you can't be queer can you, you can be bi-, but you can't be queer. And the next step was to have a kid with her. ... I did want to because, you know, even after Robert ... it wasn't the baby, it was just what a baby stands for ... producing a baby is what males are for ... so, you know. I didn't really see myself as a full male until I had a kid ... it was a mirage ... wishful thinking, like it didn't change anything. Trying to prove to myself, proving to everybody outside and inside. Saying to the world, 'I'm not queer because I've got a kid' and the same to myself. But, no, it doesn't work.*

Paul's experiences were similar in that he would often question his feelings and memories about being abused and consider his own sexuality. He strictly maintained what he considered to be an appropriate 'normal' social image, in order to detract any attention away from his private fears. Paul also believed he could sort himself out by engaging in a heterosexual experience. Both Paul and Colin found it necessary to use relationships with women to bolster their masculine identity, and both were disappointed and ended up with further and more complex difficulties.

> **PAUL:** *There were times when I thought about it and I thought I don't feel sick, I don't feel ill about this. Am I gay, you know, did I enjoy it? I mean, you know, I didn't enjoy it and, you know, 'cos I enjoyed the kindness of it and I did worry about that I would become homosexual. I didn't know about homosexuality then. I didn't know that it was something that you either are or you're not. I thought it was something that people made you. ... I had to stay on top of the situation, and if I got so much as the wrong sort of look from somebody I'd have to rush out and do something about it, like go and run up to a girl and give her a hug or something like that to say, 'I'm normal' ... I didn't want to have sex, but these fears were still with me about being homosexual. I didn't want to have sex, but I felt I had to. Almost driven to it to prove that I am not, you know, to prove that I am heterosexual.*

Justin went through a similar struggle, the experience of child sexual abuse had an impact on his self-confidence and his interest in sexual relationships, but this often brings him back to being confused about whether or not he is gay, or whether other people see him as being gay. When he considers the possibility of having a gay sexual relationship himself, he immediately remembers being abused, particularly when considering the safety of his own children. He associates risk with gay sexuality.

> **JUSTIN:** *It's always there in the back of my head. Am I gonna turn out, you know. One day I am, 'cos there are days when I don't feel like I'm interested in women or nothing like, you know I'm not interested in nothing basically. Then I sometimes prefer the company of other blokes, but not in that way. Just to be around to talk to and things like. And there's times I prefer the company of women ... It's just a nagging fear in your little mind, what are other people going to think. If I wanted to be gay, I'd be gay and I wouldn't be ashamed of being gay neither, if I was gay ... if all of a sudden I totally lost interest in women, then maybe I would try and see what being gay was like, just try it. ... Some of my best friends are gay, I've got no problems with gays ... if they want to do that let them do that. If they try it on with me it would be a different case. I know that for a fact. It would be a different case if it's my own friends that tried it on with me. 'Cos of me having my kids and everything, I wouldn't freeze now, I'd end up doing time.*

Many internal fears and concerns have been expressed in relation to perceptions of peers and in relation to behaviours deemed to be acceptable within the parameters of an outwardly perceived masculinity. Some of the young men discussed difficulties they were having with their sexual functioning and the strain it was having on their intimate relationships. These difficulties interacted with some of the other concerns about sexuality and masculine image already discussed. Colin spoke about his reaction to being touched and the fact that he often found it difficult to enjoy sex.

> **COLIN:** *Initially, I'd freeze and my stomach would start doing somersaults and I'd twinge. Like whatever part of my body had been touched would twinge and like I'd get a really weird, it's like a stitch sensation in my lower back and kidneys, my whole body just tensed up. Afterwards I would then have memories of the abuse going through my head. ... Then I think there must be something wrong with me.*

Justin's experiences were similar, his enjoyment of sex was disrupted by flashbacks and recurring memories.

JUSTIN: *To begin with there would be all the excitement, but then when I get down to doing anything, it would just pop like in the back of my head. . . . It's there in the head. . . . The brain wants to do it, but the body is numb. You know, you could stand there and slam it in the door and you wouldn't feel it, you know. It's numb. That's how it was, how it felt when it happened.*

Paul also had flashbacks, sometimes these would be triggered by newspaper articles or television programs about sexual abuse. When this happened his mood would change and he was unable to explain or communicate his feelings. This often caused considerable tensions between himself and his partner. He also had fears that sexual experiences would lead to him being hurt again.

PAUL: *. . . I felt so sick with myself and felt so sick about my body that . . . that I just didn't want to be touched. And also there was always a niggling that—it wasn't a big feeling, just a little one—that I was gonna get hurt. That was what my body was there for. It was to be hurt, because Raith had hurt it. This bloke had hurt it in a different way.*

Sean, although having difficulties, never really felt that he wanted to receive any help in coming to terms with his experience and wanted to be left to 'just get on with it'. He believes he sorted the situation out for himself mainly by getting older and having experiences that he thought were more appropriate and he had a choice about. At the time, however, he did share some of the concerns of the other young men in the study.

SEAN: *Well, to be perfectly honest, when it all started I thought I wasn't going to be straight when I left the place. I thought, 'Oh, no,' when I left the place I thought, 'now what.' I thought it was going to happen to me that I was going to become gay, blokes and men and stuff. When I left the school, the next sexual thing I had was with Helen, but it was with a woman this time and I thought, yes, I like this much better . . . even though I'm 21, I still get a bit dubious with females, you know. I think I don't know whether I want to do this sort of thing. It makes me feel like when I do go out with some-body or have an affair with somebody, it makes me feel as if, you know, I shouldn't be doing this. It makes me want to hold back sort of thing. Not because I think I'm becoming gay, but full stop basically. Having any sort of sexual relationship with anyone. . . . I like to be seen as somebody who knows what he's doing, knows how to handle it, and really be the person to be with sort of thing.*

FEARS OF ABUSING

The potential connection between having been sexually abused and subsequently sexually abusing others was discussed in Chapter 2. It was established that this was more of a problem for males than females and that there was a significant majority of males and females who have been sexually abused who do *not* sexually abuse others. It was identified that there was a social mythology or popular misunderstanding about this correlation and that this could be harmful and damaging for people who had been sexually abused. This was both in terms of their private feelings and of the assumptions other people made about them. Justin, Colin, and Paul had fears that they themselves would become abusers. This was partly based on what they felt, partly on what they had read or heard from others and partly what they understood to be the beliefs of some of their peers. Some of their comments exemplify the power and influence of popular mythology on privately held feelings and beliefs and how this internal consequence of having been sexually abused manifests itself in day-to-day relationships and peer group circumstances.

> **COLIN:** *Well, I thought that like, you know, I've been sexually abused. So, you know. So, I didn't know whether it was possible that I'd do that. . . . I've heard that abused become abusers . . . after reading that I was pretty paranoid for a couple of months or so . . . it just raised doubts for myself. . . . I mean if I was changing, say, John's nappy* [second child], *then I wouldn't touch his genitalia at all . . . I thought it would be interpreted as abuse or, you know. . . . Staff at Sycamores Clinic helped . . . they just said that basically it's got to be done, otherwise you'll get it infected. . . . I haven't got any problems with it now.*

Fears of abusing also came to a head for Justin, when he became involved in the care of his own children, partly because of his own fears, the fact that his children were male, he was male and he was abused by a male, and because of how he felt he would be seen by his peers. This situation led to a strain in his relationship, as he was unable to explain why he was afraid to become involved in the close personal caring of his children. To some extent he was able to make up for this by giving them attention through play, but he felt deprived of the closeness he could have with them. In discussing this, his manner of description (phrase underlined) illustrates how readily he conflates gay sexuality with child sexual abuse, placing himself in a position of agency and responsibility for being sexually abused. These comments were the first time Justin had ever spoken about these fears.

> **JUSTIN:** *I've heard so many cases where people who been abused go on to abuse, that scares me all the time . . . and that would kill me if I ever, ever*

abuse my own kids. I'd kill myself, I know I would, I couldn't do it. . . . I won't even bath them. . . . I shouldn't be worried about what other people are going to say, but I just don't want to be accused of touching up my own kids. . . . Before Leo was born I said I'll do everything. . . . I changed him in front of one of my friends that knew that I was sort of queer and it was the look he gave me when, you know, I put the baby wipe over his willy and across his bum. It was the look I got off my friends and that sort of made me think now I'm gonna get accused of touching these up and everything 'cos of what's happened to me, and don't you think that upset me.

When Paul was interviewed, he made it clear that he had never previously discussed being sexually abused with anybody in any detail. During the interviews, his feelings were raw and disturbing to himself. They also make disturbing reading and demonstrate the destructive power of compulsory heterosexism. His experiences have left him with fearful thoughts, anxieties, and impulses that have made him ambivalent about his actions. These feelings have to be constantly managed and have created difficulties in his personal relationships. Paul's deep sense of shame, guilt, and responsibility has prevented him from being able to share these feelings and anxieties. Paul has lived his life through the lens of having been sexually abused, and many of his personal relationships and sexual experiences have been distorted by the anxieties that have subsequently remained.

PAUL: *When I did feel dirty and ashamed, it was easier to have sex with somebody that didn't mean that much. . . . When I felt bad about myself because of what happened, it seemed OK to have sex with somebody else because you can pass those feelings on to them and get rid of them from yourself a bit. . . . I didn't see myself as an abuser. I think it did concern me that I was passing over negative feelings I was having to them. . . . When I first started to build up my sex drive and I really felt I wanted to have sex, but there weren't any people round to have sex with, I almost felt at times like I could go out and rape somebody. You know I never did, but I felt like I could, and that scared me, which is what stopped me, because it scared me. I knew that it was wrong and that that was unfair. I mean I never thought of things like I could go out and have a go at a kid, it was always like adults, women older than myself and I thought I could go out and rape somebody and I'd never get caught.*

Paul was also concerned about what he had read and heard about the relationship between the experience of abuse and subsequent abusing.

PAUL: *But I do worry what they say in the media. He abused this child, but he was abused himself. Because it spooked me when I was younger, you know, it really got me worried that I was going to be a sexual abuser, or a violent abuser, because that is just the way that I perceived it and also the fact that it happened so much with Raith and with the sexual abuse. It happened so much and so frequently that it did seem normal. Although I knew it was wrong it still seemed like that was the way things were done. You know, as if that's what people do. I'm glad that I don't think like that now, because otherwise I'd be a write-off, I'd probably be inside now.*

CONCLUSIONS

This chapter has considered the young men's perceptions of the impact of child sexual abuse on their sexuality, friendships, and peer relations. The young men's concerns centre around their perception of having 'co-operated' in a sexual relationship with an adult male, without having full awareness of how the adult male had constructed the relationship to invoke such feelings in an attempt to ensure silence. Remaining silent was supported by an oppressive social context of compulsory heterosexism and homophobia, which had been internalised by the young men. Many of the young men in this study were separated or estranged from their families, so the peer group became particularly significant as their main point of reference.

The experiences described by the young men confirmed that their increasing awareness of their sexuality was fraught with difficulty. It is difficult to assess the extent to which some of these problems may have already existed, if we accept that adolescence is a turbulent period for many people. However, many of the comments were directly related to the aftermath of child sexual abuse, and there was evidence that many of the young men did in fact have significant concerns about their sexuality and were very concerned about this being discovered by their peers. This often had an impact on the manner in which they behaved, portraying images that were consistent with their received beliefs about hegemonic masculinities. In Liam's phrase, this was 'acting the homophobic'. The young men felt marginalised in terms of their beliefs and perceptions about their masculinities. This meant that these behaviours became very transparent, and some of the young men's perceptions were quite extreme. For example, the idea was widespread that others could tell that they had been sexually abused and that therefore they were gay, by simply looking at them in a public bar or seeing their genitals in the shower at school. Paul's description of the attitudes of his peers at school, and Liam's description of some of the attitudes of his friends that have motivated him not to share information about his experiences are examples of this. Colin and Liam felt that they had to be careful about how their close supportive friendships with males were perceived and were concerned about the 'fine line' that existed in such relationships. The accounts show that, although certain aspects of behaviour were embarked upon, for the sake of image and for the sake of not being seen as gay the young men themselves continued to have private fears and self-doubt, some of which continue to present day. The solution was to behave in a certain way in which they could be seen as being a 'full male'. As a result, it appears that to some extent these friendships suffered.

The impact on their sexuality for most of the young men seemed to have lasting significance and was the area that they most wished to talk about and that, prior to these interviews, they had least talked about, if at all. It was necessary for them to perceive a degree of safety before discussing such privately held fears. The power and hold these fears have over the young men is illustrated by the fact that in most cases they continue to be hidden from their peers.

In discussing their sexuality, some of the young men described how their sexual functioning had been disrupted by being sexually abused. This sometimes resulted in difficulties with their partners and spoilt their enjoyment of intimate sexual relationships, through having to constantly struggle in private with disturbing thoughts and memories. Some of the young men spoke about having concerns about sexually abusing others, making reference to comments from peers and information they had collected from public sources, newspapers, and television. The mythology of the abused becoming abusers instigated further processes of internalised oppression. For some of the young men, a whole range of private fears and social myths interacted to cause considerable private suffering.

The experience of child sexual abuse has had a significant negative impact on the young men's perception, experience, and awareness of their sexuality. The detailed comments from the young men vividly reveal some of the processes of patriarchal gender construction. In particular, they have shown that they have sometimes conflated the experience of being sexually abused with being gay and have found themselves taking a homophobic stance in situations where they feel threatened. Some of this is fear based on peer group identities, but it is also fear based upon privately held beliefs and feelings from the sexual nature of the experience of being sexually abused, alongside other more generalised difficulties relating to adolescent sexuality. The experiences are shaped by their social context, but through some of the consequential behaviours become the context and carry forward the discourse of compulsory heterosexuality and homophobia.

8

STILL LIVING WITH THE CONSEQUENCES OF ABUSE

> **PAUL:** *I used to think about it and it was as if I could feel it all physically as well as mentally, you know, my body used to ache, even as I was a lot older, even now.*

INTRODUCTION

Strategies of resistance and coping employed by survivors of sexual abuse may in the long term cause problems, both personal and for others. Some of the comments from the young men show that they were having to cope with memories and flashbacks on a daily basis. Sometimes this had a significant influence on their behaviour and created preoccupations and moodiness, which they were unable to understand themselves or explain to others. This chapter shows how some of these experiences interacted with other difficult aspects of the young men's lives; for example, being 'in care' and living with foster carers, or being away from home in a boarding school.

The experience of ongoing flashbacks, where there was an uncontrollable flooding of vivid memories of sexual abuse sometimes followed by a blocking or constriction of memory (symptoms consistent with Post Traumatic Stress Disorder [PTSD]—Briere, 1992; Friedrich, 1995), was referred to by all the young men to varying degrees. For some they were more pervasive and ongoing than for others. This was particularly true of Paul, Ryan, and David, and it is interesting to note that their sexual abuse was pre-pubescent. It is also interesting to note that the abuse suffered by Colin, Paul, David, and Justin entailed significant threats of physical violence. Sean and Liam were both post-pubescent when they were sexually abused, and there were no significant threats of physical violence. Neither of them reported any critical difficulties with flashbacks or constriction of memory, and were both in some ways relatively more able than the rest of the sample to accommodate and cope with the abuse. They both, nevertheless, had critical anxieties about their sexuality and had significant fears about how they would be perceived and responded to by their male peer group, should information about their sexual abuse be discovered.

Some of the young men came to rely on the use of drugs and alcohol. Some of the accounts show a direct relationship between the abuse and the use of stimulants to block out memories and feelings and show how these escalated out of control, causing considerable harm to health and rapidly deteriorating circumstances. Other accounts showed how the memories resulted in powerful expressions of anger and temper, absconding and petty offending, strained family relationships, isolation and unimaginable depths of deep private sadness.

FLASHBACKS

Colin had many problems in trying to manage the uncontrollable, intrusive memories of his abuse and describes some of the circumstances that trigger them. Some of Colin's problems were discussed in Chapter 7, in terms of being triggered by specifically sexual experiences. He is aware of having these memories, but struggles to understand some of the processes of constriction and flooding and how he is able to store and hide away these memories, to the extent that when they return he is often caught off guard and has panic attacks.

> **COLIN:** *Mainly, just thoughts, but occasionally it would be like flashing, flashbacks very quick ... quite a lot of it is buried now and if I try to have an in-depth conversation about it, I can't, because a lot of it has gone back in my subconscious somewhere. But I know I do get some memories back, some thoughts, occasionally when I've had too much to drink, you know, or if I've been thinking about the 'four days'* [the period when the abuse took place]. *Anyway, I would just get the occasional flashback. Or if I've had a really stressful day, I'll sometimes get a flashback then. ... Crowded rooms sometimes, I don't know where it's from, it still happens regularly. I mean walking to the town centre on Saturday, I can't stand it, I can't handle it at all. I have real panic attacks. I started feeling claustrophobic, I just wanted to get out of there, my heart rate went straight up and I couldn't breathe too good, I just panicked. People all around and you can't move anywhere, trapped almost.*

Justin describes similar processes and refers to disturbing nightmares in which he experiences an ongoing pervasive presence of his abuser.

> **JUSTIN:** *I had one* [nightmare] *the other week. That was just like the school and things like that. ... Austin would be there in my dreams. You know, he'd just be there, he'd just be him. ... You'd be dreaming and you'd lose control of your dreams. You'd get all these little bad things happening and when I get like that I wake up in a cold sweat.*

David was sometimes so afraid of his abuser returning in his dreams that he would force himself to stay awake. He has little recall of the details of his nightmares, but associates the feelings they created with his abuse. He also refers to having flashbacks when handling his genitals when washing himself.

> **DAVID:** *There used to be some times that I wanted to stay up all night. . . . They were horrible, too horrible to describe. . . . I can't really remember the horrible ones, but I know I had them. I had some dreams about telling my parents. The first one they didn't believe me, then there was another one and I kept telling and telling them. That was one of the last ones. . . . I never used to wash down there [pointing] because it used to make me think about the abuse, so I just use to miss it out. I never used to touch it.*

Paul describes himself as having lived in a constant sea of memories, triggers, and day-to-day reminders of his abuse.

> **PAUL:** *There's not a day goes past when I don't think about my past in general. But specific aspects and details of it I can usually put away, but it can take . . . there's so many things that can trigger it off that it can take, like I can read an article on abuse in a magazine or a newspaper. For Raith, I can see somebody with a beard like his, and it comes back. I can see somebody I knew as a kid or go near the places I knew as a kid, and they'll bring it back. They weren't so much flashes, than they were images, pictures, all the time. I used to have nightmares about it. I used to think of it probably a lot more constantly than I do now, because they weren't just flashes of images, they would be there for longer periods. I would probably see whole day's events, rather than just a flash of one image. I was always all right if my mind was occupied, if I was busy doing something, but as soon as I started to slow down, like night time, I would think about the day that I've had and then something would trigger it off and then I will start getting the repeat of what happened.*

FEELINGS AND EMOTIONS

These comments speak of the intense pain and emotional turmoil the young men went through day and night and show how isolated they felt with their feelings. This comment from Justin shows that at the heart of everything that has been discussed so far is an individual who feels lost and broken in every way possible.

> **JUSTIN:** *Sometimes I sit at home and I have a little cry to myself, because I do feel better after having a cry. . . . If someone's there, like if we're watching telly and all of a sudden I feel so depressed, so I just go off to the bathroom and have a cry . . . all of a sudden you'd be really enjoying yourself, you know, having a wail of a time and all of a sudden bang! It just happens, it's just there. . . . I can remember the very first day it happened, November 23rd, that's a real shit day for me. I feel dirty all day, all that day. That's why I was in bits when you turned up yesterday. I was getting myself totally mashed up.*

The same was true for Paul: his comment demonstrated the immensity of his isolation, the depth of his sadness, how his memories would return him to the physical pain of his experiences, and how his pain sometimes turned into anger.

> **PAUL:** *When I was on my own I used to cry endlessly. . . . I'd either wait until everybody had gone out or I just go up to my room or I'd go for a long walk. There's one thing about being in a village: it's in the country, you can just walk. I'd just walk to the middle of a field and I would cry and cry and cry and I would get up and I would scream and I would shout. I'd scream just things like, you know, 'I hate you' at the top of my voice and I would scream things like 'I'm gonna get you for this', all at this bloke and Raith. Privately, I was a mess because it used to screw me up so much, but looking back on it now I can't believe just how much time I did spend crying, 'cos I never sit down and rationalise it with myself. If I was on my own and I thought about it, it would upset me and all the feelings, the shame, the guilt, being dirty, it would all come back and I would feel like I wanted to get my revenge. . . . I think anger, pain, probably the biggest feelings I had when I was on my own, physical and emotional pain. . . . I used to think about it and it was as if I could feel it all physically as well as mentally, you know. My body used to ache, even as I was a lot older, even now. I remember it all so vividly as it was like yesterday and that hurts because I can feel. Not only can I see what was happening in my mind, but I can feel it as well. And there's been times when it's been that bad that I've wanted to kill myself because I feel so ashamed of myself. There's times when I've felt very suicidal. There's times when I've been very close to doing it.*

BEHAVIOUR

For some of the young men, containing, trying to forget, or coping with the consequences of abuse had a significant impact on their behaviour. Unfortunately, this would then become the focus of the attention the young men would receive. Colin experienced placement disruptions in care, to the point that he would abscond for long periods of time, often being caught up in the destructive relationship with Penny, who at the time he considered to be his partner, that resulted in him being further sexually abused. Justin ended up in court following petty offences, leading to a period of homelessness, until he was taken in by Sally, a neighbourhood friend. Paul used to have massive rows with his foster parents, as a result of his anger building up over time. Colin describes how he resisted being controlled by adults and had a pressing need for controlling situations himself, but would often end up losing control and become angry.

COLIN: *I had a massive appetite for gaining control of situations. . . . I just got totally obsessed with power over my own life and any situation I felt lost in. I'd just give them hell. Sometimes I had quite powerful surges of anger which I had no control over. I was scared, I felt stunned, it took me back. I can remember hitting a door in an argument with my mum, and that just like really stunned me, because I'm not an aggressive person. That sort of way for me to act was like I didn't know myself and I didn't like it.*

Paul would hold on to feelings of anger, particularly in school (we have already heard how scared he was of his abuse being discovered by his peers), but periodically he would let these feelings out.

PAUL: *I used to have an amazing temper, it never used to let go. It took a lot to build me up to it, but once I was going that was it. . . . Like when I'd been teased at school, and because I never used to release how I feel about everything I used to keep it inside. It's like a bottle of champagne, if you shake it up, the cork's going to explode eventually and that's what it was like. It all just exploded in one go and then things would go quiet for a while and then it would all explode all over again. . . . It was a test for my foster parents and a way I could release things without going completely off the rails. If I hadn't have done that I would have probably ended up completely in a mess.*

Sean described how he used manage his feelings and anger through recklessly driving fast, which culminated in an accident.

SEAN: *I don't really like hurting anybody or anything. I used to. I used to take it out on my car, before I had my smash. I used to drive fast to scare myself, to calm myself down. . . . I've just forgotten about it all. I'd like to*

> *know what happened to him. As far as I'm concerned now, I'm just a 21-year-old bloke . . . I didn't want any help, I just wanted to get on with it.*

DRUGS AND ALCOHOL

Colin and Justin spoke about how and why they would use alcohol, gas, solvents, and cannabis to help block out their memories and feelings about their abuse. They felt that the consequences of not using these substances were at the time too painful to bear.

> **COLIN:** *It's mainly a form of escape. If I'm thinking about it and it's doing my head in, I'd reach for the nearest thing that I'd get a buzz out of: petrol, gas, draw, or drink. It's not as bad as it was, but, anyhow, I still do that. . . . Looking back they didn't do anything for me at all, just confused me more, but at the time they just like settle your thoughts. Like you've just got this buzz in your head and this ringing, that's all you can hear and all you can concentrate on, so I did that to escape thinking about the 'four days', just to get it from my mind, 'cos it was on my mind quite a lot at the time. It still haunts me now.*

For Justin the use of gas and cannabis was more long term and he suffered severe health consequences. He had serious lung and liver damage. He sees a direct connection between sniffing large amounts of butane gas and being sexually abused.

> **JUSTIN:** *Last time I had a sniff of gas was 1992. . . . I ended up doing 18 tins a day just to get a buzz. . . . That just helped me forget about it. That just helped me forget about everything, just about life. I was just in my own world, the one that I wanted to be in. You know, which was just following foot-prints, sea monsters, a permanent trip. It helped me to forget. If I'd stopped sniffing, I'd start thinking about it. I knew one day I'd have to cope with it, but, you know, I weren't ready to cope with it then. . . . I know I smoked cannabis before I went to the school, but it was the gas that messed up my insides and my mind. It was the gas that did that, but that was due to the school, because it helped me forget about the school. . . . It would just help me forget how I was feeling. I'd just feel so numb and totally out of it. I was just in a world of my own, and that went on for a long time.*

Justin is aware now that to sniff any more butane gas would be life-threatening. Only the threat of death is worse than his memories.

> **JUSTIN:** ... I used to get up at 3 or 4 in the morning to have a sniff of gas just to get back to sleep. I used to wake up in that much pain. ... The addiction's still there, I just don't do it anymore 'cos as far as I'm concerned when you look at yourself and your 10 stones and then, when you go past this mirror ... and then all of a sudden all you see is skin and bones it shocks you. ... And that was it, I said to myself if I pick up another tin of that and put it in my mouth again I'll die, and ever since that day I've never touched it. ... Once I packed that in, the amount of cannabis I started smoking just to get a buzz like, it was mad, it was, it was ridiculously mad.

FAMILY RELATIONSHIPS

Colin, Paul, and Sean were the subjects of care orders and had lived most of their lives in foster care, or in Sean's case in foster care and residential school. Justin and Liam lived in residential schools. A significant feature of the life-story interviews for all these young men was that they spoke little about either their birth families or their foster families. They all related to and judged themselves by their peer group. Neither their families nor their peer group were allowed true access to the private world of fear and doubt that these young men were living in. Continuous attempts were made to prove to their peers that they were healthy, 'normal' young men, capable of all the behaviours and attitudes they perceived to be expected of them. The significance of the peer group could be attributed not only to the age of the young men, but also to the absence or distance of family support. Justin had particularly strong feelings about his mother and stepfather, as he feels they were instrumental in his initial withdrawal of his statement. He believes that they have never really fully appreciated the extent to which he has suffered as a result of being abused. His comments show how destructive child sexual abuse can be to family relationships, especially when the abuser has known the parents and successfully masked his intentions of sexually abusing their children.

> **JUSTIN:** I didn't even want my mum at the fucking trial, I don't get on with my mum. I live less than five minutes away from her, I don't go. ... I do take Leo sometimes, I just find it hard to communicate to my mum. All this abuse and everything's only really just sunk in to my mum's head in the last couple of weeks as it goes. ... You know what I mean, it's took her this long just to. ... I see her trying to make up for things she didn't do years ago. You know, believe me when I told her the fucking first time, and that upsets me a great deal. But she knows that hurt me a lot, her and Joe

> *making me change that statement and going back to the school and getting abused again afterwards. That hurt me a great deal and I've never forgiven her for that. . . . I feel guilty for making her feel guilty, but it makes me feel better for making her feel guilty.*

David had some ambivalence toward his mother, particularly when he was being abused, on the basis that his mother made the decision for him to have contact with Harry, even when he said that he did not wish to go. In looking back, David is able to rationalise that his mother was not to blame for what happened.

> **DAVID:** *My mum feels a bit guilty, but I know that she wouldn't have sent me if she knew what was happening. I'm not blaming her. My tempers used to be really bad at home, and they're not anymore. . . . I had some after the abuse was stopped, but they weren't as bad as the ones when the abuse was going on. They used to really get mum upset. I used to have a go at her sometimes. I didn't want to know her, for making me go, I suppose. . . . She's talked to me about it and asked me why I had all the tempers, and I said because I didn't want to go and you did, so I used to have to go. I don't think that no more and I don't blame my mum at all.*

Paul had similar feelings toward his own mother, who died while he was in foster care.

> **PAUL:** *. . . I mean I know I shouldn't feel disrespect for my mum, and I still love her, but I don't think you can hide. There's no point in hiding and masking the truth and making excuses for people. . . . Just living with it, yeah, it upsets me and stuff, it's just one of those things that happened and I can't change it now. There's no point in hating my mum for it. . . . I suppose that deep down I know that my mum loved me or loved us.*

Sexual abuse caused significant strains between Ryan and his mother, who was very angry with Harry, the man who abused her son, but struggled to understand Ryan's apparent lack of anger. There were also tensions in that Ryan did not wish to attend a court trial, which in the event never took place, although Harry was convicted for sexually abusing David and several other boys.

> **RYAN:** *It dragged us apart when it all started happening, now it's brought us back together again kind of perhaps in a way. Me and my mum are always arguing, we don't agree on anything.*

CONCLUSIONS

This chapter has shown how for the young men the experiences of being sexually abused has continued to have a deep and pervading impact on many areas of their lives. In many ways they have had to live out their lives through the lens of sexual abuse, always fearing discovery, always anticipating the potential negative appraisal of others, and as a consequence feeling unable to communicate directly their anxieties and fears. Suddenly, there would be a flooding of vivid memory and feeling, other times there would be numbness and forgetting, with memories being repressed and pushed out of reach. This would be a normal day, perhaps in many ways a relatively good day. On a bad day the feelings would take over and dominate everything, reducing the young men to depths of unimaginable sadness, grief, and isolation. For Justin and Colin particularly, this would lead to binges of alcohol and drug abuse, in vain attempts to block out their memories and feel good. The young men would often scrutinise themselves, their feelings, their actions, and constantly ask the question why were they abused, what could they have done to stop it, why were their parents unable to see what was happening to them, and why they were unable to understand how they were feeling now, even after having told and so many months and years after it had happened. The words of these young men speak loudly and leave the reader in no doubt about the harmful impact of child sexual abuse.

9

BEING A PARTICIPANT

> **DAVID:** *I don't mind talking about the abuse as long as it gets it out of me, the stuff that's embarrassing what was done to me, the abuse. The whole thing. I was trapped.*

INTRODUCTION

This study has purposefully sought to ensure that a secure and safe (anti-hegemonic) context was set up for all the interviews with the young men. In being able to tell their stories in such detail, it is possible that the telling of the story has validated the experience, and that perhaps the young men are able to reflect on their experiences in a changed manner, hopefully with an improved insight. During the interviews, comments were made by some of the young men about how they felt about taking part in the study and whether or not they feel they have either benefited or enjoyed the process. Benefiting largely refers to the impact of talking through difficult experiences and whether or not a level of improvement of well-being has been achieved, perhaps by expressing emotions that have been held on to or by developing a better understanding of private fears and doubts that have hitherto not been shared to any significant degree. Enjoying the process refers to the level of enjoyment received by virtue of receiving positive attention and taking part in something that could be of benefit to others. The young men also expressed a view that knowing me from before was helpful, in that a level of trust was established and they knew what to expect.

FEELINGS ABOUT TAKING PART IN THE STUDY

In my discussion of the methodology in Chapter 3, I expressed caution about the use of the term 'empowerment' in research reports, arguing that the term could sometimes be used to facilitate a 'feel good' factor for the researcher and that in the current study it was important to remember that taking part in the research will not have significantly changed the material lives of the participants. It could, however, be argued that, by breaking down some of the hegemonic myths through the manner in which their stories were shared and the responses that the young men received, a level of personal empowerment through insight may have taken place. Consider the comments from Paul about his changed feelings of responsibility.

> **PAUL:** *Nobody else knows how I felt and how I feel about Martin and Kevin. . . . I know it's irrational. I know it now, you know like talking about it and stuff, because like I say nobody's ever known how I felt and how I feel about them times, so nobody's ever been there to say it's all right, it's not your fault, there was nothing you could have done. I mean that's my fault for not telling anybody. . . . The time has come that it's got to be let go because somebody else finally knows what I went through during that time and that person can turn round to me and say there was nothing you could have done, you were too young, and you did what you thought was right at the time and that is OK. . . . The fact that I've never told anybody, nobody could ever help me out. I just needed somebody to lift it off. . . . It's just like lifting a huge, great, big weight off me. . . . To know that I haven't been judged and that it is irrational to think the way I have thought is a good feeling. It really is, it's kind of emotionally exhausting in a way, but it makes me feel good. It makes feel as if there is some other purpose to my life. . . . You don't need to feel guilty. You don't need to feel ashamed. . . . But the feeling of, you know, feeling dirty and cheap, them sort of feelings, they're not so easy to get rid of, because they're not the sort of things that somebody can say, 'it's not your fault.'*

Justin commented on the extent to which he trusted me, even though he is often wary toward males. His comments highlighted the importance and significance of the ongoing support offered through a research agreement. Since the end of the research and support period, my contact with Justin has significantly faded, in that he rarely contacts me now, although he has a long-term interest in the outcome of the research. Prior to the research period he maintained a level of informal contact. This was partly due to the fact that there was a long waiting period for his compensation hearings and that his life was in turmoil. When Justin talked about his fear of abusing his children, he stated why he felt able to tell me about it and related it to the day he first told me about his abuse over five years ago.

> **JUSTIN:** *. . . You know I get nervous of things like that, but I've never told that to anyone before. . . . You can see I should really tell Ruth, but I can't because I know she wouldn't take it serious . . . but I seem to be able to tell you virtually everything. . . . You're really understanding. You see like that day when I rode over in the rain. I had to tell somebody and I thought well*

> *who can I tell, I'll go and see Andrew, he's a man I can talk to and it's been like that ever since. From the first day I met you, when I was in foster care, I thought you were somebody I can talk to. . . . It helps quite a lot, I've enjoyed doing the talking, getting it off my plate . . . that's helped relieve a bit of pressure as it goes.*

David and Ryan expressed similar views about the benefit of being able to talk through their difficult experiences.

> **DAVID:** *I don't mind talking about the abuse as long as it gets it out of me, the stuff that's embarrassing what was done to me, the abuse. The whole thing. I was trapped.*

> **RYAN:** *I don't really speak to people, you're the only person that like since I've known you that I've really spoken to about this kind of thing.*

Liam and Sean commented on the fact that the research process had enabled them to remember and discuss matters that they had either forgotten or blocked out.

> **LIAM:** *It's hard for me to remember this because basically I've blocked it out for many years. I don't talk about it or anything. You know, it's only just now that it's coming back. I trust you, this is basically the reason why I came today, trust somebody and talk about it, openly. Like I think I've told somebody, you're not the only person that's going to read this, if it gets published or anything, you know. So I mean what the hell, you know. If I talk about it it's in the tape machine, on the paper, and not stuck in here, in me anymore.*

> **SEAN:** *It's bringing up stuff that I thought I'd forgotten about . . . it was all right, I felt comfortable talking about it, it's not as if I didn't want to talk about it. . . . It's OK, I'm not bothered about talking to you about it.*

Colin saw the research as an opportunity to sort himself out and come to terms with needing to talk through his experiences. He was concerned about remembering things he had blocked out.

> **COLIN:** *I still had and still have some anxieties, so I thought it would be good to discuss those so I could get them out in the open. It's the first step,*

> *anxieties about going to the bog and getting close to other males. So I*
> *thought: well, the first step to recovery is to discuss it, go in the open and*
> *admitting it as a problem. I thought it would be a good opportunity to get it*
> *sorted really and ... that helped, the fact that I know you from before and*
> *trust you ... I had some doubts about whether or not it would bring up some*
> *things I didn't want to remember. ... Well, if it will help somebody, even if*
> *it only helps one person, that's fine.*

A draft of the study, including this chapter, was shared and discussed on separate occasions with Colin and Liam. They have maintained an ongoing interest in the progress of the research and have often contacted me. They were pleased with the manner and extent to which their identities had been concealed. They enjoyed seeing their own contributions being used and expressed agreement with the overall approach to the research and its conclusions.

WRITING AND DRAWING—NON-VERBAL ACCOUNTS

David and Ryan were 15 years old when they were interviewed and were within three years of their experience of being sexually abused. They were very keen to take part in the research and saw it as part of their recovery process. Telling their stories further validated their experiences, while at the same time they felt they received further help and support. They were young, their experiences were recent, and they sometimes found it difficult to express their feelings in words. They were, however, able to express their feelings in a non-verbal manner, using poetry, art, writing, and drawing. Most of this was produced during the interviews as a means of assistance to verbal communication, but the poetry was written in solitude, outside the interviews. These non-verbal accounts from Ryan and David amounted to dramatic condensations of their experiences and feelings, complemented and added weight to their verbal accounts, and helped them to make a distinctive and valuable contribution to the research. This supplemented the more extensive verbal accounts of the older participants and underlined the importance and value of recognising and not prioritising verbal accounts to the exclusion of non-verbal communication in research methodology. These methods and their outcome are discussed and presented in Chapter 11, alongside other materials for assisting therapeutic practice.

BEING A RESEARCHER

Conducting a research study of this nature will inevitably have an impact on the researcher (Kelly, 1988b). From my previous social work experience, I was aware that working with young people who have been sexually abused would be challenging and stressful but also that assisting their recovery was not unrewarding. In conducting the interviews, I felt a level of personal responsibility to ensure that the participants did not suffer and that in some way they would benefit from the experience. My sense of responsibility and emotional investment deepened as the research progressed and as the extent to which some of the young men had suffered became clear. Listening to these seven stories first-hand and in parallel was very stressful. For a period it placed me alongside the young men and these experiences, and deepened my understanding of what had and was happening to them. Throughout the research, I have felt very close to the transcripts, to the extent that even now as I read them I can remember the individual voices, diction, intonation, and so on. My formal supervision at the university and from my employment in social services has therefore been very important to me. Not necessarily in terms of talking to any great extent about this personal impact, but more in maintaining an ongoing supportive awareness of the potential stresses involved. I will always remember the young men who took part in this study and wonder how their lives have progressed.

CONCLUSIONS

The young men who took part in this study have stated that they felt supported in being able to share sensitive information about their experiences of child sexual abuse. Some of the young men clearly stated that they felt they had benefited from taking part and had been able to let go of fearfully held feelings. Finally, it was noted that conducting a research study of this nature will have an impact on the researcher and that supportive supervision was essential.

Part III

IMPLICATIONS FOR PRACTICE

10

A FRAMEWORK FOR THERAPEUTIC PRACTICE

INTRODUCTION

This chapter examines the implications of the study for providing direction in developing new and more child- and young person-centred therapeutic practices. The young men's accounts challenge the current legalism of the childcare arena and emphasise the need for the criminal justice system to exercise greater sensitivity in responding to the needs of children and young people. They highlight the need for social work intervention to challenge the mechanistic procedures of investigation and prosecution that have become enshrined legally into formal policies and practices. These approaches have been matched by a dominance of potentially pathologising psychiatric and psychological symptomology and 'treatment' procedures. The experiences of the young men do not (and should not be made to) fit into medicalised, diagnostic categorisation. Such approaches not only locate both the problem and its solution within the individual but also divert attention away from seeking social solutions to what this study has shown to be a widespread social problem.

There are significant structural dimensions to the problem of child sexual abuse that this study has sought to address, in terms of challenging oppressive gender construction, heterosexism, and the social construction of childhood. However, sociological approaches that take a purely structural perspective will potentially homogenise the individual experience and launder out difference and diversity. Alternatively, a post-structural approach will allow an analysis of the individual experience and will centralise issues of language, power, gender, and sexuality. However, there is a danger that focusing on the individual experience could again be pathologising. Common experiences of the impact of widespread social oppression could be misinterpreted as being individual factors.

This chapter presents an analytical practice framework that has sought to overcome many of these problems. This framework has informed the analysis of the study and consequently has important and significant implications for better and more helpful therapeutic practice with children and young people who have been sexually abused (and others). The framework allows a socially contextual analysis of the individual experience that recognises the role of language in creating and carrying forward oppression, alongside recognising the importance of power and sexuality. It does not exclude consideration of individual psychological factors, such as trauma responses and dissociation, but enables these factors to be considered as part of the individual's socially lived-in world.

A NEW PRACTICE FRAMEWORK

In establishing the essential importance of a sensitive approach to studying the impact of child sexual abuse, we argued in Chapter 3 that ethnography and feminist research practice recognise the importance of individual experiences and that an anti-oppressive approach seeks to account for the power differentials in research. These approaches are consistent with post-structural perspectives that emphasise diversity and individual experiences and recognise the importance of power. Jackson (1992) identifies three main themes of post-structuralism. First, language is seen as constructing and not transmitting meaning, and subjectivity is constituted through language. Second, there is a denial of the existence of an essential self outside culture and language. Third, there is no possibility of an objective scientific truth, and knowledges are seen as 'discursive constructs' (p. 26) produced from particular positions.

This research study has been essentially post-structuralist in its method and analysis, in that an emphasis was placed on diversity and the uniqueness of individual experiences. However, as the research unfolded, across this uniqueness, the young men were found to have had experiences, beliefs, and feelings that they held in common. This did not deny or compromise the uniqueness of each young man's experience, but rather served to highlight common struggles, concerns, and fears. While post-structuralism presents a challenge to the essentialist nature of structuralist theory, arguing that it homogenises groups of people and launders out diversity, it has been noted that it has the danger of unseating some of the classic analytical concepts: woman, class, and 'race'. In this respect it has been criticised for breaking down and fragmenting the solidarity of oppressed groups, allowing space for traditional or classic oppressive relationships to establish increased potency, through being hidden within the tapestry of difference (Barrett and Phillips, 1992).

The statements from the young men also present a challenge to the post-structural notion of reality being mediated by language. It became important to note that the extent to which this occurs is related to and often dependent on the social context in which the language is used. In an oppressive social context of patriarchal relations, the use of particular types of language can invoke and carry forward social oppression and thereby significantly influence interpersonal power relationships. In this sense, language potentially becomes a tool of oppression. This study has shown how simple statements or even words can embody significant meanings that directly relate to widespread and socially embedded and supported oppression. It was shown, for example, that the use of the word 'queer' in the context of adolescent peer group relations has a particularly powerful impact (Nayak and Kehily, 1997). It can make some people significantly more powerful and others significantly less powerful. The use of this word was shown to be capable of invoking multiple oppressive discourses about personal identity and social misconceptions about the nature and impact of child sexual abuse.

In seeking a rapprochement that allows us in some way to reconcile these theoretical inconsistencies (essentially, the contradiction between post-structural and structural approaches) and hold on to both common and unique experiences at the same time, a new approach for therapeutic practice and research is implied. This approach seeks to allow diverse interpersonal language and individual experiences to be considered in a context of social oppression. This approach utilises Cooper's (1995) concept of 'organising principles', to allow for multiple dimensions of inequality and social oppression:

> Rather than basing analysis on axes of oppression, gender, class and race can be conceived as 'organizing frameworks' or less systematically 'principles' that over-determine each other in their operation and effects. (Cooper, 1995, p. 11)

Racism, for example, is considered as its interacts with other structures of social oppression, such as age, gender, or sexuality. No single aspect of social oppression is seen as an absolute determinant of social power. It therefore becomes easier to account for the complexities of interpersonal relationships; for example, between a White woman and a Black man, or between a White child and a Black woman. The White woman may have less power by virtue of being a woman, but may have more power through being White. Similarly, a White child may have more social power than a Black adult or, in certain circumstances, than a gay man. The location and social context of these power relationships can also be highly significant in determining their outcome.

I have drawn some of these theoretical considerations together to form the analytical framework that is represented in Figure 10.1. The framework allows a study of power relationships at different interrelated levels of social interaction, in the context of widespread oppressive social and political influences. At the centre of the framework, the individual is an agent of choice and action, with wishes, desires, and beliefs. Individual experience, however, is subject to and created by interactions with others. Each level of interaction constitutes a site of learning and influence. Each individual is a member of each level and so not only receives its influence but contributes to its influence on others as well. This may, for example, be at a peer group level or at the level of the wider political and social context, where processes of hegemony and consensus involve each individual in receiving beliefs, carrying them forward within themselves, passing them on to others, and so forth. The extent of the influence will vary according to many factors, some of which may relate to class, 'race', gender, sexuality, age, or ability. The influence of each level is interdependent and will vary according to the individual's circumstances, age, and development.

The most immediate level of this interaction is family and kinship. In most circumstances, for a young child this is the site of initial interactions, relationships, and learning, and continues to have a varying influence over time. The next level of interaction is the social network of extrafamilial relationships and interactions. Within this network is located the peer group and access to other close and

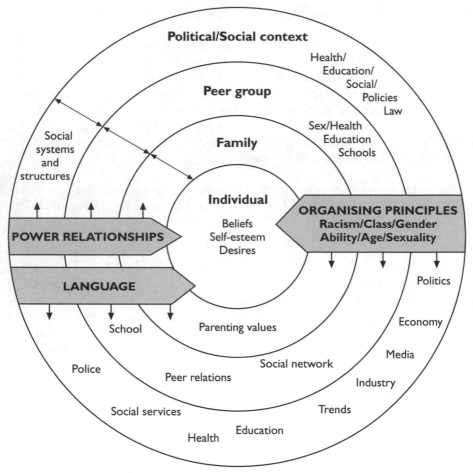

Figure 10.1   Analytical practice framework.

intimate relationships, experienced through schools and possibly pre-school net-works, social and leisure contacts, work, or college. The three levels—individual, family, and peer group—are located in the wider social and political context, which again influences and interacts with each level and contributes to the determination of interactions between the different levels.

The framework has been advanced in terms of its specific usefulness in under-standing male-child sexual abuse and how feelings and beliefs during and after such an event are constructed in a relationship with wider social forces and interaction. It allows an analysis of interpersonal power relationships and high-lights the significance of language in mediating, carrying forward, supporting, and being supported by oppressive discourses. The framework has usefulness for a wide range of therapeutic practice and is a valuable tool for the analysis of oppression in changing circumstances. It has a fluidity that makes it immedi-ately applicable to the turbulent arena of childcare and other therapeutic practice.

In applying the framework to the young men's stories, the particular focus has been the common experiences relating to perceived masculinities and sexual identity. These have been examined through the lens of this framework, whereby it has been established that there have been common forces of oppression shaping each young man's unique experience. Sexuality, for example, has been identified as a significant form of disciplinary power (Foucault, 1976), especially in a social context where sexual desire and attraction is strongly regulated to create a social climate of compulsory heterosexism and homophobia. Particular attention was paid to hegemonic masculinities and the possibility that the experience of child sexual abuse has led some of the young men to believe themselves to be in a subordinate position in relation to other males, particularly their peers, whom they see and believe to be living a life more consistent with received beliefs about hegemonic masculinities. Some of this subordination was evidenced by not only actual life experiences, but through the choice of language used to describe their experiences. In trying to limit, deny, or change the extent of this perceived subordination, some of the young men adopted behaviours perceived to be consistent with the masculinities (hegemonic) they believed they should aspire to. In effect, they themselves began to carry and perpetuate the discourse that was hurting them. In the case of Justin and Liam this involved acting tough and 'acting the homophobic'. In Colin's case this involved being led into another sexually abusive situation, but this time by a woman.

Some of the experiences of the young men from this study are represented collectively in Figure 10.2. This portrays a discourse of male-child sexual abuse, showing how many of the young men's experiences and beliefs have been socially constructed throughout the course of their lives, with the young men themselves playing their own part in carrying forward beliefs and expectations. In applying the framework to an individual person's experience, it will allow a unique construction of the personal, family, social, and political influences on how experiences have been understood and interpreted. It will be useful to a young person to be helped in understanding how the abuser may have purposefully invoked oppressive (traditional) understandings of gender and sexuality, so as to instil a sense of that young person feeling responsible for the abuse. This may involve distorting the young person's sense of normality: a girl or a young woman may be told that the sexual abuse is about 'being a real woman' alongside a paradoxical implication that telling would cause people to question the young girl's 'femininity'. For a boy or a young man, the abuser may make reference to homophobia in responding to arousal, 'you're aroused, you must want this to happen, so if you tell, then what will people think of you—you're gay, so it must be your fault.' The study has demonstrated these processes taking place and the devastating impact they have had on the young men. The framework effectively gives the young person a map through which to interpret and negotiate the past, present, and future landscape of having been sexually abused.

CHILD AND YOUNG PERSON-CENTRED PRACTICE

The link between research and practice is further sustained through the study's sensitive methodology, which has implications for future practice. There are strong connections between how this research was conducted and how sensitive

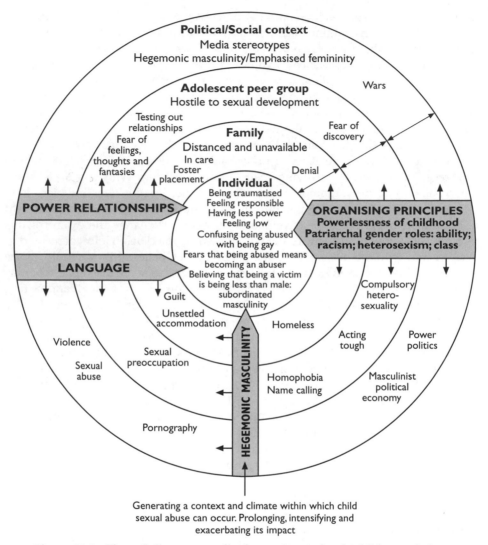

Figure 10.2   The socially contextualised experience of male-child sexual abuse.

therapeutic practice should proceed. In both arenas, there is a need for a knowledgeable and perceptive approach that takes full account of the needs and wishes
of the child or young person and the impact of social oppression.

There is a need to go beyond a simple adoption of the term 'child-centred',
which has been used in a neutral and moralistic sense to justify varied adult-
centred practices that fail to establish any significant detail of children's perspectives (Macleod and Saraga, 1991). Approaches to practice need to incorporate a
critique of dominant social constructions of childhood that emphasise innocence
and powerlessness, moving toward alternative discourses of empowerment and
children's competencies, recognising their strategies of resistance, struggle, and
survival, helping them to name their own oppression (Kitzinger, 1997). This

research study has shown that it is important to approach practice from a perspective that empowers the child or young person, by allowing him (her) to theorise his (her) own experience. This involves paying careful attention to the words used by the young person, to explain and describe experiences that have taken place. This allows the young person's 'story' to unfold in a manner that has personal and private meaning and texture, elucidating the day-to-day realities of their lives. As this research has shown, in order to facilitate the unfolding of the story it is necessary to create the right environment in which to engage the young person in a positive and supportive manner. Such an environment would need to be anti-oppressive (anti-hegemonic, anti-homophobic, anti-heterosexist, anti-racist, etc.) and would need to involve supportive, caring, and appropriately defined relationships to allow the young person to feel safe in letting go of fears and anxieties that may have been long and deeply held on to. As the study has shown, many of these fears are likely to be based on the nature of the abusive experience itself. They may additionally be based on subsequent personal and social experiences, including inappropriate and unhelpful professional responses that may have in themselves further constructed and compounded the initial impact of the abuse.

This study has shown the importance of taking care to listen for clues in the language and the manner in which the young person describes his experiences. Single words or phrases can reveal complex social pressures, peer group fears, and internalised oppression. An example of this was given by Justin's use of the phrase 'one of my friends who knew that I was sort of queer'. Through this phrase, Justin invoked the intersecting discourses of homophobia, of children and young people being responsible for being abused, and of the misconceived link between being abused and abusing others. He had carried and internalised the implications of these discourses for many years, which influenced how he saw himself, how he managed his relationships and interactions with others, causing considerable pain, struggle, and suffering. As we have seen above, the analytical practice framework allows these words and experiences to be placed in their context, in a manner that captures the interpersonal power relationships and the daily dynamics and textures of a young person's individual life, in an overarching context of social oppression. The framework can be used to help us understand these experiences and to help us convey a helpful insight to the young person.

This approach allows an exploration that appreciates the young person's positive use of personal power, no matter how great or small that may be, in struggling to survive day-to-day experiences. The young person is not and was not powerless, although he did have significantly less power than the person who abused him. He may have significantly less personal and social power than those who continue to oppress him, but he is not utterly powerless. The study has shown how the young men used the small amounts of power they had, in varied ways, to resist and survive the experiences they suffered. The study has shown how the abusers manipulated the young men's existing social exclusion to create sustained opportunities to sexually abuse. The framework allows an insight into the social circumstances and 'normal' power relationships that allowed an adult or other person to feel able to make the decision to sexually abuse. It reveals the discourses that supported that person's authority, abuse of power, and 'rightness' about what was to take place, often in a manner that engendered the young person's 'wrongness' for 'allowing' it to happen. These distortions are supported by the use of social oppression and popular mythology to reinforce these feelings and beliefs and to further silence the young person into shame and feeling responsible. Through this framework, a young person can be helped to understand how and where the adult was situationally located, in terms of being able to use his social and personal power in planning the abuse, and, as we have already said, how the abuser was able to support his activities by calling on multiple aspects of oppression, based on age, class, ability, gender, 'race', sexual orientation, heterosexism, homophobia, and so on. For example, an abuser may have told a Black child that if he or she told, he or she would never be believed by a White person or that a child's word would never be believed against that of an adult. The abuser may tell a boy that if he told, then his friends would think that he was gay. To the child, statements like this are likely to have resonance with other life experiences. The framework would allow the practitioner to draw out and explain the social origins of some of these beliefs and fears and explore with the child or young person how they may have been internalised; for example, drawing out a framework of the young person's own beliefs and feelings, possibly accompanied by looking through newspapers and magazines and discussing images of gender and sexuality. Similarly, the framework could be used to explore the influences on peer group experiences.

The sensitive approach established by this research has the potential of narrowing the power differential in the adult–young person relationship, toward a greater equality that allows personal feelings, fears, and anxieties to be expressed. Through the process of telling the story, with the power and expertise in the hands of the teller, the young person may have a better and more helpful conversation and consequently gain a different perspective. This may lead to greater insight, with the young person being helped to see where he is located and to see the multiple range of influences and discourses that have shaped his fears and stifled and smothered his hopes. He can be helped to recognise how the words he has 'chosen' to use have wide-ranging social meanings and have become vehicles of prolonged internalised oppression. These suggestions have consistencies with some of the narrative approaches to practice suggested by White and Epston (1992) and the broader based approach to identifying links between a wide range of (male) gender-based violences suggested by Wolfe et al. (1997).

The analytical framework gives both young people and practitioners insight into the personal and social circumstances of the young person's experiences of sexual abuse. It provides the practitioner with a starting point and a framework for supportive and sensitive intervention, in helping young people recover from sexual abuse. It allows an approach that uses an analysis of narrative in a contextualised manner, accounting for the uniqueness of the individual experience, without losing sight of how those experiences are shaped by social circumstances. This approach allows many of the young person's problems to become externalised. It provides a deep understanding that centralises gender, sexuality, and power within helping strategies for work with boys and young men, in a similar manner to the work Kelly (1988b) has undertaken in relation to women and sexual violence.

The study's methodology strongly suggests a practice approach toward young people who have been sexually abused that significantly moves away from the pathologising framework of adult-centred psychological and legal practice frameworks. Such an approach is consistent with that suggested by Butler and Williamson (1994), being child and young person-centred. This involves recognising the impact of adult power, making every attempt to establish and respond to the child or young person's view of the experiences being discussed, addressing and validating the trauma, without imposing adult interpretations and distortions of meaning; it also involves recognising the importance of trust and confidentiality, involvement of the young person, offering choice and autonomy, in a context of having an understanding of why they are telling. This is a skilled and knowledgeable approach, equally relevant to research and practice, that is able to clearly convey to the child or young person a sense of being in control and being safe.

PROVIDING HELPFUL SERVICES

The young men's experiences presented in this research have significant implications for the nature and type of services that need to be set up, in order to help and support young people who have been sexually abused. The research has shown that the current legalism of the childcare system is harmful and that significant improvements could be made. The stories also suggest that there needs to be a wider and more flexible range of services that are able to meet young people's longer term needs.

The research has shown the lengths to which abusers are prepared to go in order to gain access to children and young people and make sure that their abusing remains undetected. The majority of the abusers were adults who were known to the children, often holding positions of trust and formal responsibility. This is not to forget the risks presented by strangers, which as Colin's case has shown can be substantial. Equally, it is important not to forget that there are many circumstances of sexual abuse being committed against children and young people by members of their families. The research highlights the diversity of circumstances through which children and young people can face risks of being sexually abused. This underlines the importance of preventive programmes to provide full information about the wide range of circumstances through which abusers may operate and the wide variation of their social background. Broader media campaigns, making links with sexual abuse and domestic violence, would challenge myths and stereotypes about abusers and would raise people's awareness of the widespread nature and prevalence of sexual abuse. These would further contribute to environments that break down silences and ensure greater protection, increasing the readiness of adults and others to listen to what children and young people may be trying to say (Mullender and Morley, 1994; Bagley and Thurston, 1996a; Wolfe et al., 1997).

The study underlines the need for more to be done to ensure that people with intentions to sexually abuse do not get into positions that provide them with

formal or professional access to children and young people. The recent setting up
of the national Criminal Records Bureau and the use of the Sex Offenders Register
will contribute to this. However, this still leaves the problem of abusers who have
never been prosecuted and are therefore not listed on any register. This could
therefore lull some people (including children and young people) or organisations
into false senses of safety and security. The research also highlights the importance
of appropriate training for members of staff in residential and other childcare
institutions, so as to enable them to become aware of the nature and impact of
child sexual abuse. It would also lead to improvements in the detection of ongoing
abuse from adults or peers either from within or outside the institution (Green and
Parkin, 1999). The study also shows how important it is for childcare institutions
to have policies that define sensitively and appropriately the boundaries of the
professional relationships between children and staff. Such institutions need to
have frequent and thorough inspections that should ideally include substantial
independent contact with the children and young people living in them.
Inspections should ensure that they have support and safety networks, including
unfettered regular access to confidential telephone helplines, such as Childline or
the NSPCC Child Protection Helplines (Butler and Williamson, 1994). Greater
child protection would more generally be achieved by an approach that promotes
an increased consultation and participation of children and young people in the
running of the institution and other matters concerning their lives, based on a
children's rights perspective, that challenge the adult–child power relationship
and extend the voice of the child (Myers et al., 1999).

The study has shown how difficult it is for children and young people to tell
about being sexually abused and how unhelpful some professional responses have
been, particularly within the legal and criminal justice system. This suggests a
need for a radical rethink about the procedures to which children and young
people are subjected, when all they may really want to do is tell and/or possibly
simply gain access to some form of help. This study suggests the need for children
and young people to be provided with these opportunities, without necessarily
having to fully go through the processes of a formal investigation. This suggests a
need for a more diverse range of services that may or may not necessarily involve
legal processes, or perhaps delay the involvement of legal processes, to a point
where the child or young person feels stronger and more able to cope. When it is
necessary to involve legal processes, the study suggests that they need to be
significantly amended to become more 'child-centred', taking account of what
young people have said about being on the receiving end, making sure that
every effort is made to prevent them from experiencing further harm. This
study challenges the fairness of the requirement for a child or young person
who has been sexually abused to appear in court. It has shown that when this
does happen the potential for further harm is great.

The study has provided ideas for helpful and supportive therapeutic intervention, regardless of the stage at which an investigation has reached (Durham,
1997a). It has been shown that there are significant aspects of harm that are
either generated or exacerbated by the wider social context in which the sexual
abuse has occurred. The wider and more generalised beliefs that are likely to have
been oppressively internalised have been shown to have a notable and detrimental

impact on the young person's self-esteem and feelings of social, sexual, and personal competence. The study has shown how these factors may also contribute to a child or young person's sense of being responsible for having been abused. By helping a young man gain an insight that breaks down some of these beliefs and socially generated myths, he can be helped in an indirect way to develop a better, more balanced and less harmful understanding of his experiences. In other words, the young person can be helped to develop strategies to dismantle the more generalised apparatus of his internalised oppression. This would potentially lead the young person into having an improved insight and ability to survive and sustain himself through a difficult stage of his life; this may be a stage where he is having to anticipate the likely oppressive outcome of having to appear as a witness in a court case. This work could be undertaken without discussing the factual details of the young person's abuse, until it had been presented in court as evidence. Taking this indirect approach is a compromise, in response to what the research has shown to be an unhelpful legal context, that often places evidential requirements before needs and wishes of the child or young person. This is not to deny the importance of prosecution, but to question the means by which it is currently achieved. These approaches are consistent with the recent Home Office et al. (2001a) *Provision of Therapy for Child Witnesses prior to a Criminal Trial—Practice Guidance*. In this study, Justin and David received a level of validation through being believed at a court trial. Prosecution was important for Colin, despite his anxieties about the investigation procedures, especially his forensic medical examination. He stated that '. . . if there was anything that could have nailed him I'd have done it.'

The study has challenged a linear model of recovery. It has shown how prolonged the impact of sexual abuse can be and how, after periods of recovery and survival, young people *may* experience setbacks and the return of abuse-related problems. This may occur, for example, when significant life events are faced, such as becoming involved in consenting sexual relationships, or becoming a father, or perhaps a family bereavement, or an anniversary of when the abuse took place. The young men's accounts of extensive and ongoing difficulties challenge the wisdom of time-limited, post-abuse services that are often a response to organisational demands and priorities and often a far cry from the needs of the child or young person. The expectation of recovery after a short time-limited intervention, if not fulfilled, may in itself convey a sense of failure. A young person, having gone through such a programme, may still feel the impact of being abused and may well be in need of further help and support. The research suggests a need for the provision of a diverse range of flexible specialist services that are user-friendly and non-pathologising, with less strictly defined cut-off points. These services would allow a young person to have access to ongoing support, additionally providing security in the knowledge that they are available, even if not used. It would be helpful for these services to include aspects of peer support and the involvement of other survivors of child sexual abuse (Scott, 1992; Durham, 1997a, 2000). This means thinking beyond current organisational structures within statutory agencies (particularly the divisions between adult, mental health, and children's services), so as to be able to provide appropriate support across the lifespan (NCH Action for Children, 1994).

CONCLUSIONS

This study has significant implications for the development of future forms of therapeutic practice that are potentially less pathologising than many existing services and forms of practice, which are dominated by either a medical (and) or legal framework. The research has provided a framework for future therapeutic practice that recognises the significance of narrative and discourse, in a context of social oppression. It has highlighted the need for an extremely sensitive therapeutic approach to the needs of children and young people who have been sexually abused. It has provided an important starting point of listening very closely and fully to what is communicated by the child or young person, verbal and non-verbal, and holding on to and responding to their needs and wishes as far as possible.

The research has shown how relevant and important it is for social work intervention to allow the young person to have the maximum possible control over the consequences of reporting sexual abuse. Without this, telling may ultimately amount to secondary abuse. Listening to the young men's stories has provided clues as to how to negotiate, advocate, and meet the therapeutic needs of the child or young person, alongside his (or her) involvement in difficult and often traumatic investigative and legal proceedings. The research has shown the complexities of surviving and recovering from sexual abuse and has highlighted the need for a more flexible approach to the provision of therapeutic services across the lifespan.

11

ASSISTANCE IN RECOVERY

INTRODUCTION

This chapter presents a plan for therapeutic work with children and young people who have been sexually abused. The plan is presented as a programme of work to be undertaken with an individual child or young person, but can be adapted easily to become part of a group work plan. Strong emphasis is placed on the plan being flexible and transparent, allowing the child or young person a maximum level of awareness and control. The plan allows the child or young person to become the expert in their recovery from sexual abuse and places the practitioner into the role of being a facilitator in assisting the child or young person to gain access to and develop personal competencies.

The chapter also presents further ideas, techniques, and materials that can be used as part of a therapeutic plan. This includes detail of some of the techniques of work undertaken with the research participants David and Ryan:

- *Road to Recovery* (see p. 135) is a pavement drawn out with David, on a large roll of wallpaper, as a path of his journey to recovering from being abused.
- *Feelings and Colours* (see p. 137 and the cover to this book) is a painting by David used as a visual technique to help him express his mixed feelings and understand how they interacted and sometimes contradicted each other.
- *Ryan's Poetry* (see p. 138) was produced spontaneously by Ryan during the course of the study.
- *Thoughts and Feelings Sort Cards* (see p. 141 and Appendix A) represent a helpful starting point for the therapeutic work, allowing the child or young person to be introduced to some difficult aspects of how they may feel about the abuse, by considering some of the thoughts, feelings, and anxieties expressed by other children and young people.
- *Keeping Safe Plan* (see p. 142) is a plan of work for helping children and young people keep themselves safe and feel more confident about telling.
- *Why Young People Find It Hard to Tell about Sexual Abuse* (see p. 143) is a useful summary, listed under three headings: Fear of the Consequences; Problems in Trying to Tell; Worries and Fears about Themselves.
- *Abuser–Victim Flow Chart* (see p. 145 and Appendix B) is a chart to help clarify how an abuser may construct an abusive relationship with a child or young person.

- *Feeling Safe and Being Safe (Information for Young People about Healthy Relationships)* (see p. 145 and Appendix C) is a leaflet to be used with young people, when discussing sexual relationships and sexuality.
- *Information About Child Sexual Abuse* (see Appendix D) is a useful summary leaflet.

A PLAN FOR FLEXIBLE THERAPEUTIC WORK

Below is an outline of suggestions for a flexible therapeutic plan for assisting a child or young person in their recovery from sexual abuse. This is not an exhaustive plan and should not be considered to be exclusive of other aspects of therapeutic support not included in the plan. This study has highlighted the importance of allowing children and young people the maximum possible control over any plan for their recovery. In this respect, the word 'flexible' is not used lightly, and a transparency of approach should be maintained throughout the entire process of the work. The order in which the work is undertaken will of course vary with the individual needs and circumstances of the child or young person. It would also be possible to adapt many aspects of this plan for group work. The timescale of this work will vary considerably between individual children. Where possible, the child or young person should be offered a choice about the gender of the therapeutic practitioner.

The plan will be discussed under the following headings:

- Being Safe—Feeling Safe—Keeping Safe
- Telling, Being Heard, Listened to, and Believed
- Placing Total Responsibility with the Abuser
- Telling Family
- Help with Legal Processes—Police—Court—Compensation
- How It Happened
- Why It Happened
- Understanding Gender Myths and Oppression
- Memories, Flashbacks, and Fears
- Anger and Feelings
- Sex and Sexuality Education and Knowledge
- Physical Pleasure
- Fears of Abusing Others
- Friendships and Peer Relations
- General Support

Being Safe—Feeling Safe—Keeping Safe

The initial phase of post-abuse therapeutic intervention should focus on the safety of the child or young person. Beginning with safety in the here and now, it is important to demonstrate that this has been considered in a manner that is understood, believed, and felt by the child or young person. This is why a transparency of approach is absolutely essential—it extends an opportunity of being in control and demonstrates that there are no hidden intentions. This is an aspiration, as it may take some considerable time for a child or young person to feel able to trust both the practitioner and the therapeutic process. He or she may have already been let down and betrayed by the person who committed the sexual abuse, so being asked to trust another person at this stage may at the very least be ambitious.

In maintaining a transparency of approach, the practitioner will have already met with the child or young person and somebody already known to them, whom they can accept day-to-day support from and whom hopefully they are able to trust. This becomes more difficult to achieve if the child or young person has recently moved out of home into public care. It is important that the principles and ideas behind a proposed plan of therapeutic work are declared and shared openly with the child or young person, alongside someone with whom they may at least have established some level of trust, and that they are offered an informed choice about taking part. There may be difficulties here if a child or young person is clearly having difficulties in coming to terms with being sexually abused, but at the same time is saying that he or she does not wish to talk or engage in receiving therapeutic support. It has to be remembered that many children and young people who have been sexually abused never report their abuse, never receive direct help and support, and manage to survive. A child or young person should not be pushed, pressured, or forced into post-abuse therapeutic work, as this will be experienced as an immediate loss of control and will run the risk of further compounding the impact of the abuse. For the child or young person it will become a further consequence of having been sexually abused.

If the child or young person chooses to enter into the therapeutic work, the sensitivity of this initial engagement will have to be maintained as he or she continues to assess, weigh up, and test out the process. Clearly stated ground rules that highlight safety and restate the choices and options will help maintain the young person's sense of being in control. Some children and young people will welcome a written and signed set of ground rules, others may find this intimidating and feel safer with a verbal process. As a starting point, the practitioner will need to gauge and assess the most appropriate way in which to proceed, the aspiration being that the child or young person feels central and in control. At this stage, the issue of confidentiality will need to be discussed, in terms of maintaining the safety of the child or young person and any other person who may be at risk of harm. There will be particular issues about this if the child or young person is waiting to appear as witness to their abuse in an impending court case and details of the therapeutic work may have to be disclosed.

Building on this process, the child or young person can then be helped to explore his or her feelings about safety in other areas of their life, informed about what they should expect for the future in terms of keeping safe, and told what he or she could do in the event of not feeling safe (see the *Keeping Safe Plan* on p. 142).

Telling, Being Heard, Listened to, and Believed

As a practitioner, it is likely that you will have heard already some of the details of the sexual abuse that has taken place. The child or young person may have given basic information in a formal interview with the police, you may have even been part of this process. This research has shown how difficult it is for a child or young person to make a 'disclosure' in the formal setting of a police interview or in a court cross-examination and how, in essence, this can be experienced as a loss of control. The child or young person is now in a position of being in control and telling the story in a manner closer to his or her choosing, and the practitioner at this stage is there to listen and provide sensitive and understanding responses.

Once safety has been established and tested out, some children and young people will be able to tell their story in an off-loading manner, with little prompting. Others will require more directive help and support in unfolding their story. The *Thoughts and Feelings Sort Cards* (discussed on p. 141 and displayed in Appendix A) are very helpful in this respect and can also be used to help the child or young person set a therapeutic agenda. There are also other materials presented later in the chapter and the appendices that may be useful at this stage. It is essential that in telling his or her story, the child or young person feels that he or she has been heard and believed. Many aspects of the process and outcome of this storytelling have been discussed at length in previous chapters and have been demonstrated by the methodology of the research study, which sought to maintain principles of good therapeutic practice throughout.

Placing Total Responsibility with the Abuser

In having listened to the story, it is important for the practitioner to emphasise strongly that the child or young person is not responsible for being sexually abused. This is a message that needs to be repeated at every opportunity, in a manner that has meaning for the child or young person. I have found it helpful to use a simple mathematical equation: 'There is only one hundred per cent of responsibility, and the abuser is one hundred per cent responsible, so what does that leave for you?' For younger children I have used word- guessing games with the answer being: 'it was not my fault' or 'I was made to believe it was my fault and now I know that it wasn't'. Writing these and other messages in multiple colours alongside doodles on flip chart paper is also helpful. For other children and young people, the process of feeling responsible may have to be explored more specifically and more explicitly in relation to the details of the abuse and the feelings involved. The term 'spellbound' can be a useful analogy in helping a child or young person understand how they may have been tricked into actions in situations and circumstances that were really well beyond their control. Looking back they may feel that there are many courses of action they feel they should have taken. Being under a 'spell' and 'breaking a spell' by telling may for some children and young people be a helpful concept.

It is also helpful to look at the abuse in terms of the young person having less power than the abuser, but not being completely powerless after all; by virtue of being in the room with the practitioner, the child or young person will have already told somebody about the abuse, and here they are now, taking further control, by getting help and assistance. The concept of powerlessness is therefore in many respects unhelpful. In hearing the child or young person's story in detail, there will be many examples of resistance and attempts to limit the impact of the abuse: 'I hid', 'I closed my eyes', 'I didn't go back', 'I went back so that I wouldn't be dragged there', 'I told my mum', and so on. These need to be identified and built on, with an emphasis on the child or young person's competency and survival.

At early stages of post-abuse, therapeutic work, the practitioner may be hearing the rationalisations of the abuser, through the words of the victim—the abuser in the victim's head—and these will have to be explored fully, in a manner that allows the child or young person to understand how these instilled rationalisations may have caused him or her to feel responsible for the abuse. There needs to be a return to the simple equation that the abuser was totally responsible. If he (she) was not there, it would not have happened.

Telling Family

Once the child or young person has told about their sexual abuse, depending on the circumstances, there may be significant changes to his or her family relationships that will need to be explored and discussed. It is often difficult for families to hear that their children have been sexually abused, particularly if the abuse has been committed by a family friend or a family member. Families may often have mistaken beliefs about sexual abuse—as this study has shown the causes and nature of sexual abuse is often misrepresented in the media. Some preparatory work with family members may therefore be necessary. The child or young person may wish to tell their family in their own time, or not at all. Here it may be necessary to explore with the child how a wish for privacy, or more accurately secrecy, may be related to notions of feeling responsible and how secrecy can maintain and propagate these feelings and beliefs. Being believed and understood by a practitioner is often a small step in comparison to being believed and understood by close family members. The child or young person may wish to tell their family in your presence, or may wish you to tell them in his or her presence, or in his or her absence. They may wish for some family members to know and for others not to know. Essentially, as far as possible, in terms of safety and protection, it has to be the choice of the child or young person.

Help with Legal Processes—Police—Court—Compensation

This study has shown how difficult and threatening the legal processes can be for children and young people who have been sexually abused and the extent to which they require support and advocacy in negotiating these complex and challenging circumstances. Some children and young people will have completed their involvement with the legal system by the time they have chosen to receive therapeutic support; for example, the abuse may have happened in earlier childhood, or a decision may have been taken not to prosecute. Here there may be a wish to look back and discuss these processes, either in a search for information, understanding, and meaning or as part of a need for support and recovery. Children and young people often have difficulties with their cross-examination, where they may feel that they have been intimidated and accused publicly of telling lies.

Quite often, for a child or young person who has been sexually abused a court trial is a no-win situation. If a prosecution has not succeeded, the child or young person is left with fears about not being believed and private speculations as to who else may follow suit. If the prosecution has been successful, he or she may have to come to terms with somebody they know and trusted, and possibly loved, having to face a prison sentence. Children and young people may not necessarily hate their abusers or even wish for them to come to harm, they may simply want the abuse to be stopped. Losing a parent or a sibling may have an equal or worse impact than being sexually abused, particularly if the abuser is the main caregiver. It is therefore very important for a child or young person to have choice about how their abuse is reported and whether or not they wish to attend a court trial. If he or she wishes to attend the trial, then it must be made clear that the outcome may not be what the child wishes, that there is a difference between believing something has happened and proving it beyond reasonable doubt in a court of law, and that the secrecy and hidden nature of child sexual abuse militates against the latter. There are many cases of child sexual abuse that do not even reach the court trial stage.

Recent government guidance, *Achieving Best Evidence in Criminal Proceedings* (Home Office et al., 2002) has made improvements to the involvement of children, young people, and vulnerable adults in court trials and has set out a range of recommendations for witness support throughout all stages of a trial, and afterwards. The guidance includes an implementation plan for the video recording of cross-examinations prior to a court trial. This would prevent the need for the child or young person to appear in court. It remains to be seen whether or not this proposal advances beyond its piloting phase. A related government document is *Provision of Therapy for a Child Witness Prior to a Criminal Trial* (Home Office et al., 2001a). This document was produced in response to concerns that child witnesses were being denied 'therapy' pending the outcome of a criminal trial for fear that evidence could be tainted and the prosecution lost. This concern may conflict with the need to ensure that child victims are able to receive, as soon as possible, immediate and effective therapeutic intervention to assist their recovery. It is also recognised that many child victims express the wish to see their abuser convicted and punished. The primary conclusion of this guidance states that those involved in the prosecution of an alleged abuser have no authority to prevent a child from receiving therapy. In Chapter 10 we discussed how therapeutic work could proceed, while at the same time maintaining the admissibility of the child's or young person's evidence (see also Durham, 1997a, 2000). A reordering of the therapeutic programme would allow factual details of the child's or young person's abuse to be discussed at a later stage, after the court trial, while allowing many of the contextual impact issues relating to sexuality and other fears and anxieties to be addressed more immediately, alongside providing support, building self-esteem, and establishing trust. In undertaking such work, it may be necessary for the practitioner to produce reports and explain his or her actions at the court trial. The fact that it has been necessary to provide such help and support may in itself serve as an important contribution to the court trial, particularly if the practitioner is asked to give an opinion on the state and well-being of the child or young person.

Following a criminal trial, or in the absence of a criminal trial, it may be possible for the child or young person to apply to the Criminal Injuries Authority for compensation. In the absence of a satisfactory outcome to criminal proceedings, this process can serve as an official validation of the abuse taking place. As with a criminal trial, it needs to be explained to the child or young person that applying for compensation involves risk, in that the application may not be successful.

How It Happened

It is helpful for the child or young person to understand the processes that the abuser went through in making the decision to sexually abuse. If it can be seen that the abuser's decision to abuse has a history that the child or young person was not part of, and for the most part not aware of, then this will help break down his or her sense of feeling responsible. It may be helpful to discuss Finkelhor's (1984) 'Four Preconditions to Sexual Abusing', perhaps in more simple terms of being the 'Four Steps to Committing Sexual Abuse':

1 wanting to do it;
2 thinking it's OK to do it;
3 finding an opportunity to do it;
4 getting the child or young person to go along with it.

The Abuser–Victim Flow Chart (see p. 145 and Appendix B) can also be used to assist some of this explanation of how the child or young person may have been targeted and groomed by the abuser. The detail and complexity of the explanations will of course have to vary in accordance with the child or young person's age and understanding, particularly in relation to the sexual content. Some young people may wish to discuss the sexual motivations of the abuser.

Why It Happened

In simple terms, the abuse happened because the abuser was present with the motivation and desire to abuse. The child or young person was targeted purposefully by the abuser. If the abuser had chosen not to abuse, then it would not have happened. It may also be helpful to discuss some of the contextual issues that have led to the prevalence of sexual abuse in our society.

Understanding Gender Myths and Oppression

The sexual abuse is likely to have an impact on how the child or young person feels about himself as a boy or herself as a girl. The abuse will likely be experienced as an assault on his or her 'masculinity' or femininity' and sexuality. Boys who have been abused may fear that they are gay or that they will become abusers; girls may fear that their femininity has been destroyed or damaged, and turn inward against themselves, and may feel that the only way they can relate to men is through their bodies. It is important to explore myths and false beliefs about gender and sexuality, as they may exacerbate significantly the impact of the abuse and serve as a vehicle to prolong and precipitate that impact into the child or young person's day-to-day living experiences. These issues have been discussed at length in previous chapters and form the centre of a narrative approach that helps the child or young person to externalise many of the issues that are causing concern, assisting him or her to challenge the dominant story with a more informed and insightful personal story, moving on toward an emphasis on new competencies in new contexts through being empowered by the light of this new information, and moving away from the passengerhood of a disabling pathology that maintains the child or young person as the essential centre of the problem. A personal framework, based on the diagram of analytical framework in Chapter 10, could be drawn out on a flip chart with the help of the child or young person, in accordance with his or her individual circumstances, feelings, and beliefs.

Memories, Flashbacks, and Fears

Chapters 2 and 8 explained how and why children and young people who have been sexually abused may be prone to an oscillation of flooding (flashbacks) and constriction (blocking) of memory, leading to dissociative states. This usually happens when memories of the trauma have been repressed so that they are not generally accessed by the conscious mind. Subconscious memories invade the conscious mind in a fragmented sense. Sounds, sights, tastes, smells, and touch can transport the child or young person back in their mind to their experience of being sexually abused; they have little control over this and often have little understanding of why or how these thoughts and feelings can be triggered. The thoughts and feelings can be extremely powerful and devastating. The child or young person will need some short-term help in coping with the immediate impact of flashbacks and further help in trying to prevent flashbacks occurring in the longer term. In coping with the immediate flashbacks, cognitive behavioural techniques are helpful in building-in alternative consequences and endings to the content of the flashback.

For example, one young person was helped by transforming into a 'super hero' who was able to interrupt the abusive process and take control saying, 'Not so fast! Now that I have told, you cannot do this to me anymore!' Other scenarios could involve interruption by police or parents and so on. In order to establish a meaningful interruption, the child or young person has to be engaged in describing the details of the flashback, which in itself will help to limit its intensity by confronting the details in the conscious mind. Again the issues about feeling safe are very important here, and it is likely that this work can only be done when trust and safety has been adequately established within the therapeutic process. These techniques are described more fully by Deblinger and Heflin (1996); also helpful are techniques described by Wasserman (1998).

The longer term problem of flashbacks is likely to be alleviated by the whole process of the therapeutic work being undertaken. A crucial aim of this work would be to assist the child or young person in becoming able to confront and fully comprehend the details and circumstances of his or her abuse and reintegrate visual images, physical sensations, and physiological responses—tastes, sounds, sights, smells, feelings—into their conscious mind. This would allow the child or young person to become able to ground themselves and distinguish past from present and, through being encouraged to access and develop personal competencies, become empowered toward taking control and rebuilding his or her life.

Anger and Feelings

Throughout many aspects of the therapeutic work, the child or young person is likely to require support and guidance in managing anger and in expressing feelings and emotion. It is important for the child or young person to find ways to express emotions and feelings in manners that are constructive and not disruptive to their lives. Sometimes this may be a high aspiration, as taking control can be very challenging and difficult to achieve. Feelings, thoughts, and anger need to be explored and discussed as much as possible, in a search for appropriate expression and solutions. The child or young person will need to know that it is important to be in touch with how their actions may affect other people and may sometimes alienate potential sources of help. Key people in the child or young person's life will need to be helped to have understanding about some of these processes and how best to be able to respond and provide appropriate support. For the child or young person, expression of feelings, which are quite often very powerful, is an essential part of the telling of the story and may sometimes be the only medium through which he or she feels able to communicate.

Sex and Sexuality Education and Knowledge

It is important to establish for the child or young person an age-appropriate level of understanding of sexual knowledge and an ability to be able to discuss his or her own sexuality. In helping young people understand issues about sexuality and sexual behaviour, it is important to have clearly stated values that take a holistic view of sexuality. Children and young people should be encouraged to understand that sexual behaviour is not just about physical or genital contact, but includes physical, mental, emotional, individual, social, cultural, religious, and political components, and that it is not necessary to have sex in order to express sexuality. They should be helped to understand that all forms of sexuality are equally valid: heterosexuality, lesbian and gay sexuality, celibacy. In discussing these issues, it is important to challenge oppression, misinformation, and stereotyping.

Physical Pleasure

The experience of physical pleasure while being sexually abused can quite often be one of the child or young person's most deeply held anxieties and can be a significant cause and rationale for feeling guilty and thereby responsible for the abuse. It can also cause considerable fears about sexuality and future sexual motivations. The abuser may well have made reference to the child or young person's physical response to the abuse as a calculated means of gaining simultaneously their 'co-operation' and silencing. These fears tap into many of the myths and oppressions that have been discussed fully in this study. It is essential for the practitioner to discuss this aspect of the abuse with the child or young person. Sometimes the fears may be so great that the child or young person will avoid or resist their discussion. It is also a potential source of great relief for the child or young person to have this aspect of the abuse analysed and explained in terms of anatomy and physiology: how the human body is constructed in terms of nerve cells and biological responses to genital touching and intercourse and how it is very hard for these experiences not to encounter pleasurable physical sensations.

Fears of Abusing Others

The fear of abusing others is another issue that may not, through fear and anxiety, be directly raised by the child or young person. As most abusers are male and because of the oppressive social construction of masculine sexuality and sexual behaviour, this is more likely to be a problem for boys and young men than for girls and young women, but not exclusively. Some young women who have been sexually abused have significant fears about the harm they may do to their own children, others may have powerful feelings of wishing to seek revenge. However, as this study has established, there are widespread misconceptions about the 'cycle of abuse', and many adult males who have sexually abused make reference to having been sexually abused themselves, which creates particular fears for boys and young men. The study has also discussed society's homophobic misconceptions and misunderstandings about connections between gay sexuality and paedophilia. This study directs the practitioner toward the need to disentangle all these misconceptions for and with the child or young person and to make the point strongly, clearly, and firmly that most people who have been sexually abused do not sexually abuse others.

Friendships and Peer Relations

The child or young person may have significant fears about how their close friends and acquaintances may react to finding out about the sexual abuse. The first point is that the child or young person should be selective in who he or she tells about the sexual abuse. It is essentially a private and personal matter that does not have to be shared. Sometimes, it may be helpful to assist the child or young person in constructing a cover story that can adequately explain any visible changes in his or her circumstances. Sometimes, close friends can be an essential source of help and support. The child or young person should be encouraged to discuss and plan out whom they may wish to tell about the abuse and be assisted in speculating what their reaction might be and, importantly, in assessing how well a confidence may be maintained. The child or young person will need to know that the information they may give may in itself be very distressing and difficult for their friend to manage and that this person may have a need for help and support from some-body else. This study has shown that peer group relations can be a significant catalyst to the child or young person's fears and anxieties about being sexually abused. It would therefore be helpful for these issues to be discussed throughout the various stages of the therapeutic work.

General Support

Through the provision of the therapeutic work, the child or young person will be receiving general ongoing support that, while working through specifically identified topics, will also involve the practitioner in the ups and downs of his or her daily life. Space should be provided within each session for discussion of day-to-day problems and their possible solutions. This space should also allow the sharing and celebration of day-to-day achievements and successes. Throughout the work, the child or young person should be nurtured into positive thinking, in a manner that builds persistently on self-esteem and personal competencies and gives a clear vision of being able to heal and to move on.

DAVID'S ROAD TO RECOVERY

During the course of my conversations with David, I had used the phrase 'on the road to recovery', which, in response, David had suggested could be sketched. This was done jointly. Using a large roll of wallpaper, a pavement was drawn: at the beginning was the date David remembered the abuse as starting and at the end was the present day. Major events were denoted by pelican crossings or traffic lights. The events that had taken place were listed in chronological order, with David's memories or thoughts and feelings associated with the events alongside. This enabled David to construct a visual picture of the process he had been through, how he had survived difficult experiences, and was able to reflect on his achievements, comparing past and present feelings.

The picture shows the turbulence in David's life: getting through one stage, such as the court appearance; feeling better; only to be later besieged by the onset of further nightmares or name-calling at school. Gradually, David was able to shun his feelings of responsibility and develop an improved insight into what had happened to him. David's experiences, thoughts, and feelings reflect Sanford's 'checkerboards of strengths and weaknesses' (1990, p. 16) and demonstrate the complexity of recovering from child sexual abuse. There have been many low points for David over the past few years, but these have been interspersed with positive achievements, events, and experiences. David's account shows the amount of work he has had to do in order to get over his abuse and concludes with a positive sense of his recovery and moving on. What follows is a transcript of what was written on the wallpaper, alongside the road drawing.

Year 1

- Going to his house, being abused.
- Being frightened to tell anyone.

Year 2 to 3

- Joining the group. Meeting the other boys, making friends.
- Going to the group each week.
- Bad feelings while waiting to go to court.
- Feeling that I have done something wrong.
- Getting angry about it.
- Worrying a lot.
- Learning that it was not my fault.
- Talking about court.
- Talking about how I feel in the group with the others.
- Feeling better in the group.
- Going to court, getting it over with.

Year 4 to 5

- Leaving the group, being back on my own again.
- I was all right at first, but then I started to worry again.
- Thinking he might come and get me.
- Or that I might meet him.
- Talking to mum about it.
- Applying for the money (compensation).
- Having trouble with school.
- Bad times coming back again. Being called names.
- Worrying about being gay and getting the names I was called.
- Thinking about the abuse again and Harry.
- Getting annoyed and angry about everything.
- Having arguments at home.
- Bad moods and losing my temper.
- Getting compensation money.
- Worrying that if I talk about it I will have to go to court again.
- Getting more help and planning it.
- Talking about bits of the abuse I hadn't been able to remember or tell anyone about before.
- Knowing that I definitely won't be going back to court.
- Having plenty of time to talk about what happened.
- Starting to work on my memory blocks.
- Talking about my bad dreams.
- Talking about the abuse in more detail.
- Asking questions about sex and sex education at school.
- Feeling better about me.
- Feeling better about my body.
- Understanding my body and how it makes me feel.
- Beginning to do better at school.
- More sex education and reading the book *Out in the Open* (Bain and Sanders, 1990) about other young people who were abused.
- Looking at why I couldn't tell at the time it happened.
- Becoming more able to talk about it and how I feel about it now.

- Being more able to talk about my worries about being gay.
- More help with my memory blocks.
- More talking about what happened and my memory blocks.
- Talking about friendships and relationships.
- Asking more questions about sex education and borrowing some more books on it.
- Understanding about being able to choose my friendships and my relationships if I want any.
- Knowing that the abuse hasn't made me gay.
- Understanding privacy and closeness between people.
- Being able to help protect my younger brothers.
- Not having to block everything out because of being afraid.
- Not losing my temper too much.
- Feeling able to make new friends.
- Not worrying about name-calling anymore.
- Feeling happier and more relaxed.
- Feeling good about myself and my future.
- Continuing with my life.
- Feeling OK about all of this.
- My future will be Great.

David (research participant)

David's account compliments many of the verbal comments from the other participants. When he was sexually abused, he was taken away and isolated. He was frightened to tell and felt responsible for what had happened. Going to court was a difficult experience for David and caused him considerable anxiety. He feels he benefited from meeting others with similar experiences in a group, which helped him through the court experience. After a while he began to feel better, but this was short-lived, and he began to ruminate over some of his memories, and began to have fears that when Harry was released from prison he would come and look for him. At school, his anxieties and experiences were similar to some of those experienced by the other participants, a hostile peer group that was quick in accusations and sexual name-calling. Like the others, David had a sensitive antenna to these comments and developed private fears about being gay. He had nightmares and was prone to mood swings and temper outbursts that he was unable to explain or understand.

Through talking, writing, and drawing, David was able to look back and understand some of these feelings and began to be able to accept that he was not responsible for the abuse. This allowed David to confront some of his fears and talk about some of his dreams and flashbacks, which in turn enabled him to talk more about what had happened to him.

THE MIXED FEELINGS PAINTING

David found it difficult to express some of his feelings, but it was clear that he did have feelings about what had happened to him and was showing a great amount

of confusion and ambivalence. As a medium of expression, I introduced David to
the idea of associating different colours with different feelings: that different
feelings could be experienced at the same time in a similar way to different
colours being seen simultaneously. David had very mixed feelings about the
man who abused him, brought on by memories of treats and positive experiences
alongside the abuse. He is aware that the experiences and treats took place so as to
make the abuse possible, but nonetheless struggles with a mixture of good and
bad feelings.

As a starting point, I painted a red margin and a blue margin and asked David
to identify the difference in associated feelings between the two colours. Blue was
identified as cold, and red as hot. Using a feelings chart (showing facial expressions) David was asked to select the ones that applied to the way he felt and
identify a colour he could associate with the feeling. David moved from selecting
solid colours and, jointly with myself, painting them on to the paper in separate
blocks, to mixing his own colours and painting them to overlap and cover existing
colours. Between us, an abstract picture of swirling and changing colours
emerged: a unique drawing, in which David selected more and more feelings
and obtained a wide range of colours.

The drawing was specifically produced in relation to David's feelings about
Harry, the man who had abused him. Once painted, no additional attempt at
interpretation is made, beyond this understanding and explanation of how and
why the painting was produced. David has asked for it to be included as part of
his contribution to the research. The painting appears on the cover of this book.
The initial colour key was:

Red : Warm	Blue : Cold	Brown : Unhappy/Sad
Yellow : Sick	Green : Good	Black : Scared/Bad
Red : Excited	Purple : Worried	Orange : Happy/Warm
Blue : Hurt	White : Hopeful	

RYAN'S POETRY

Ryan's feelings were most vividly expressed through his poetry, which he wrote
during the period in which he was taking part in the research interviews. Writing
these poems had a therapeutic value for Ryan, allowing him to express hidden
and hitherto unexpressed emotions. He was very pleased with them and very
positive about the prospect of them being published for others to see. The
poems demonstrate the extremity of some of his feelings, which he often finds
difficult to get in touch with in normal day-to-day interactions. During the research, Ryan explained that there are often large parts of the day that he would
forget and that he seemed to have an ability to block out difficult or challenging
experiences. He is unsure as to whether he wishes these experiences to be blocked
out or whether he has no choice about it. Some of these experiences appear to have
features of dissociation. If this is the case then they are likely to be a coping

mechanism. There are large parts of the abuse Ryan suffered that he can't remember, and the details he can remember sometimes vary from day to day. The poetry indicates the presence of deeply held feelings that are not easily accessed by Ryan, exemplified by sharp metaphors: edge; ledge; pain; private hell; bottomless well; sorrow trap; wreckage at the bottom of the bay; barren land; unspoken words hidden from light; punch and bash; always awake. The poems stand as a vivid testament to the experiences of all seven of the young men who took part in this research:

Who Me!
People say I can write
verse!
To me it sounds bad!
Don't try, if you read,
To understand me.
The verses I write
think how they feel,
Deep inside!

Far Too Late
Is it too late?
This feeling I hate.
My fate contemplate
on the edge
on this ledge.
My only way barred by a hedge.
Now I pledge
on this ledge.
Far to late
to contemplate.

I Wish You Could See
As you sit and stare through the
mirror you don't hear my thoughts.
If you could only see what you mean
to me, it would fill me with glee.
To take your hand and take you on a tour through this barren land of my
mind, from front to behind, inside you
would find the unspoken truth of
this matter, the unspoken words which
have lay so long, hidden from the light
of day which I long to say! To this day
I have found no way (?) In the wreckage
at the bottom of the bay, these words I long
to say.

My Hell

Locked in these four walls
chained in this cell, I've got
my own private Hell.
Like a bottomless well,
Never ending the drop of my
moral. Will you help me break this spell?
As you walk down the hall
be careful not to fall into
the sorrow trap.

Fear

That immortal scream
in dreams it came
it made me afraid.
Each raid my cave saved,
and aided me sometimes it
seemed to fade but I'm
Still afraid!

Always Awake

As I sit here in the sun,
I start to wonder through my mind.
I laugh and joke with my pride.
Punch and bash my dignity.
I then find an emotion I can't
understand, so I observe
and try to understand!
What are these feelings?
Sometimes harsh (?)
Sometimes soft (?)
Cold, warm too (?)
This emotion I can't control
for many years it takes
It forms, but in all its
Varying states hard to see but
always awake.

Help

How can I stop this pain?
Please tell me!
Can I stop the pain?
It hurts so bad!
Help me stop the pain!
My soul is sore!
Help me stop the pain!

THOUGHTS AND FEELINGS SORT CARDS

These sort cards (see Appendix A) are largely based on the experiences and comments the young men made during the course of this study. They would therefore best be introduced to the child or young person undergoing therapeutic post-abuse work as comments made by young people who have themselves been sexually abused and have expressed a wish to help others by sharing their thoughts, feelings, and experiences.

By using these cards, the child or young person is introduced safely to the thoughts and feelings of others. This will help break down feelings of isolation and will assist in helping the child feel less responsible for what has happened. Sometimes, it may be easier for children and young people to sort through a pack of cards, rather than reading a book. The card format allows the practitioner to be selective in what is presented, in accordance with the child or young person's age and understanding and how they may be feeling at the time.

The cards can be presented to the child or young person to look at without comment, or he or she can be asked to select which cards they may feel are relevant to their own experiences, thoughts, and feelings. Many of the comments on the cards are in themselves sensitive and may be controversial or challenging for the child or young person. They raise topics that, while relevant, may be fear-provoking. They nonetheless allow these fears to be named, without necessarily being directly verbalised; this is likely to act as a prompt for the young person. The young person could then be asked to form, from the cards, a hierarchy of concerns, which will then form the basis of a plan for further therapeutic work. Importantly, the child or young person must be asked if he or she feels that there are aspects for discussion beyond what is presented by the cards. The cards can be helpful in assisting the child in setting an agenda for therapeutic support, but they must not in themselves become the agenda, as the child or young person may feel they have lost or are losing control over the process.

It is important that these cards are used skilfully by a practitioner, who will need to have the experience and resources to respond to the emotions and reactions they are likely to precipitate from the child or young person. It is not advisable for these cards to be handed to the young person in circumstances where they will not receive appropriately informed support and therapeutic guidance.

The cards can be used to introduce topics as a vehicle for discussion with perhaps safer reference to a third person: 'Why do you think this person may have felt like this or made this particular comment?' It is sometimes safer for a child or young person to talk about someone else's experiences, rather than their own, with connections to their own experiences and feelings being made later through the therapeutic process.

Quotation cards

In a similar way, more detailed quotations from the main text of the young men's stories can be copied and made into cards. Again, a card format will allow the practitioner to be selective, timely, and sensitive in presenting particular aspects of the young men's stories to the child or young person. Often, on hearing these quotations, children and young people will want to know more about the person behind the quotation, how they were abused, how old they were, and so on. There is sufficient information in the text for these questions to be answered.

KEEPING SAFE PLAN

Initial phase

- Establish the child's understanding of the need for safety work.
- Discuss ground-rules about confidentiality, stating that where possible an appropriate level of confidentiality will be maintained, but that information relating to the actual or potential harm of the child or another person may have to be shared with others in sufficient detail as to ensure safety and protection. It may be helpful to give concrete examples of circumstances where information would have to be shared and why.
- Create opportunities for the child to say anything they wish—good and bad.
- With the child identify important people in his or her life—use an ecomap (a diagram drawn out on a flip chart highlighting people and activities in the child's life). A drawing of the child, preferably by the child, is at the centre, with lines drawn to aspects of home, school, friendships, and leisure pursuits, with comments from the child about the relative importance of each aspect and the quality of relationships with the key people involved.
- Identify whom the child feels safe about.
- Identify anyone whom the child may have difficulties with.
- Move on to some more specific questions about the child's life. These could include questions about: which people the child spends time with; whose company he or she likes the most; how the child spends time at home; where time is spent; perceptions of risk and safety.
- Ask if there is anything specifically bothering or worrying the child.
- Encourage the child to talk about life at home and school.
- Introduce the idea of safety—being safe—feeling safe—keeping safe.

Introduce 'protective behaviours'[1] concepts

- We all have the right to feel safe all the time.
- There is nothing so awful we can't talk about it with someone.
- Understanding and experiencing feelings—safe—scary—fun—unsafe.
- OK and NOT OK touching.
- Privacy and secrecy—good secrets—bad secrets.
- Body awareness—private parts.

---

[1] Based on materials developed from the Australian Protective Behaviours Programme, 'Protective Behaviours' is about empowerment, communication, self-esteem, and other life skills. It is an internal process where each person applies the ideas and concepts to their own unique experience (further details are available from www.protectivebehaviours. co.uk).

Telling

- What to tell—discuss circumstances where the child may feel uncomfortable, unsafe, or feels unhappy about. Give concrete examples of inappropriate touching and inappropriate conversation or threats. Remind the child that he or she can tell about anything that he or she is unhappy about or unsure of.
- How to tell—rehearsals and role-plays with the child, discussing the language he or she may use to tell. Help the child to identify safe circumstances and scenarios of telling.

Telling group

A list of people whom the child would feel safe about telling to:

- Draw out hand and list five people, one on each finger.
- Discuss what would be expected of a person whom was told something.
- Rules for 'telling people' in 'telling group': (1) they would listen; (2) they would act—do something to help; (3) they would tell someone else—teacher/policeman/parents, etc.
- Check out by asking questions such as: Have you ever tried to tell somebody about something you were not happy with? What happened?
- Have you ever wanted to tell somebody about something, but felt unable to. What happened?
- Emphasise the importance of persistence—if the child is not happy with the outcome of telling, then he or she could tell somebody else.
- Emphasise the potential good outcome of telling: (1) it's not your fault; (2) you won't be in trouble; (3) something will be done to change whatever you are unhappy about.

Closure phase

- Check out how much information the child or young person has retained and get him or her to recall the five 'telling people' in their 'telling group'.

WHY YOUNG PEOPLE FIND IT HARD TO TELL ABOUT SEXUAL ABUSE

This summary of possible reasons why a child or young person may have difficulty in telling about or reporting sexual abuse has been drawn and developed from the young men's accounts in the research. It has many potential uses. For the practitioner, it can serve as a checklist that can be applied to thinking about a particular child or young person and may prompt particular questions based on those circumstances. It also serves as a reminder of the range of considerations a child or young person may be facing in reaching a decision to tell. It can be used directly with the child or young person, in a similar manner to the 'Thoughts and Feelings Sort Cards'. For some, this may be a preferred format to the sort cards. It is a very useful document for parents and carers. I have used it to good effect many times in providing training courses for foster carers. It helps carers to think more laterally about their child's circumstances and actions, on which they can base thoughtful and sensitive responses. It will generally add to their understanding about the impact of child sexual abuse.

Fear of the consequences

- Being physically and emotionally harmed by the abuser.
- Being threatened themselves, or threats to other family members.
- Feeling worried about what people will think of them.
- Not wanting to cause trouble for their family.
- Not wanting the person who abused them to get into trouble.
- Protecting brothers and sisters from the consequences of telling.
- Fears about not being believed.
- Knowing that the abuser will deny that it happened.
- Fears about being seen as an abuser.
- Fears about involving the police.
- Fears about racism.
- Fears about their friends finding out.

Problems in trying to tell

- Being made to promise to keep a secret.
- Having already tried and not being heard.
- Being paid money or given treats not to tell.
- Not knowing which words to use.
- Being unable to find an opportunity to tell.
- Not knowing who is a safe person to tell.
- Not knowing that something could be done to stop it happening again.
- Being isolated.
- Simply wanting to forget about it.

Worries and fears about themselves

- Being tricked into believing it was their fault.
- Feeling guilty, embarrassed, and ashamed.
- Feeling responsible for being abused, believing they were the abuser.
- Feeling dirty.
- Fears about having flashbacks.
- Being worried about experiencing physical pleasure when it happened.
- Fears about health and physical injuries.
- Fears about sexually transmitted diseases.
- Fears that they may have done something to attract the abuse.
- Fears about being a 'prostitute'.
- Fears about pregnancy.
- Fears about future sexual relationships.
- Fears about being gay or being seen as being gay.

- Fears about never being able to be a real or true 'woman' or 'man'.
- Fears about abusing others.
- Fears about not doing anything to stop it.
- Fears about being sexually ruined.
- Fears about thinking about sex too much.
- Overall fears about how they will be viewed by other people.

ABUSER–VICTIM FLOW CHART

This flow chart (see Appendix B) summarises some of the processes of child sexual abuse and further illustrates how the abuser takes control and makes the child or young person feel responsible for the abuse. It highlights how little the child or young person knows about the abuser's intentions, how trapped he or she would feel, and how difficult it would be to tell. As with 'Why Young People Find It Hard to Tell About Sexual Abuse', this document lends itself to a range of uses: for practitioners, for their own understanding, and for use with carers and young people. For a child or young person who has been sexually abused, a personalised set of boxes could be compiled. It would also be helpful for the child or young person to be given a printed sheet with this flow chart on it (p. 171), so as to help him or her understand that many other young people in similar circumstances may have the same feelings. This would help to break down feelings of shame and isolation.

FEELING SAFE AND BEING SAFE

Sex education is an important aspect of post-abuse work. *Feeling Safe and Being Safe* (see Appendix C) is a leaflet I have developed for working generally with young people, in helping them with their understanding of a range of peer-related issues about sexual behaviour. It helps them to consider the wider influences on their received beliefs and understandings about how men and women (or boys and girls) should behave toward each other and how they should portray their sexuality. It invites the young person to look beyond these images and develop the confidence to be whom they want to be, rather than whom they feel they ought to be. It deals with homophobia, peer pressure, and informed consent and reminds everybody that they have a right to feel safe.

As a leaflet, it can be distributed to young people for them to read themselves, but its greatest use is as an agenda for planned sessions of therapeutic work. Each section can be developed, expanded, and supplemented with other materials as appropriate to develop a comprehensive programme of work.

INFORMATION ABOUT CHILD SEXUAL ABUSE

This is a leaflet (see Appendix D) giving basic initial information about child sexual abuse. The information is both helpful to parents and to children and young people.

12

CONCLUSIONS

This book has centralised and validated seven young men's accounts of experiences of child sexual abuse and has contextually analysed its impact in close detail. The study has explored common and diverse experiences, attempting to capture the texture and meaning of the unique integration of the impact of child sexual abuse into each of the young men's lives. The study emphasised the issue of participant support, recognising the extreme sensitivity of child sexual abuse as a research topic. An attempt was made to create a safe research environment that has been described as being 'anti-hegemonic', allowing the young men to feel safe in expressing sensitive and raw feelings, in the knowledge that they would receive appropriate and supportive responses, before, during, and after the life-story interviews. The majority of information generated was verbal, but this was not prioritised to the exclusion of non-verbal accounts and therefore included poetry and artwork. The theoretical perspective of the study allowed the development of a new analytical practice framework that has provided new and exciting ideas for non-pathologising therapeutic practice with children and young people who have been sexually abused.

WHAT THE STORIES HAVE TOLD US

The study has shown how and why experiences of child sexual abuse have had a serious and long-lasting, harmful impact on the lives of the young men who were interviewed. The young men, having already lived through difficult and disadvantaged childhood circumstances, were subsequently sexually abused through asymmetrical power relationships constructed by adults in positions of formal, official, or social authority. Often, the adults commanded social circumstances that allowed them to have significant degrees of control over the young men's lives and allowed them to abuse and subsequently silence them. The young men were made to feel guilty and ashamed of being sexually abused and were warned that telling would be met by criticism, blame, or disbelief. The young men's accounts revealed their many and varied strategies of resistance in surviving these adverse circumstances. Those who formally reported being sexually abused found their involvement with the legal system distressing. Those who did not formally report their abuse found the prospect of being involved with the legal system potentially stressful.

Further theoretical connections have been made between the centrality of sexuality and power in post-structuralism and the nature of experiences of child sexual abuse. It was recognised through the work of Foucault (1976) and others (Weedon, 1987; Cooper, 1995) that sexuality is a central locus of power in post-structural theory. Compulsory heterosexuality, homophobia, and eroticised power are also recognised as being central to patriarchal constructions of masculinities (Kaufman, 1987; Connell, 1989; Seidler, 1989) or, more accurately, men's practices (Hearn, 1996).

The experiences of the young men were analysed in relation to these social constructions, which were identified as being a social context that allows the sexual abuse of women and children to happen. The young men's experiences showed that the manner in which they perceived their masculinities had a significant exacerbating influence on the impact of being sexually abused. There was evidence of internalised oppression based on beliefs about experiences of sexual abuse not being consistent with social constructions of hegemonic masculinities (dominant forms of men's practices). The young men carried homophobic fears that were daily reinforced by their peer group experiences.

The research and literature (Bremner and Hillin, 1993; Nayak and Kehily, 1997) established that homophobia and internalised oppression were not uncommon among male adolescent peer groups. It was shown that these beliefs had become more threatening and pronounced as a result of the young men's experiences of being sexually abused. There was evidence that, through privately held fears and misinformation, the young men conflated their experiences of sexual abuse with gay sexuality. Consequently, all the young men developed fears of being gay or being 'accused' of being gay. Additionally, some of the young men took this further and lived in fear of abusing others or being accused of abusing others. In particular, some of the young men commented specifically on how they felt being abused had caused them to worry about how they would be perceived as fathers, caring for their own children. All the young men's accounts showed that they were oppressively affected by their peer group interactions, living in fear of 'discovery'. In order to evade this discovery, some of the young men embarked on patterns of behaviour that they perceived to be a conformity to dominant social constructions of men's practices (as Liam said, 'acting the homophobic'). In a circular manner, this served to reinforce patterns of hegemonic masculinity and heightened their fears of 'discovery'. The research recognised that, in a context of patriarchal relations, these fears were reinforced by the media, in its responses to gay sexuality, child sexual abuse, and sexual offending and more generally in its portrayal of masculinities through imagery and popular culture.

In the months and years that followed the sexual abuse, the young men continued to have difficulties with their lives. Social pressures and flashbacks kept the wounds open and once again drove some of the young men into silence and secrecy, concealing their memories and feelings. In surviving and resisting social pressures, some of the young men used drugs and alcohol to block out memories and get through the days. However, and improbably, the stories have also shown perspectives of hope and resistance. The research reminds us that it is important to recognise that those who live their lives out on the margins often have prodigious strengths and that what is amazing is not that they fail, but how often they triumph (Sanford, 1990).

Two of the young men had not previously discussed or reported their abuse, taking their research participation as an opportunity to finally relieve themselves of the burden they had been carrying for many years. All the young men welcomed the opportunity to share their thoughts and feelings about being sexually abused and stated that they felt they had benefited from taking part in the research. A cautious approach is taken to drawing conclusions about how much the young men benefited, and the extent to which they experienced any form of empowerment. This is in recognition of their continuing disadvantaged lives, not helped by the impact of child sexual abuse and its interaction with other life experiences. This challenges a linear model of recovery. It was recognised that the young men had different and changing experiences, having good days and bad days, ups and downs, sometimes being able to move on into new experiences and phases of their lives, other times falling back into the pains of the past.

A NEW FRAMEWORK FOR NON-PATHOLOGISING THERAPEUTIC PRACTICE WITH YOUNG MEN

This research has recognised that existing services are overly legalistic and mechanistic and that psychological 'treatment' procedures are pathologising in their reference to 'diagnosis', 'symptoms', and 'characteristics'. These approaches have the potential to compound inadvertently the child or young person's oppressively internalised understanding of how and why they have been sexually abused. This underlines the need to develop forms of therapeutic practice that consciously seek to externalise the problem from the young person, in a manner that unequivocally places the responsibility for the abuse where it belongs: with the abuser.

While there has previously been significant gender-centred research and practice in relation to work with women and girls who have been sexually abused (Kelly, 1988b; Hall and Lloyd, 1989), this has not been the case in relation to males. This research has attempted to provide new ideas for therapeutic practice with boys and young men that centralise issues of gender and power. It has drawn attention to the importance of these issues to be considered for all young men, through a wide range of practices; for example, in their schooling, their general health, and social education (Wolfe et al., 1997). In particular, the anti-oppressive methodology and the analysis has provided a practical and theoretical framework for non-pathologising therapeutic practice with sexually abused young men (the study has maintained throughout that many of these suggested approaches to practice are transferable to girls and young women). This is an approach that has an emphasis on supporting, empowering, and assisting a child or young person's recovery, recognising their strengthening through survival. It provides the space for a young man to gain insight into how his hopes, fears, and beliefs have been socially constructed. It provides a starting point for the practitioner, in terms of approaching the provision of assistance from the perspective of the young man. This involves paying careful attention to the words used by the young man to explain and describe his experiences, taking time to pick up on the important clues they may give about internalised oppression and distorted beliefs about responsibility and about what a young man may think being abused means.

This study has highlighted the need for services to be more flexible and child- and young person-centred. It has shown how harmful and traumatic the mechanistic procedures and the current legalism of the childcare arena can be for those on the receiving end of investigation procedures. While recognising the urgent need for radical changes in the legal system, the study has provided helpful ideas for supporting children and young people caught up in the unacceptable delays and traumas of the current system.

The study has shown the important need for appropriate training for staff members of childcare institutions. It has demonstrated the urgency of ensuring that those with intentions to abuse do not get into positions where they have power and authority over children and young people, underlining the need for regular and unfettered inspection. It has shown the importance of providing a range of supportive opportunities for telling and the need for ongoing flexible services to be provided across the lifespan.

Finally, it is hoped that the young people who have contributed to the knowledge generated by this study and others who in some way become aware of it will benefit. It is also hoped that future research and other professional practices will become more anti-oppressive and allow the voices of children and young people to be heard, fully understood, and responded to in a more helpful manner. The last word should be with one of the participants, Justin, who, in a very deep and searching reflection, attempting to salvage something positive from what he has been through, told me:

> I don't think it was my fault, what happened. What's happened has happened, I can't turn nothing back. If I could I would, but I can't. But then if I turned it back my life wouldn't be what it is . . .

BIBLIOGRAPHY

Abel GG, Becker JV, and Cunningham-Rathner J (1984) 'Complications, consent, and cognitions in sex between children and adults.' *International Journal of Law and Psychiatry*, **7**, 89–103.

Abercrombie N, Hill S, and Turner BS (eds) (1990) *Dominant Ideologies*. London, Unwin Hyman.

Acker J, Barry K, and Esseveld J (1983) 'Objectivity and truth: Problems in doing feminist research.' *Women's Studies International Forum*, **6**(4), 423–35.

Adams J (1995) 'Kinsey report based on pervert's files.' *The Sunday Times*, 10 December, p. 18.

Ahmad B (1990) *Black Perspectives in Social Work*. Birmingham, Venture Press.

Aldridge J and Freshwater K (1993) 'The preparation of child witnesses.' *Journal of Child Law*, **5**(1), 25–7.

Aldridge M, Timmins C, and Wood J (1997) 'Children's understanding of legal terminology: Judges get money at pet shows, don't they? *Child Abuse Review*, **6**(2), 141–6.

Anderson K (1997) 'Uncovering survival abilities in children who have been sexually abused.' *Families In Society*, November–December, 592–9.

Angelou M (1969) *I Know Why the Caged Bird Sings*. London, Virago Press.

Araji SK (1997) *Sexually Aggressive Children—Coming to Understand Them*. Thousand Oaks, CA, Sage Publications.

Arber S (1993) 'The research process'. In N Gilbert (1993) *Researching Social Life*. London, Sage Publications.

Archard D (1993) *Children: Rights and Childhood*. London, Routledge.

Asdigian NL and Finkelhor D (1995) 'What works for children in resisting assaults?' *Journal of Interpersonal Violence*, **10**(4), 402–18.

Babiker G and Herbert M (1996) 'The role of psychological instruments in the assessment of child sexual abuse.' *Child Abuse Review*, **5**, 239–51.

Bagley C and Thurston W (1996a) *Understanding and Preventing Child Sexual Abuse*. Aldershot, UK, Arena.

Bagley C and Thurston W (1996b) *Understanding and Preventing Child Sexual Abuse*. Aldershot, UK, Arena.

Bain O and Sanders M (1990) *Out in the Open. A Guide for Young People Who Have Been Sexually Abused*. London, Virago Press.

Barrett M and Phillips A (1992) *Destabilizing Theory*. Cambridge, Polity Press.

Bartholow BN, Doll LS, Joy D, Douglas Jr JM, Bolan G, Harrison JS, Moss P, and McKirnan D (1994) 'Emotional, behavioural, and HIV risks associated with sexual abuse among adult homosexual and bisexual men.' *Child Abuse and Neglect*, **18**(9), 747–61.

Bates J, Pugh R, and Thompson N (eds) (1997) *Protecting Children: Challenges and Change*. Aldershot, UK, Arena.

Bean B and Bennett S (1993) *The Me Nobody Knows*. New York, Lexington.

Becker JV, Kaplan MS, Tenke CE, and Tartaglini A (1991) 'The incidence of depressive symptomatology in juvenile sex offenders with a history of abuse.' *Child Abuse and Neglect*, **15**, 531–6.

Beitchman JH, Zucker KJ, Hood JE, DaCosta GA, and Akman D (1991) 'A review of the short-term effects of child sexual abuse.' *Child Abuse and Neglect*, **15**, 537–56.

Beitchman JH, Zucker KJ, Hood JE, DaCosta GA, Akman D, and Cassavia E (1992) 'A review of the long-term effects of child sexual abuse.' *Child Abuse and Neglect*, **16**, 101–18.

Belitz J and Schacht A (1992) 'Satanism as a response to abuse: The dynamics and treatment of satanic involvement in male youths.' *Adolescence*, **27**(108), 853–72.

Bell V (1993) *Interrogating Incest*. London, Routledge.

Bendixen M, Muus KM, and Schei B (1994) 'The impact of child sexual abuse—A study of a random sample of Norwegian students.' *Child Abuse and Neglect*, **18**(10), 837–47.

Bennetts C, Brown M, and Sloan J (1992) *AIDS—The Hidden Agenda in Child Sexual Abuse*. Harlow, UK, Longman.

Benoit JL and Kennedy WA (1992) 'The abuse history of male adolescent sex offenders.' *Journal of Interpersonal Violence*, **7**(4), 543–8.

Bentovim A, Vizard E, and Hollows A (eds) (1991) *Children and Young People as Abusers*. London, National Children's Bureau.

Berliner L and Conte JR (1990) 'The process of victimisation: The victims' perspective.' *Child Abuse and Neglect*, **14**, 29–40.

Berliner L and Saunders BE (1996) 'Treating fear and anxiety in abused children: Results of a controlled 2-year follow-up study'. *Child Maltreatment*, **1**(4), 294–309.

Bibby PC (ed.) (1996) *Organised Abuse*. Aldershot, UK, Arena.

Black CA and DeBlassie RR (1993) 'Sexual abuse in male children and adolescents: Indicators, effects and treatments.' *Adolescence*, **28**(109), 123–33.

Black M, Dubowitz H, and Harrington D (1994) 'Sexual abuse: Developmental differences in children's behaviour and self-perception.' *Child Abuse and Neglect*, **8**, 85–95.

Bly R (1990) *Iron John*. Shaftesbury, UK, Element.

Bolton Jr FG, Morris LA, and MacEachron AE (1989) *Males at Risk*. Beverly Hills, CA, Sage Publications.

Bowen D (1993) 'The delights of learning to apply the life history method to school non-attenders.' In B Broad and C Fletcher (eds) (1993) *Practitioner Social Work Research in Action*. London, Whiting and Birch.

Bowl R (1985) *Changing the Nature of Masculinity*. Norwich, UK, University of East Anglia.

Bradley AR and Wood JM (1996) 'How do children tell? The disclosure process in child sexual abuse.' *Child Abuse and Neglect*, **120**(9), 881–91.

Brannan C, Jones JR, and Murch JD (1991) *Castle Hill Report* (Practice Guide). Shrewsbury, UK, Shropshire County Council.

Brannan C, Jones JR, and Murch JD (1993) 'Lessons from a residential special enquiry: Reflections on the Castle Hill Report.' *Child Abuse Review*, **2**(4), 271–5.

Brannen J (1993) 'The effects of research on participants: Findings from a study of mothers and employment.' *The Sociological Review*, 328–48.

Brayden RM, Dietrich-MacLean G, Dietrich MS, Sherrod KB, and Altemeier WA (1995) 'Evidence for specific effects of childhood sexual abuse on mental well-being and physical self-esteem.' *Child Abuse and Neglect*, **19**(10), 1255–62.

Bremner J and Hillin A (1993) *Sexuality, Young People and Care*. London, Central Council for Education and Training in Social Work.

Briere J and Runtz M (1988) 'Post sexual abuse trauma.' In GE Wyatt and GJ Powell (eds) *Lasting Effects of Child Sexual Abuse* (pp. 85–99). Beverly Hills, CA, Sage Publications.

Briere J, Smiljanich K, and Henschel D (1994) 'Sexual fantasies, gender, and molestation history.' *Child Abuse and Neglect*, **18**(2), 131–7.

Briere JN (1992) *Child Abuse Trauma*. Beverly Hills, CA, Sage Publications.

Briggs F (1995a) *From Victim to Offender*. St Leonards, Australia, Allen & Unwin.

Briggs F (1995b) *Developing Personal Safety Skills in Children with Disabilities*. London, Jessica Kingsley.

Briggs F and Hawkins RMF (1996) 'A comparison of the childhood experiences of convicted male child molesters and men who were sexually abused in childhood and claimed to be nonoffenders.' *Child Abuse and Neglect*, **20**(3), 221–33.

British Sociological Association (1994) *British Sociological Association Statement of Ethical Practice* (Equality of the Sexes Committee, Appendix 4). Durham, UK, BSA.

Broad B and Fletcher C (eds) (1993) *Practitioner Social Work Research In Action*. London, Whiting & Birch.

Brown HC (1998) *Social Work and Sexuality*. London, Macmillan.

Browne J (1996) 'Unasked questions or unheard answers? Policy development in child sexual abuse.' *British Journal of Social Work*, **26**, 37–52.

Burgess RG (1984) *In the Field*. London, Routledge.

Burgess RG (ed.) (1982) *Field Research*. London, Routledge.

Burke M (1995) 'Identities and disclosures. The case of lesbian and gay police officers.' *The Psychologist*, December, 543–7.

Burman E (1994) *Deconstructing Developmental Psychology*. London, Routledge.

Butler I (1996) 'Children and the sociology of childhood.' In I Butler and I Shaw (eds) *A Case of Neglect?* (pp. 1–18). Aldershot, UK, Avebury.

Butler I and Shaw I (1996) *A Case of Neglect?* Aldershot, UK, Avebury.

Butler I and Williamson H (1994) *Children Speak*. Harlow, UK, Longman.

Cain M (1990) 'Realist philosophy and standpoint epistemologies or feminist criminology as a successor science.' In L Gelsthorpe and A Morris (eds) *Feminist Perspectives in Criminology*. Buckingham, UK, Open University Press.

Calvi B (1994a) 'The sexual abuse of males: Current literature and research recommendations, Part One.' *Treating Abuse Today*, **4**(5), 16–21.

Calvi B (1994b) 'The sexual abuse of males: Current literature and research recommendations, Part Two.' *Treating Abuse Today*, **4**(6), 28–33.

Campbell D (1994) 'Breaching the shame shield: Thoughts on the assessment of adolescent child sex abusers.' *Journal of Child Psychotherapy*, **20**(3), 309–26.

Capra F (1975) *The Tao of Physics*. Bungay, UK, Fontana.

Carballo-Dieguez A and Dolezal C (1995) 'Association between history of childhood sexual abuse and adult HIV—Risk of sexual behaviour in Puerto Rican men who have sex with men.' *Child Abuse and Neglect*, **19**(5), 595–605.

Carrigan T, Connell B, and Lee J (1987) 'Hard and heavy: Toward a new sociology of masculinity.' In M Kaufman (ed.) *Beyond Patriarchy*. Toronto, Open University Press.

Cawson P (2002) *Child Maltreatment in the Family: The experience of a National Sample of Young People*. London, National Society for the Prevention of Cruelty to Children.

Cawson P, Wattam C, Brooker S, and Kelly G (2000) *Child Maltreatment in the United Kingdom* (a study of child abuse and neglect). London, National Society for the Prevention of Cruelty to Children.

CCETSW (1995) *Dip SW: Rules and Requirements for the Diploma in Social Work* (Paper 30). London, Central Council for Education and Training in Social Work.

Cermak P and Molidor C (1996) 'Male victims of child sexual abuse.' *Child and Adolescent Social Work Journal*, **3**(5), 385–400.

Chandy JM, Blum RW, and Resnick MD (1996) 'Gender-specific outcomes for sexually abused adolescents.' *Child Abuse and Neglect*, **20**(12), 1219–31.

Chandy JM, Blum RW, and Resnick MD (1997) 'Sexually abused adolescents: How vulnerable are they?' *Journal of Child Sexual Abuse*, **6**(2), 1–16.

Clifford D (1994) 'Critical life-histories: Key anti-oppressive research methods and processes.' In B Humphries and C Truman (eds) *Re-thinking Social Research*. Aldershot, UK, Avebury.

Coffey P, Leitenberg H, Henning K, Turner T, and Bennett RT (1996) 'Mediators of the long term impact of child sexual abuse: Perceived stigma, betrayal, powerlessness, and self-blame.' *Child Abuse and Neglect*, **20**(5), 447–55.

Connell RW (1987) 'Theorising gender.' *Sociology*, **19**(2), 260–72.

Connell RW (1989) *Gender and Power, Society, the Person and Sexual Politics*. Cambridge, Polity Press.

Connell RW (1995) *Masculinities*. Cambridge, Polity Press.

Conte JR and Schuerman JR (1987) 'Factors associated with an increased impact of child sexual abuse.' *Child Abuse and Neglect*, **11**, 201–11.

Cooper D (1995) *Power in Struggle*. Buckingham, UK, Open University Press.

Cornwall A and Lindisfarne N (eds) (1994) *Dislocating Masculinity*. London, Routledge.

Cornwell N (1993) 'The crucial issue: Obtaining agreement for practitioner research.' In B Broad and C Fletcher (eds) *Practitioner Social Work Research in Action*. London, Whiting & Birch.

Cowburn M (1996) 'The black male sex offender in prison: Images and issues.' *Journal of Sexual Aggression*, **2**(2), 122–42.

Craig S (ed.) (1992) *Men, Masculinity and the Media*. London, Sage Publications.

Creighton SJ (1993) 'Organized abuse: NSPCC experience.' *Child Abuse Review*, **2**(4), 232–42.

Cunningham C and MacFarlane K (1996) *When Children Abuse*. Brandon, VT, Safer Society Press.

Cunningham RM, Stiffman AR, Dore P, and Earls F (1994) 'The association of physical and sexual abuse with HIV risk behaviours in adolescence and young adulthood: Implications for public health.' *Child Abuse and Neglect*, **18**(3), 233–45.

Dahlheimer D (1990) 'Creative approaches to healing sexual abuse trauma.' In M Hunter (ed.) *The Sexually Abused Male* (Vol. 2). New York, Lexington.

Dallam SJ (1997) 'Is there a false memory epidemic?' *Treating Abuse Today*, **7**(3), 29–38.

Daly M (1978) *Gyn/Ecology*. London, The Women's Press.

Darlington Y (1993) 'The experience of childhood sexual abuse: Perspectives of adult women who were sexually abused in childhood.' PhD Thesis, Brisbane, University of Queensland.

D'Augelli AR and Patterson CJ (eds) (1995) *Lesbian, Gay and Bisexual Identities over the Lifespan*. New York, Oxford University Press.

Davenport C, Browne K, and Palmer R (1994). 'Opinions on the traumatizing effects of child sexual abuse: evidence for consensus.' *Child Abuse and Neglect*, **18**(9), 725–38.

Davies G (1992) 'Protecting the child witness in the courtroom.' *Child Abuse Review*, **1**(1), 33–41.

Davis GE and Leitenberg H (1987) 'Adolescent sex offenders.' *Psychological Bulletin*, **101**(3), 417–27.

Deblinger E and Heflin AE (1996) *Treating Sexually Abused Children and Their Nonoffending Parents*. Thousand Oaks, CA. Sage Publications.

Dempster HL and Roberts J (1993) 'Child sexual abuse research: A methodological quagmire.' *Child Abuse and Neglect*, **15**, 593–5.

Denzin NK (1997) *Interpretive Ethnography: Ethnographic Practices for the 21st Century*. Thousand Oaks, CA, Sage Publications.

De Young M (1997) 'Satanic ritual abuse in day care: An analysis of 12 American cases.' *Child Abuse Review*, **6**(2), 84–93.

DOH (1991) *Working Together under the Children Act*. London, Her Majesty's Stationery Office.

DOH (1992) *Memorandum of Good Practice on Video Recorded Interviews with Child Witnesses for Criminal Proceedings*. London, Her Majesty's Stationery Office.

DOH (1995) *Child Protection—Messages from Research*. London, Her Majesty's Stationery Office.

DOH (1999) *Working Together To Safeguard Children* (a guide to inter-agency working to safeguard and promote the welfare of children). London, Her Majesty's Stationery Office.

DOH (2002) *Achieving Best Practice in Criminal Proceedings*. London, Her Majesty's Stationery Office.

Dollimore J (1991) *Sexual Dissidence*. Oxford, Clarendon Press.

Doran C and Brannen C (1996) 'Institutional abuse.' In PC Bibby (ed.) *Organised Abuse*. Aldershot, UK, Arena.

Douglas A, Coghill D, and Will D (1996) 'A survey of the first five years' work of a child sexual abuse team.' *Child Abuse Review*, **5**, 227–38.

Doyle C (1996) 'Sexual abuse by siblings: The victims' perspectives.' *The Journal of Sexual Aggression*, **2**(1), 17–32.

Dreyfuss DJ (1989) 'Understanding the cycle of child sexual abuse: A comparison of moral reasoning and coping styles among victimising versus nonvictimising abused children.' PhD Thesis, Los Angeles, California School of Professional Psychology.

Driver E and Droisen A (eds) (1989) *Child Sexual Abuse: Feminist Perspectives*. Basingstoke, UK, Macmillan.

Dubowitz H, Black M, Harrington D, and Verschoore A (1993) 'A follow-up study of behaviour problems associated with child sexual abuse.' *Child Abuse and Neglect*, **17**, 743–54.

Durham AW (1993) 'From victim to survivor.' Unpublished M.A. Dissertation, Warwick, UK, University of Warwick.

Durham AW (1997a) 'The groupwork support of sexually abused boys.' In J Bates, R Pugh, and N Thompson (eds) *Protecting Children: Challenges and Change*. Aldershot, UK, Arena.

Durham AW (1997b) 'The SIBS Survey 1997.' In *SIBS Annual Report*, Internal Report, Warwick, UK, Warwickshire Social Services Department.

Durham AW (1999) 'Young men living through and with child sexual abuse: A practitioner research study.' PhD thesis, Warwick University, UK.

Durham AW (2000) 'From victim to survivor: The groupwork support of sexually abused boys.' In N Baldwin (ed.) *Protecting Children Promoting Their Rights*. London, Whiting & Birch.

Durham, AW (2002) 'Developing a sensitive practitioner research methodology for studying the impact of child sexual abuse.' *British Journal of Social Work*, **32**, 429–42.

Durham AW, Beasley CI, Samson DM, and Ryan H (1995) *The SIB's Project Survey*. Warwick, UK, Warwickshire County Council and North Warwickshire Health Trust Internal Report.

Dziuba-Leatherman J and Finkelhor D (1994) 'How does receiving information about sexual abuse influence boys' perceptions of their risk.' *Child Abuse and Neglect*, **18**(7), 557–68.

Eagleton T (1991) *Ideology*. London, Verso.

Edwards R (1993) 'An education in interviewing: Placing the researcher and the research.' In CM Renzetti and RM Lee (eds) *Researching Sensitive Topics*. Newbury Park, CA, Sage Publications.

Elliot M (ed.) (1993) *Female Sexual Abuse of Children*. Harlow, UK, Longman.

Elliot M, Browne K, and Kilcoyne J (1995) 'Child sexual abuse prevention: What offenders tell us.' *Child Abuse and Neglect*, **19**(5), 579–94.

England SE (1993) 'Modelling theory from fiction and autobiography.' In CK Riessman (ed.) *Qualitative Studies in Social Work Research*. Thousand Oaks, CA, Sage Publications.

Ennis J and Williams BK (1993) *Practice Issues in work with Perpetrators of Child Sexual Abuse*. Dundee, UK, Department of Social Work, University of Dundee.

Etherington K (1995) *Adult Male Survivors of Childhood Sexual Abuse*. London, Pitman Press.

Etherington K (1997) 'Maternal sexual abuse of males.' *Child Abuse Review*, **6**(2), 107–17.

Everitt A (1998) 'Research and development in social work.' In R Adams, L Dominelli, and M Payne (eds) *Social Work*. Basingstoke, UK, Macmillan.

Everitt A, Hardiker P, Littlewood J, and Mullender A (1992) *Applied Research for Better Practice*. Basingstoke, UK, Macmillan.

Faller KC (1989) 'Characteristics of a clinical sample of sexually abused children: How boy and girl victims differ.' *Child Abuse and Neglect*, **13**, 281–91.

Featherstone B (1997) 'What has gender got to do with it? Exploring physically abusive behaviour towards children.' *British Journal of Social Work*, **27**, 419–33.

Featherstone B and Lancaster E (1997) 'Contemplating the unthinkable: Men who sexually abuse children.' *Critical Social Policy*, **17**(4), 51–71.

Fegan L, Rauch A, and McCarthy WB (1993) *Sexuality and People with Intellectual Disability*. Artarmon, Australia, MacLennan & Petty.

Feiring C, Taska L, and Lewis M (1996) 'A process model for understanding adaptation to sexual abuse: The role of shame in defining stigmatization.' *Child Abuse and Neglect*, **20**(8), 767–82.

Feiring C, Taska L, and Lewis M (1998) 'Social support and children's and adolescent's adaptation to sexual abuse.' *Journal of Interpersonal Violence*, **13**(2), 240–60.

Ferguson I and Lavalette M (1999) 'Social work, postmodernism, and Marxism.' *European Journal of Social Work*, **2**(1), 27–40.

Finkelhor D (1984) *Child Sexual Abuse—New Theory and Research*. New York, Free Press.

Finkelhor D (1993) 'Epidemiological factors in the clinical identification of child sexual abuse.' *Child Abuse and Neglect*, **17**, 67–70.

Finkelhor D (1994) 'The international epidemiology of child sexual abuse.' *Child Abuse and Neglect*, **18**(5), 409–17.

Finkelhor D and Browne A (1986) 'The traumatic impact of child sexual abuse: A conceptualization.' *American Journal of Orthopsychiatry*, **55**(4), 530–41.

Finkelhor D, Araji S, Baron L, Browne A, Peters SD, and Wyatt GE (1986) *A Sourcebook on Child Sexual Abuse*. Newbury Park, CA, Sage Publications.

Finkelhor D, Hotaling G, Lewis IA, and Smith C (1990) 'Sexual abuse in a national survey of adult men and women: Prevalence, characteristics and risk factors.' *Child Abuse and Neglect*, **14**, 19–28.

Fisher D (1994) 'Adult sex offenders.' In T Morrison, M Erooga, and C Beckett (eds) *Sexual Offending against Children*. London, Routledge.

Fletcher C (1993a) 'An agenda for practitioner research.' In B Broad and C Fletcher (eds) *Practitioner Social Work Research in Action*. London, Whiting & Birch.

Fletcher C (1993b) 'An analysis of practitioner research.' In B Broad and C Fletcher (eds) *Practitioner Social Work Research in Action*. London, Whiting & Birch.

Foucault M (1976) *The History of Sexuality* (Vol. 1). Harmondsworth, UK, Penguin.

Foucault M (1979) *Discipline and Punish* (transl. by AM Sheridan-Smith). London, Penguin.

Freeman-Longo RE (1986) 'The impact of sexual victimisation on males.' *Child Abuse and Neglect*, **10**(3), 411–14.

Freire P (1985) *The Politics of Education*. Basingstoke, UK, Macmillan.

Freud S (1973) *Introductory Lectures on Psychoanalysis*. Harmondsworth, UK, Penguin.

Friedrich WN (1993) 'Sexual victimization and sexual behaviour in children: A review of recent literature.' *Child Abuse and Neglect*, **17**, 59–66.

Friedrich WN (1995) *Psychotherapy with Sexually Abused Boys*. Thousand Oaks, CA, Sage Publications.

Friedrich WN, Beilke RL, and Urquiza AJ (1988a) 'Behaviour problems in young sexually abused boys. A comparison study.' *Journal of Interpersonal Violence*, **3**(1), 21–8.

Friedrich WN, Berliner L, Urquiza AJ, and Beilke RL (1988b) 'Brief diagnostic group treatment of sexually abused boys.' *Journal of Interpersonal Violence*, **3**(3), 331–43.

Friedrich WN, Luecke WJ, Beilke RL, and Place V (1992) 'Psychotherapy outcome of sexually abused boys.' *Journal of Interpersonal Violence*, **7**(3), 396–409.

Friedrich WN, Jaworski TM, Huxsahl JE, and Bengtson BS (1997) 'Dissociative and sexual behaviours in children and adolescents with sexual abuse and psychiatric histories.' *Journal of Interpersonal Violence*, **12**(2), 155–71.

Fromuth ME and Burkhart BR, (1989) 'Long-term psychological correlates of childhood sexual abuse in two samples of college men.' *Child Abuse and Neglect*, **13**, 533–542.

Fromuth ME, Burkhart BR and Jones CW (1991) 'Hidden child molestation. An investigation of adolescent perpetrators in a nonclinical sample.' *Journal of Interpersonal Violence*, **6**(3), 376–84.

Frosh S (1993) 'The seeds of masculine sexuality.' In JM Ussher and CD Baker (eds) *Psychological Perspectives on Sexual Problems*. London, Routledge.

Frude N (1982) 'The sexual nature of sexual abuse.' *Child Abuse and Neglect*, **6**(2), 211–23.

Fryer P (1988) *Black People in the British Empire*. London, Pluto.

Fuller R and Petch A (1995) *Practitioner Research*. Buckingham, UK, Open University Press.

Furniss T (1991) *The Multi-professional Handbook of Child Sexual Abuse*. London, Routledge.

Garfinkel H (1967) *Studies in Ethnomethodology*. Englewood Cliffs, NJ, Prentice Hall.

Gelsthorpe L and Morris A (eds) (1990) *Feminist Perspectives in Criminology*. Buckingham, UK, Open University Press.

Gil E (1996) *Treating Abused Adolescents*. New York, Guilford Press.

Gil E and Johnson TC (1993) *Sexualised Children*. Rockville, MD, Launch Press.

Gilbert N (ed.) (1993) *Researching Social Life*. London, Sage Publications.

Gilgun JF (1990) 'Factors mediating the effects of childhood maltreatment'. In M Hunter (ed.) *The Sexually Abused Male* (Vol. 1). New York, Lexington.

Gilgun JF and Reiser E (1990) 'The development of sexual identity among men sexually abused as children.' *Families in Society*, November, 515–23.

Gill M and Tutty L (1997) 'Sexual identity issues for male survivors of childhood sexual abuse: A qualitative study.' *Journal of Child Sexual Abuse*, **6**(3), 31–47.

Gill P (1996) 'Organised abuse and Asian communities.' In PC Bibby (ed.) *Organised Abuse*. Aldershot, UK, Arena.

Gilligan C (1997) 'Getting civilised.' In A Oakley and J Mitchell (eds) *Who's Afraid of Feminism*. London, Hamish Hamilton.

Gilroy P (1993) *Small Acts*. London, Serpent's Tail.

Glaser BG and Strauss AL (1967) *The Discovery of Grounded Theory*. Chicago, Aldine.

Glasgow D, Horne L, Calam R, and Cox A (1994) 'Evidence, incidence, gender and age in sexual abuse of children perpetrated by children. Towards a developmental analysis of child sexual abuse.' *Child Abuse Review*, **3**, 196–210.

Gold SR (1991) 'History of child sexual abuse and adult sexual fantasies.' *Violence and Victims*, **6**(1), 75–82.

Gonsiorek JC (1995) 'Gay male identities: Concepts and issues.' In AR D'Augelli and CJ Patterson (eds) *Lesbian, Gay and Bisexual Identities over the Lifespan*. New York, Oxford University Press.

Gonsiorek JC, Bera WH, and LeTourneau D (1994) *Male Sexual Abuse*. Thousand Oaks, CA, Sage Publications.

Gorey KM and Leslie DR (1997) 'The prevalence of child sexual abuse: Integrative review adjustment for potential response and measurement biases.' *Child Abuse and Neglect*, **21**(4), 391–98.

Gough DB (1996) 'An overview of the literature.' In PC Bibby (ed.) *Organised Abuse*. Aldershot, UK, Arena.

Graham H (1984) 'Surveying through stories.' In C Bell and H Roberts (eds) *Social Researching*. London, Routledge & Kegan-Paul.

Gramsci A (1971) *Selections from the Prison Notebooks of Antonio Gramsci*. London, Lawrence & Wishart.

Green L and Parkin W (1999) 'Sexuality, sexual abuse and children's homes—Oppression or protection?' In The Violence Against Children Study Group (eds) *Children, Child Abuse and Child Protection*. Chichester, UK: John Wiley & Sons.

Griffin C (1995) 'Feminism, social psychology and qualitative research.' *The Psychologist*, **8**(3), 119–21.

Grubin D (1998) Sex Offending against Children: Understanding the Risk (Police Research Series Paper 99). London, Her Majesty's Stationery Office.

Grubman-Black SD (1990) *Broken Boys/Mending Men*. New York, Ivy Books.

Hall ER (1987) 'Adolescents' perceptions of sexual assault.' *Journal of Sex Education and Therapy*, **13**(1), 37–42.

Hall L and Lloyd S (1989) *Surviving Child Sexual Abuse*. London, Falmer Press.

Hammersley M and Atkinson P (1983) *Ethnography—Principles in Practice*. London, Tavistock.

Hampton RL (1991) *Black Family Violence*. New York, Lexington.

Harder M and Pringle K (eds) (1997) *Protecting Children in Europe*. Aalborg, Denmark, Aalborg University Press.

Harding S (1987) 'Introduction. Is there a feminist method?' In S Harding (ed.) *Feminism and Methodology*. Buckingham, UK, Open University Press.

Harlow E, Hearn J, and Parkin W (1992) 'Sexuality and social work organisations.' In P Carter, T Jeffs, and M Smith (1992) *Changing Social Work and Welfare*. Buckingham, UK, Open University Press.

Harper J (1993) 'Pre-puberal male victims of incest: A clinical study.' *Child Abuse and Neglect*, **17**, 419–21.

Haugaard JJ and Emery RE (1989) 'Methodological issues in child sexual abuse research.' *Child Abuse and Neglect*, **13**, 89–100.

Hazzard A (1993) 'Trauma-related beliefs as mediators of sexual abuse impact in adult women survivors: A pilot study.' *Journal of Child Sexual Abuse*, **2**(3), 55–69.

Hazzard A, Celano M, Gould J, Lawry S, and Webb C (1995) 'Predicting symptomology and self-blame among child sex abuse victims.' *Child Abuse and Neglect*, **19**(6), 707–14.

Hearn J (1996) 'Is masculinity dead? A critique of the concept of masculinity/masculinities.' In M Mac an Ghaill (ed.) *Understanding Masculinities*. Philadelphia, Open University Press.

Hearn J (1998) *The Violences of Men*. London, Sage Publications.

Hendry J (1989) 'Sexual abuse of boys, the "sexual assault cycle" and the implications for social work practice.' *Child Abuse Review*, **3**(1), 13–16.

Henry J (1997) 'System intervention trauma to child sexual abuse victims following disclosure.' *Journal of Interpersonal Violence*, **12**(4), 499–512.

Henwood K and Pidgeon N (1995) 'Grounded theory and psychological research.' *The Psychologist*, **8**(3), 115–18.

Hepburn JM (1994) 'The implications of contemporary feminist theories of development for the treatment of male victims of sexual abuse.' *Journal of Child Sexual Abuse*, **3**(4), 1–180.

Herman JL (1990) 'Sex offenders. A feminist perspective.' In WL Marshall, DR Laws, and HE Barbaree (eds) *Handbook of Sexual Assault*. New York, Plenum Press.

Herman JL (1992) *Trauma and Recovery*. London, Harper-Collins.

Hilton NZ, Jennings KT, Drugge J, and Stephens J (1995) 'Childhood sexual abuse among clinicians working with sex offenders.' *Journal of Interpersonal Violence*, **10**(4), 525–32.

Holmes G and Offen L (1996) 'Clinicians' hypotheses regarding clients' problems: Are they less likely to hypothesize sexual abuse in male compared to female clients?' *Child Abuse and Neglect*, **20**(6), 493–501.

Home Office (1997) *Criminal Statistics for England and Wales 1996*, London, Government Statistical Service.

Home Office, Crown Prosecution Service, and Department of Health (2001a) *Provision of Therapy for Child Witnesses prior to a Criminal Trial* (Practice Guidance). London, Crown Copyright.

Home Office, Lord Chancellor's Office, Crown Prosecution Service, Department of Health and the National Assembly For Wales (2002) *Achieving Best Evidence in Criminal Proceedings: Guidance for Vulnerable or Intimidated Witnesses, Including Children*. London, Home Office Communication Directorate.

Hooks B (1984) *Feminist Theory—From Margin to Centre*. Boston, South End Press.

Hooks B (1989) *Talking Back—Thinking Feminist—Thinking Black*. Boston, South End Press.

Horne L, Glasgow D, Cos A, and Calam R (1991) 'Sexual abuse of children by children.' *Journal of Child Law*, September–December, 147–51.

Hudson A (1990) 'Elusive subjects: Researching young women in trouble.' In L Gelsthorpe and A Morris A (eds) *Feminist Perspectives in Criminology*. Buckingham, UK, Open University Press.

Hudson A (1992) 'The child sexual abuse "industry" and gender relations in social work.' In M Langan and L Day (eds) *Women, Oppression and Social Work*. London, Routledge.

Humphries B (1994) 'Empowerment and social research: Elements for an analytical framework.' In B Humphries and C Truman (eds) *Re-thinking Social Research*. Aldershot, UK, Avebury.

Humphries B and Truman C (eds) (1994) *Re-thinking Social Research*. Aldershot, UK, Avebury.

Hunter Jr JA (1991) 'A Comparison of the psychosocial maladjustment of adult males and females sexually molested as children.' *Journal of Interpersonal Violence*, **6**(2), 205–17.

Hunter JH (1995) 'Victim to victimizer: Identification of critical victimization variables predictive of later sexual perpetration in juvenile males' (Final Report, Grant No. 90-CA-1454). Report presented at the one-day conference *Juveniles Who Sexually Abuse, 23 April 1996, University of Keele, Staffordshire, UK*.

Hunter M (1990a) *Abused Boys: The Neglected Victims of Sexual Abuse*. New York, Fawcett Columbine.

Hunter M (ed.) (1990b) *The Sexually Abused Male—Prevalence Impact and Treatment* (Vol. 2). New York, Lexington.

Hunter M (ed.) (1990c) *The Sexually Abused Male—Application of Treatment Strategies* (Vol. 2). New York, Lexington.

Hunter M (1995) *Child Survivors and Perpetrators of Sexual Abuse—Treatment Innovations*. Thousand Oaks, CA, Sage Publications.

Hyde C, Bentovim A, and Monck E (1995) 'Some clinical and methodological implications of a treatment outcome study of sexually abused children.' *Child Abuse and Neglect*, **19**(11), 1387–99.

Ireland K (1993) 'Sexual exploitation of children and international travel and tourism.' *Child Abuse Review*, **2**(4), 263–70.

Itzin C (1996) 'Pornography and the organisation of child sexual abuse.' In PC Bibby (ed.) *Organised Abuse*. Aldershot, UK, Arena.

Itzin C (1997) 'Pornography and the organisation of intrafamilial and extrafamilial child sexual abuse: Developing a conceptual model.' *Child Abuse Review*, **6**(2), 94–106.

Jackson S (1992) 'The amazing deconstructing woman.' *Trouble and Strife*, **25**(Winter), 25–31.

Jackson V (1996) *Racism and Child Protection*. London, Cassell.

James CLR (1980) *The Black Jacobins*. London, Allison & Busby.

Jaudes PK and Morris M (1990) 'Child sexual abuse: Who goes home?' *Child Abuse and Neglect*, **14**, 61–8.

Jenkins A (1990) *Invitations to Responsibility*. Adelaide, Dulwich Centre.

Jenson JM, Jacobson M, Unrau Y, and Robinson RL (1996) 'Intervention for victims of child sexual abuse: An evaluation of the children's advocacy model.' *Child and Adolescent Social Work Journal*, **13**(2), 139–56.

Jezl DR, Molidor CE, and Wright TL (1996) 'Physical, sexual and psychological abuse in high school dating relationships: Prevalence rates and self-esteem issues.' *Child and Adolescent Social Work Journal*, **13**(1), 67–87.

Johnson TC (1989) 'Female child perpetrators: Children who molest other children.' *Child Abuse and Neglect*, **13**, 571–85.

Joll J (1977) *Gramsci*. Glasgow, Fontana.

Jones DPH and Ramchandani P (1999) *Child Sexual Abuse*. Abingdon, UK, Radcliffe Medical Press.

Jubber K (1991) 'The socialization of human sexuality.' *South African Sociological Review*, **4**(1), 27–49.

Jumper SA (1995) 'A meta-analysis of the relationship of child sexual abuse to adult psychological adjustment.' *Child Abuse and Neglect*, **19**(6), 715–28.

Kahn TJ (1990) *Pathways*. Brandon, VT, Safer Society Press.

Kamsler A (1992) 'Her story in the making: Therapy with women who were sexually abused in childhood.' In C White and M Durrant (eds) *Ideas for Therapy with Sexual Abuse*. Adelaide, Dulwich Centre.

Kaplan MS, Becker JV, and Tenke CE (1991) 'Influence of abuse history on male adolescent self-reported comfort with interview gender.' *Journal of Interpersonal Violence*, **6**(1), 3–11.

Karp CL and Butler TL (1996) *Treatment Strategies for Abused Children*. Thousand Oaks, CA, Sage Publications.

Karp CL, Butler TL, and Bergstrom SC (1998) *Treatment Strategies for Abused Adolescents*. Thousand Oaks, CA, Sage Publications.

Kassim K and Kasim MS (1995) 'Child sexual abuse: Psychosocial aspects of 101 cases seen in an urban Malaysian setting.' *Child Abuse and Neglect*, **19**(7), 793–99.

Katz I (1996) 'How do young Asian and white people view their problems? A step towards child-focused research.' In I Butler and I Shaw (eds) *A Case of Neglect?* Aldershot, UK, Avebury.

Kaufman M (1987) 'The construction of masculinity and the triad of men's violence.' In Kaufman M (ed.) *Beyond Patriarchy*. Toronto, Open University Press.

Kelly L (1988a) 'How women define their experiences of violence.' In K Yllö and M Bograd (eds) *Feminist Perspectives on Wife Abuse*. Thousand Oaks, CA, Sage Publications.

Kelly L (1988b) *Surviving Sexual Violence*. Cambridge, Polity Press.

Kelly L (1990) 'Journeying in reverse: Possibilities and problems in feminist research on sexual violence.' In L Gelsthorpe and A Morris A (eds) *Feminist Perspectives in Criminology*. Buckingham, UK, Open University Press.

Kelly L (1992) 'The connections between disability and child abuse: A review of research evidence.' *Child Abuse Review*, 1, 157–67.

Kelly L (1994) 'The extent and nature of organised and ritual abuse—DOH Report Reviewed.' *Childright*, No. 111, 7–8.

Kelly L (1996) 'Weasel words: Paedophiles and the cycle of abuse.' *Trouble and Strife*, 33(Summer), 44–9.

Kelly RJ, Macdonald V, and Waterman J (1990) 'Research: Adult male victims of child sexual abuse.' *Advisor*, 3(1), 5.

Kelly L, Regan L, and Burton S (1991) *An Exploratory Study of the Prevalence of Sexual Abuse in a Sample of 16–21 Year Olds*. London, Child Abuse Studies Unit, Polytechnic of North London.

Kelly L, Wingfield R, Burton S, and Regan L (1995) *Splintered Lives*. Barkingside, UK, Barnardo's.

Kennedy M (1992) 'Not the only way to communicate: A challenge to voice in child protection work.' *Child Abuse Review*, 1(3), 169–77.

Kinzl JF, Traweger C, and Biebl W (1995) 'Sexual dysfunctions: Relationship to childhood sexual abuse and early family experiences in a nonclinical sample.' *Child Abuse and Neglect*, 19(7), 785–92.

Kinzl JF, Mangweth B, Traweger C, and Biebl W (1996) 'Sexual dysfunction in males: Significance of adverse childhood experiences.' *Child Abuse and Neglect*, 20(8), 759–66.

Kitzinger C (1989) 'The regulation of lesbian identities: Liberal humanism as an ideology of self-control.' In J Shotter and KJ Gergen (eds) *Texts of Identity*. London, Sage Publications.

Kitzinger J (1997) 'Who are you kidding? Children, power and the struggle against sexual abuse.' In A James and A Prout (eds) *Constructing and Reconstructing Childhood*. London, Falmer Press.

Klein I and Janoff-Bulman R (1996) 'Trauma history and personal narratives: Some clues to coping among survivors of child abuse.' *Child Abuse and Neglect*, 20(1), 45–54.

Koel E (1992) 'Sexually abused boys: Sexual confusion and aggression.' PhD Thesis, Los Angeles, California School of Professional Psychology.

Kweller RB and Ray SA (1992) 'Group treatment of latency-age male victims of sexual abuse.' *Journal of Child Sexual Abuse*, 1(4), 1–18.

La Fontaine JS (1993) 'Defining organised sexual abuse.' *Child Abuse Review*, 2(4), 223–31.

Lamb S and Coakley M (1993) 'Normal childhood sexual play and games: Differentiating play from abuse.' *Child Abuse and Neglect*, 17, 515–26.

Langeland W and Dijkstra S (1995) 'Breaking the intergenerational transmission of child abuse: Beyond the mother–child relationship.' *Child Abuse Review*, 4(1), 4–13.

Lawson C (1993) 'Mother–Son sexual abuse: Rare or underreported? A critique of the research.' *Child Abuse and Neglect*, 7, 261–9.

Leith A and Handforth S (1988) 'Groupwork with sexually abused boys.' *Practice*, 2(2), 166–75.

Leonard P (1984) *Personality and Ideology*. London, Macmillan.

Lew M (1988) *Victims No Longer*. New York, Nevraumont.

Ligezinska M, Firestone P, Manion IG, McIntyre J, Ensom R, and Wells G (1996) 'Children's emotional and behavioural reactions following the disclosure of extrafamilial sexual abuse: Initial effects.' *Child Abuse and Neglect*, **20**(2), 111–25.

Lynch BF, Condon RH, Newell D, and Regan M (1990) 'Positive social action in the treatment of male sexual abuse victims.' *Residential Treatment for Children and Youth*, 17(3), 59–73.

Lyon KH (1999) 'The place of research in social work education.' *ESRC-funded Seminar, Brunel University, 26 May 1999.*

Mac an Ghaill M (ed.) (1996) *Understanding Masculinities*. Philadelphia, Open University Press.

McClellan J, Adams J, Douglas D, McCurry C, and Storck M (1995) 'Clinical characteristics related to severity of sexual abuse: A study of seriously mentally ill youth.' *Child Abuse and Neglect*, **19**(10), 1245–54.

McFadyen A, Hanks H, and James C (1993) 'Ritual abuse: A definition.' *Child Abuse Review*, **2**, 35–41.

McLeod E (1994) *Women's Experience of Feminist Therapy and Counselling*. Buckingham, UK, Open University Press.

Macleod M and Saraga E (1988) 'Child sexual abuse: Challenging the orthodoxy.' In M Loney and R Bocock (1991) *The State or the Market: Politics and Welfare in Contemporary Britain*. London, Sage Publications.

Macleod M and Saraga E (1991) 'Clearing a path through the undergrowth: A feminist reading of recent literature on child sexual abuse.' In P Carter, T Jeffs, and M Smith (eds) *Social Work and Social Welfare Yearbook 3*. Buckingham, UK, Open University Press.

Maltas C and Shay J (1995) 'Trauma contagion in partners of survivors of childhood sexual abuse.' *American Journal of Orthopsychiatry*, **65**(4), 529–39.

Maltz W and Holman B (1987) *Incest and Sexuality*. Toronto, Lexington Books.

Marshall WL, Laws DR, and Barbaree HE (1990) *Handbook of Sexual Assault*. New York, Plenum Press.

Martin J, Anderson J, Romans S, Mullen P, and O'Shea M (1993) 'Asking about child sexual abuse: Methodological implications of a two stage survey.' *Child Abuse and Neglect*, **17**, 383–92.

Martinson FM (1994) *The Sexual Life of Children*. Westport, CT, Bergin & Garvey.

Masson J (1988) *Against Therapy*. London, Fontana.

McLeod E (1994) *Women's Experience of Feminist Therapy and Counselling*. Buckingham, UK, Open University Press.

Mendel MP (1993) 'Issues of particular salience to male survivors of childhood sexual abuse.' *Family Violence and Sexual Assault Bulletin*, **9**(1), 23–7.

Mendel MP (1995) *The Male Survivor*. Thousand Oaks, CA, Sage Publications.

Mennen FE (1995) 'The relationship of race/ethnicity to symptoms in childhood sexual abuse.' *Child Abuse and Neglect*, **19**(1), 115–24.

Mennen FE and Meadow D (1994) 'Depression, anxiety, and self-esteem in sexually abused children.' *Families in Society*, February, 74–81.

Mezey GC and King MB (eds) (1992) *Male Victims of Sexual Assault*. Oxford, Oxford University Press.

Miles MB and Huberman MA (1994) *Qualitative Data Analysis*. Thousand Oaks, CA, Sage Publications.

Mills CW (1959) *The Sociological Imagination*. Oxford, Oxford University Press.

Monck E (1997) 'Evaluating therapeutic intervention with sexually abused children.' *Child Abuse Review*, **6**(3), 163–77.

Monck E and New M (1996) *Report of a Study of Sexually Abused Children and Adolescents, and of Young Perpetrators of Sexual Abuse Who Were Treated in Voluntary Agency Community Facilities*. London, Her Majesty's Stationery Office.

Moore S and Rosenthal D (1993) *Sexuality in Adolescence*. London, Routledge.

Morris I, Scott I, Mortimer M, and Barker D (1997) 'Physical and sexual abuse of children in the West Midlands.' *Child Abuse and Neglect*, 21(3), 285–93.

Morris LA (1997) *The Male Heterosexual*. Thousand Oaks, CA, Sage Publications.

Morrison T and Print B (1995) *Adolescent Sexual Abusers*. Hull, UK, National Organisation for the Treatment of Abusers.

Morrison T, Erooga M, and Beckett C (eds) (1994) *Sexual Offending against Children*. London, Routledge.

Morrow J, Yeager CA, and Lewis DO (1997) 'Encopresis and sexual abuse in a sample of boys in residential treatment.' *Child Abuse and Neglect*, 21(1), 11–18.

Morss JR (1996) *Growing Critical*. London, Routledge.

Mullen PE, Martin JL, Anderson JC, Romans SE, and Herbison GP (1996) 'The long-term impact of the physical, emotional, and sexual abuse of children: A community study.' *Child Abuse and Neglect*, 20(1), 7–21.

Mullender A and Morley R (eds) (1994) *Children Living with Domestic Violence*. London, Whiting & Birch.

Mullender A and Ward D (1991) *Self-directed Groupwork: Users Take Action for Empowerment*. London, Whiting & Birch.

Munir AB and Yasin SHM (1997) 'Commercial sexual exploitation.' *Child Abuse Review*, 6(2), 147–53.

Myers J, O'Neill T, and Jones J (1999) 'Preventing institutional abuse: An exploration of children's rights, needs and participation in residential care.' In The Violence Against Children Study Group (eds) *Children, Child Abuse and Child Protection*. Chichester, UK, John Wiley & Sons.

Myers MF (1989) 'Men sexually assaulted as adults and sexually assaulted as boys.' *Archives of Sexual Behaviour*, 18(3), 203–15.

Nasjleti M (1980) 'Suffering in silence: The male incest victim.' *Child Welfare*, LIX(5), 269–75.

Nayak A and Kehily MJ (1997) 'Maculinities and schooling—Why are young men so homophobic?' In L Steinberg, D Epstein, and R Johnson (eds) *Border Patrols*. London, Cassell.

NCH (1992) *The Report of the Committee of Enquiry into Children and Young People Who Sexually Abuse Other Children*. London, NCH.

NCH Action for Children (1994) *Messages from Children*. London, NCH.

Nelson S (2000) 'Confronting sexual abuse—Challenges for the future.' In C Itzin (ed.) *Home Truths about Child Sexual Abuse—Influencing Policy and Practice*. London, Routledge.

Ney PG, Fung T, and Wickett AR (1994) 'The worst combinations of child abuse and neglect.' *Child Abuse and Neglect*, 18(9), 705–14.

Nyman A and Svensson B (1995) *Boys Sexual Abuse and Treatment*. London, Jessica Kingsley.

Oakley A (1981) 'Interviewing women: A contradiction in terms.' In H Roberts (ed.) *Doing Feminist Research*. London, Routledge & Kegan-Paul.

Oakley A (1997) 'A brief history of gender.' In A Oakley and J Mitchell (eds) *Who's Afraid of Feminism*. London, Hamish Hamilton.

O'Brien MJ (1989) *Characteristics of Male Adolescent Sibling Incest Offenders* (Preliminary Findings). Orwell, VT, Safer Society Program.

O'Callaghan D and Print B (1994) 'Adolescent sexual abusers.' In T Morrison, M Erooga, and RC Beckett (eds) *Sexual Offending against Children, Assessment and Treatment of Male Abusers*. London, Routledge.

Openshaw DK, Graves RB, Ericksen SL, Lowry M, Durso DD, Laurel A, Todd S, Jones KE, and Scherzinger J (1993) 'Youthful sexual offenders: A comprehensive bibliography of scholarly references 1970–1992.' *Family Relations*, **42**, 222–6.

Parton N (ed.) (1996) *Social Theory, Social Change and Social Work*. London, Routledge.

Parton N (1999) 'Some thoughts on the relationship between theory and practice in and for social work.' *ESRC-funded Seminar, Brunel University, 26 May 1999*.

Pellegrin A and Wagner WG (1990) 'Child sexual abuse: Factors affecting victims' removal from home.' *Child Abuse and Neglect*, **14**, 53–60.

Phillips A (1992) 'Universal pretensions in political thought.' In M Barrett and A Phillips (eds) *Destabilizing Theory*. Cambridge, Polity Press.

Pilkington B and Kremer J (1995a) 'A review of the epidemiological research on child sexual abuse—Community and college samples.' *Child Abuse Review*, **4**, 84–98.

Pilkington B and Kremer J (1995b) 'A review of the epidemiological research on child sexual abuse—Clinical samples.' *Child Abuse Review*, **4**, 191–205.

Pithers WD (1990) 'Relapse prevention with sexual aggressors.' In WL Marshall, DR Laws, and HE Barbaree (eds) *Handbook of Sexual Assault*. New York, Plenum Press.

Plummer K (1983) *Documents of Life*. London, Unwin Hyman.

Porter D (ed.) (1992) *Between Men and Feminism*. London, Routledge.

Porter E (1986) *Treating the Young Male Victim of Sexual Assault*. New York, Safer Society Press.

Pringle K (1995) *Men, Masculinities and Social Welfare*. London, Universities College London Press.

Prior V, Glaser D, and Lynch MA (1997) 'Responding to child sexual abuse: The criminal justice system.' *Child Abuse Review*, **6**(2), 128–40.

Rasmussen LA, Burton JE, and Christopherson BJ (1992) 'Precursors to offending and the trauma outcome process in sexually reactive children.' *Journal of Child Sexual Abuse*, **1**(1), 33–48.

Ray KC and Jackson JL (1997) 'Family environment and childhood sexual victimization— A test of the buffering hypothesis.' *Journal of Interpersonal Violence*, **12**(1), 3–17.

Reay D (1996) 'Insider perspectives of stealing the words out of women's mouths: Inter-pretation in the research process.' *Feminist*, No. 53(Summer), 57–73.

Rees G and Stein M (1997a) 'Abuse of adolescents.' *Children and Society*, **11**, 60–2.

Rees G and Stein M (1997b) 'Abuse of adolescents: Implications of North American research for the UK.' *Children and Society*, **11**, 128–34.

Reinhart MA (1987) 'Sexually abused boys.' *Child Abuse and Neglect*, **11**(2), 229–35.

Reinharz S (1992) *Feminist Methods in Social Research*. New York, Oxford University Press.

Renzetti CM and Lee RM (eds) (1993) *Researching Sensitive Topics*. Newbury Park, CA, Sage Publications.

Report of the National Commission of Inquiry into the Prevention of Child Abuse (1996) *Childhood Matters*, Vol. 1: *The Report*. London, Her Majesty's Stationery Office.

Ribbens J (1989) 'Interviewing—An unnatural situation?' *Women's Studies International Forum*, **12**(6), 579–92.

Rice M (1990) 'Challenging orthodoxies in feminist theory: A black feminist critique.' In L Gelsthorpe and A Morris (eds) *Feminist Perspectives in Criminology*. Buckingham, UK, Open University Press.

Richardson MF, Meredith W, and Abbot DA (1993) 'Sex-typed role in male adolescent sexual abuse survivors.' *Journal of Family Violence*, **8**(1), 89–100.

Ridgeway SM (1993) 'Abuse and deaf children: Some factors to consider.' *Child Abuse Review*, **2**(3), 166–73.

Riessman CK (eds) (1993) *Qualitative Studies in Social Work Research*. Thousand Oaks, CA, Sage Publications.

Risin LI and Koss MP (1987) 'The sexual abuse of boys. Prevalence and descriptive characteristics of childhood victimisations.' *Journal of Interpersonal Violence*, **2**(3), 309–23.

Roane TH (1992) 'Male victims of sexual abuse: A case review within a child protective team.' *Child Welfare*, **LXII**(3), 231–9.

Roberts H (ed.) (1981) *Doing Feminist Research*. London, Routledge & Kegan-Paul.

Robson C (1993) *Real World Research*. Oxford, Blackwell.

Rogers CN and Terry T (1984) 'Clinical interventions with boy victims of sexual abuse.' In IR Stuart and JG Greer (eds) *Victims of Sexual Aggression*. New York, Van Nostrand Reinhold.

Rudin MM, Zalewski C and Bodmer-Turner J (1995) 'Characteristics of child sexual abuse victims according to perpetrator gender.' *Child Abuse and Neglect*, **19**(8), 963–73.

Runyan DK, Hunter WM, Everson MD, Whitcomb D, and De Vos E (1994) 'The intervention stressors inventory: A measure of the stress of intervention for sexually abused children.' *Child Abuse and Neglect*, **18**(4), 319–29.

Ryan G (1986) 'Annotated bibliography: Adolescent perpetrators of sexual molestation of children.' *Child Abuse and Neglect*, **10**, 125–31.

Ryan G (1989) 'Victim to victimiser.' *Journal of Interpersonal Violence*, **4**(3), 325–41.

Ryan GD and Lane SL (1991) *Juvenile Sexual Offending*. Lexington, MA, Lexington Books.

Salter AC (1988) *Treating Child Sex Offenders and Victims*. Newbury Park, CA, Sage Publications.

Salter AC (1995) *Transforming Trauma*. Thousand Oaks, CA, Sage Publications.

Sanders-Phillips K, Moisan PA, Wadlington S, Morgan S, and English K (1995) 'Ethnic differences in psychological functioning among Black and Latino sexually abused girls.' *Child Abuse and Neglect*, **19**(6), 691–706.

Sanford L (1990) *Strong at the Broken Places*. London, Virago.

Sansonnett-Hayden H, Hayley G, Marriage C, and Fine S (1987) 'Sexual abuse and psychopathology in hospitalised adolescents.' *Journal of the American Academy of Child and Adolescent Psychiatry*, **26**, 262–7.

Saradjian J (1998) *Women Who Sexually Abuse*. Chichester, UK, John Wiley & Sons.

Sariola H and Uutela A (1994) 'The prevalence of child sexual abuse in Finland.' *Child Abuse and Neglect*, **18**(10), 827–35.

Savin-Williams RC (1995) 'Lesbian, gay and bi-sexual adolescents.' In AR D'Augelli and CJ Patterson (eds) *Lesbian, Gay and Bisexual Identities over the Lifespan*. New York, Oxford University Press.

Scott S (1993) 'Beyond belief: Beyond help? Report on a helpline advertised after the transmission of a Channel 4 film on ritual abuse.' *Child Abuse Review*, **2**(4), 243–50.

Scott W (1992) 'Group therapy with sexually abused boys: Notes toward managing behaviour.' *Clinical Social Work Journal*, **20**(4), 395–408.

Scraton P (1990) 'Scientific knowledge or masculine discourses? Challenging patriarchy in criminology.' In L Gelsthorpe and A Morris (eds) *Feminist Perspectives in Criminology*. Buckingham, UK, Open University Press.

Sebold J (1987) 'Indicators of child sexual abuse in males.' *Social Casework*, February, 75–80.

Sedgwick EK (1985) *Between Men*. New York, Columbia University Press.

Sedgwick EK (1990) *Epistemology of the Closet*. Berkeley, CA, Columbia University Press.

Sefarbi R (1990) 'Admitters and deniers among adolescent sex offenders and their families: A preliminary study.' *American Journal of Orthopsychiatry*, **60**(3), 460–5.

Seidler VJ (1989) *Rediscovering Masculinity*. London, Routledge.

Seidler VJ (ed.) (1992) *Men, Sex and Relationships*. London, Routledge.

Sgroi SMD (1982) *Handbook of Clinical Intervention in Child Sexual Abuse*. Toronto, Lexington.

Shaw I (1996) 'Unbroken voices: Children, young people and qualitative methods.' In I Butler and I Shaw (eds) *A Case of Neglect?* Aldershot, UK, Avebury.

Shotter J and Gergen KJ (eds) (1989) *Texts of Identity*. London, Sage Publications.

Siddall R (1994) 'The hidden taboo.' *Community Care—Inside*, 30 June.

Sigmon ST, Greene MP, Rohan KJ, and Nichols JE (1996) 'Coping and adjustment in male and female survivors of childhood sexual abuse.' *Journal of Child Sexual Abuse*, **5**(3), 57–75.

Silverman AB, Reinherz HZ, and Giaconia RM (1996) 'The long-term sequelae of child and adolescent abuse: A longitudinal community study.' *Child Abuse and Neglect*, **20**(8), 709–23.

Simpson L (1995) *Evaluation of Treatment Methods in Child Sexual Abuse* (a literature review). Bath, UK, Social Services Research and Development Unit, University of Bath and Dorset Area Child Protection Committee.

Sinason V (ed.) (1994) *Treating Survivors of Satanist Abuse*. London, Routledge.

Singer MI, Hussey D, and Strom KJ (1992) 'Grooming the victim: An analysis of a perpetrator's seduction letter.' *Child Abuse and Neglect*, **16**, 877–86.

Sivanandan A (1990) *Communities of Resistance*. London, Verso.

Smith WR (1988) 'Delinquency and abuse among juvenile sexual offenders.' *Journal of Interpersonal Violence*, **3**(4), 400–13.

Solomos J (1989) *Race and Racism in Contemporary Britain*. London, Macmillan.

Spencer JR and Flin R (1990) *The Evidence of Children*. London, Blackstone.

Steele K and Colrain J (1990) 'Abreactive work with sexual abuse survivors.' In M Hunter (ed.) *The Sexually Abused Male* (Vol. 2). New York, Lexington.

Steinberg L, Epstein D, and Johnson R (1997) *Border Patrols*. London, Cassell.

Steinman C (1992) 'Gaze out of bounds: Men watching men on television.' In S Craig (ed.) *Men, Masculinity and the Media*. London, Sage Publications.

Struve J (1990) 'Dancing with the patriarchy: The politics of sexual abuse.' In M Hunter (ed.) *The Sexually Abused Male* (Vol. 1). New York, Lexington.

Sumner C (1990) 'Foucault, gender and the censure of deviance.' In L Gelsthorpe and A Morris (eds) *Feminist Perspectives in Criminology*. Buckingham, UK, Open University Press.

Taylor-Browne J (1997a) 'Obfuscating child sexual abuse 1: The identification of social problems.' *Child Abuse Review*, **6**(1), 4–10.

Taylor-Browne J (1997b) 'Obfuscating child sexual abuse 2: Listening to survivors.' *Child Abuse Review*, **6**(2), 118–27.

Thanki V (1994) 'Ethnic diversity and child protection.' *Children and Society*, **8**(3), 232–44.

Thomas WI and Znaniecki F (1958) *The Polish Peasant in Europe and America*. New York, Dover Publications (originally published 1918).

Thompson N (1993) *Anti-Discriminatory Practice*. Basingstoke, UK, Macmillan.

Thompson R (1993) *Religion, Ethnicity and Sex Education Exploring the Issues*. London, National Children's Bureau.

Truman C (1994) 'Feminist challenges to traditional research: Have they gone far enough?' In B Humphries and C Truman (eds) *Re-thinking Social Research*. Aldershot, UK, Avebury.

Urquiza AJ and Capra M (1990) 'The impact of sexual abuse: Initial and long term effects.' In M Hunter (ed.) *The Sexually Abused Male* (Vol. 1). New York. Lexington.

Urquiza AJ and Keating LM (1990) 'The prevalence of sexual victimization of males.' In M. Hunter (ed.) *The Sexually Abused Male* (Vol. 1). New York, Lexington.

Ussher JM and Baker C (eds) (1993) *Psychological Perspectives on Sexual Problems—New Directions in Theory and Practice.* London, Routledge.

Vander Mey BJ (1988) 'The sexual victimisation of male children: A review of previous research.' *Child Abuse and Neglect*, **12**, 61–72.

Violence against Children Study Group (eds) (1990) *Taking Child Abuse Seriously.* London, Unwin Hyman.

Walby S (1992) 'Post-post modernism? Theorizing social complexity.' In M Barrett and A Phillips (eds) *Destabilizing Theory.* Oxford, Polity Press.

Warner M (1993) *Fear of a Queer Planet.* Minneapolis, MN, University of Minnesota Press.

Wasserman B (1998) *Feeling Good Again.* Brandon, VT, Safer Society Press.

Watkins B and Bentovim A (1992a) 'Male children and adolescents as victims: A review of current knowledge.' In GC Mezey and MB King (eds) *Male Victims of Sexual Assault.* Oxford, Oxford University Press.

Watkins B and Bentovim A. (1992b) 'The sexual abuse of male children and adolescents: A review of current research.' *Journal of Child Psychology and Psychiatry*, **33**(1), 197–248.

Weedon C (1987) *Feminist Practice and Post-structuralist Theory.* Oxford, Blackwell.

Weir K and Wheatcroft MS (1995) 'Allegations of children's involvement in ritual sexual abuse: Clinical experience of 20 cases.' *Child Abuse and Neglect*, **19**(4), 491–505.

Wellings K, Field J, Johnson AM, and Wadsworth J (1994) *Sexual Behaviour in Britain.* Harmondsworth, UK, Penguin.

Wellman MM (1993) 'Child sexual abuse and gender differences: Attitudes and prevalence.' *Child Abuse and Neglect*, **17**, 539–47.

West DJ (1992) 'Homophobia: Covert and overt.' In GC Mezey and MB King (eds) *Male Victims of Sexual Assault.* Oxford, Oxford University Press.

Westcott HL (1991) *Institutional Abuse of Children.* London, National Society for the Prevention of Cruelty to Children.

White C and Durrant M (eds) (1992) *Ideas for Therapy with Sexual Abuse.* Adelaide, Dulwich Centre.

White M (1989) *Selected Papers.* Adelaide, Dulwich Centre.

White M and Epston D (1992) *Experience, Contradiction, Narrative and Imagination* (selected papers of Michael White and David Epston, 1989–1991). Adelaide, Dulwich Centre.

Widom CS and Ames MA (1994) 'Criminal consequences of childhood sexual victimization.' *Child Abuse and Neglect*, **18**(4), 303–18.

Wiehe VR (1990) *Sibling Abuse.* New York. Lexington.

Wieland S (1998) *Techniques and Issues in Abuse-focused Therapy with Children and Adolescents.* Thousand Oaks, CA, Sage Publications.

Williams C (1995) *Invisible Victims.* London, Jessica Kingsley.

Wilson M (1993) *Crossing the Boundary—Black Women Survive Incest.* London, Virago.

Wolfe DA (1994) 'Preventing gender-based violence—The significance of adolescence.' *Violence Update*, **5**(1), 1, 2, 4, 8, and 10.

Wolfe DA, Sas L, and Wekerle C (1994) 'Factors associated with the development of post traumatic stress disorder among child victims of sexual abuse.' *Child Abuse and Neglect*, **18**, 37–50.

Wolfe DA, Wekerle C, and Scott K (1997) *Alternatives to Violence.* Thousand Oaks, CA, Sage Publications.

Worling JR (1995) 'Sexual abuse histories of adolescent male sex offenders: Differences on the basis of the age and gender of their victims.' *Journal of Abnormal Psychology*, **104**(4), 610–13.

Wright LB and Loiselle MB (1997) *Back on Track—Boys Dealing with Sexual Abuse*. Brandon, VT, Safer Society Press.

Wynkoop TF, Capps SC, and Priest BJ (1995) 'Incidence and prevalence of child sexual Abuse: A critical review of data collection procedures.' *Journal of Child Sexual Abuse*, 4(2), 49–66.

Wyre R (1996) 'The mind of a paedophile.' In PC Bibby (ed.) *Organised Abuse*. Aldershot, UK, Arena.

Youngson SC (1993) 'Ritual abuse: Consequences for professionals.' *Child Abuse Review*, 2(4), 251–62.

Zucker KJ and Kuksis M (1990) 'Gender dysphoria and sexual abuse: A case report.' *Child Abuse and Neglect*, 14, 281–3.

Appendix A

THOUGHTS AND FEELINGS SORT CARDS

CONTENTS OF THE CARDS

I was afraid that I might get AIDS
I was afraid that I might get pregnant
I was afraid that I might make her pregnant
I thought that people would think I was weird
I thought I would be blamed
I was afraid people would think that I was gay
I was worried that I would upset the family
I was worried I would upset the person who abused me
I felt dirty
I felt it was my fault
I was told that it was my fault
I thought I'd have to go into care
I didn't really know it was wrong when it first started
I worry that I knew it was wrong and didn't stop it
I was worried about how sometimes it felt good
I was worried because it didn't feel good
I was worried about being sexually aroused when it was happening

I cared about him/her and didn't want to get him/her into trouble
It looked as if I had agreed for it to happen
I didn't know who to tell
I was embarrassed
I was ashamed
I felt guilty
I was given things and/or money not to tell
I was told not to tell
I was too afraid to tell
I didn't think anyone would believe me
I was disgusted with myself
I thought people would be disgusted with me
I didn't want to involve the police
I didn't want to go to court
I was afraid he/she would come after me
I worry that it might mean that I am gay
I worry that it might cause me to abuse someone
I worry that I let it happen to me
I think I could have done more to stop it happening
I worry that I attract people to abuse me
I worry that I won't be able to enjoy sex when I am older
I worry that people can tell that I've been abused
I wished I hadn't told anybody
I'm really scared about it all
I keep thinking about it all the time
I was worried that I would split my parents up
I thought my brothers/sisters would have to go into care

Appendix B

ABUSER–VICTIM FLOW CHART

Abuser

Victim

Finds a child or young person, who may be vulnerable, isolated, or *may* have other difficulties and is likely to find it difficult to tell. Offers trust and friendship.	Child enjoys the friendship, the close attention, and possibly the treats being given and begins to feel special and cared about. Begins to initiate further contact.
Begins to get closer and sets up opportunities for physical contact, which becomes sexual contact, and tells the child this is part of being special and being loved.	Child becomes confused and afraid, but doesn't know what to do, and still enjoys the treats and attention being given.
You're aroused, you're enjoying this. I love you. You're special. I'm pleased that we're doing this. This is just for us, our secret. Please don't tell. You won't tell. You can't tell. If you do then I'll . . . and people will begin to think that you . . . . So let it be our secret.	I don't know why it feels good when I'm being touched. Is this because I want it to happen. I don't know why it doesn't feel good. What's wrong with me? What would people think about me? Why am I doing this? Why do I like him (her)? I'm so scared, I'm going to get into so much trouble. So I'll just keep it quiet.

Appendix C

Feeling Safe and Being Safe

(Information for Young People about
Healthy Relationships)

Images

When you look in the newspapers or on TV, what images of men and women do you see and how do they make you feel?

Newspapers present very powerful false images about the way men should be and about the way women should be and how they should manage their sexuality and their sexual identity.

Men are often portrayed as being confident, active, dominant, and in control. Women are often portrayed as being weak, passive, and dependent on men.

Often we may feel uncomfortable by these images, because we know they do not really fit with our own feelings and experiences.

When this happens we can become oppressed by these images to the point that we may even try to change our own behaviour and image to fit in with how we think we ought to be.

Sexuality

Sexuality is about our sexual feelings; toward others and how we feel about ourselves.

It's also about sexual attraction to others.

It's also about our sexual identity—how we portray ourselves to others and the messages we give out about our sexual interests.

Sexuality is really about everything in our daily lives that makes us sexual human beings: our sexual feelings, thoughts, and desires, as well as any sexual contact from sexual touching to sexual intercourse.

We cannot really control our sexual feelings, but we can control our sexual behaviours.

Sexual Feelings

Sometimes we have sexual and emotional feelings toward members of the opposite sex.

Sometimes we have these feelings towards members of our own sex.

**Sometimes we may have both; we are all capable of
having both.**

This is particularly true when we are teenagers and our bodies and sexual feelings are changing and developing very fast.

Why do you think it is that girls feel more comfortable about having emotional feelings toward each other than boys do?

Sometimes when we have these feelings, we may be worried about our sexuality and our sexual identity.

We all like to have the right image, and we sometimes believe that the right image is the one we see in the newspapers or on TV.

We should not believe the false images that we see.

**The most important thing is to be comfortable about who
we are and how we feel about ourselves and about
others.**

We Are All Still Learning!

Many teenagers think that their friends and peers know more about sex than they do.

Many teenagers think that their friends and peers are more sexually experienced than they are.

If you thought or believed this, how might it affect the way you feel and behave?

Some people make the mistake of believing that having the right image is more important than being truthful about what they know, what they don't know, and what they need to learn.

**It is important to know that you cannot always act on
your sexual feelings.**

Informed consent

It is really important that we find out how another person may feel about anything we may wish to say to or do with them.

If we would like to put our arm around another person or kiss them, we should ask for their consent (permission):

- We should not just do it and hope that they are OK about it.
- Just because you are a boy, it does not mean that you have to make the first move.
- Just because you are a girl, it does not mean that you have to say yes.
- We should never do anything sexual to another person unless they are old enough and able to give informed consent.

To give informed consent, a person has to be:

- Old enough to understand what they are consenting to.
- Have enough knowledge and information.
- Be in a situation where it is just as easy to say 'no' as it is to say 'yes'.
- They must no feel under any pressure.

Pressure

How might somebody feel under pressure?

- Being younger than the other person.
- Having less knowledge and experience than the other person.
- Having less power than the other person.
- Feel that they should say yes because this is what is expected of them.
- Feel they should say yes to maintain an image among their friends.
- Believe that they will feel ashamed and less of a man or less of a woman because they have said no.

If anybody touches you or says something to you in a way that makes you feel uncomfortable, you should tell somebody who can help you do something about it. Always try to have a list in your mind of the people you could tell.

You have a right to feel safe all the time!

Appendix D

Information about Child Sexual Abuse

When a child or young person has been sexually abused, he or she is likely to be left with many confused and distressing feelings. He or she may need help and reassurance in understanding that he or she is not responsible for what has happened and that the way he or she feels is a normal reaction.

Most children and young people will fare better with the help and support of a caring adult(s). The impact of child sexual abuse will vary between individuals and will not always become immediately evident.

Often children and young people in these circumstances will say that they are managing and will not really wish to share their feelings or discuss details of their abuse. Some will hide and disguise their feelings in a misguided attempt to protect themselves and their families.

Many children and young people deeply believe that they are responsible for being abused, or may have fears that they have cooperated, or may be worried about experiencing aspects of physical pleasure during the abuse. Some of these feelings are likely to have been set up by the abuser as a means of preventing the child or young person from being able to tell.

Some children and young people will have recurring flashbacks, brought on by senses and feelings that remind them of the abuse. Some will find it very difficult to trust others and may become withdrawn. Others may become angry and sometimes have unpredictable behaviours or losses of temper. Some may live in fear of retaliation from the abuser for telling or may worry about having to give evidence at a court trial.

Young people who have been sexually abused may have anxieties about their sexuality and future sexual behaviour. A few mischosen words can cause considerable anxiety and drive the young person into further silence and private suffering.

It is normal for young people to experience great difficulty in talking openly about their feelings, even to people who are close to them. Parents and carers can also have feelings of guilt and responsibility, forgetting that responsibility is with the person who committed the abuse.

Often survivors of abuse will say that they are OK, when really they may need help. Some children and young people can recover from sexual abuse at a greater pace than others. Some will need specialist help in coming to terms with what they have been through and in gaining a better understanding of how they were not responsible, and why their thoughts and feelings are a normal response to a very difficult experience.

INDEX

The Abuser–Victim Flow Chart 125, 131, 145, 171
abusing others 27–8, 93–5, 134, 147
Achieving Best Evidence in Criminal Proceedings
    (Home Office et al., 2002) 130
admissibility, evidence 130
adolescents
   identity 29
   language 114
   masculinities 11
   peer groups 114
   PTSD 97
   sexuality 83–4
adult power issues 64–7, 121
alcohol 102–3, 147
analytical practice framework diagram 116
anger management 101, 133
anti-oppression 35–7
appeal hearings 80
attraction 6–7
authority 55

behavioural issues
   abuse consequences 100–2
   cognitive behavioural techniques 132
   disturbed behaviours 26
   masculinities 117
   protective behaviours 142
benefits, research participation 106–10, 148
Browne, A 21–2, 26
butane gas 102–3

child-centred practices 117–21, 149
cognitive behavioural techniques 132
Colin's story 49–50
   abusing others 93
   adult power abuse 66–7
   alcohol 102
   being abused 60–2
   control issues 101

drugs 102
   flashbacks 98
   friendships 88–9
   panic attacks 98
   peer groups 89–90
   research participation 108–9
   sexual enjoyment 91
   sexual fears 89–90
   trying to tell 72–3, 78–9
   violence 61
colours 125, 138
compensation issues 48, 53, 80, 131
confidentiality 127, 142
confusion 28–30
control issues 101, 127
Cooper, D 115
court trials 130
criminal injuries 48, 53, 80, 131
criminal justice system 113, 122
Criminal Records Bureau 122
cultural factors 22–3, 83

Daly, M 4–5
data collections 17
David's story 51–2
   being abused 64
   families 104
   Feelings and Colours 125
   flashbacks 99
   nightmares 99
   non-verbal contributions 109
   research participation 108
   research techniques 125
   Road to Recovery 125, 135–7
   sexual fears 88
   trying to tell 76, 79
debriefing processes 38
definitions
   child sexual abuse 16–20

definitions (*cont.*)
  multiple/organised abuse 20
  racism 23–4
  ritual abuse 21
denial issues 18–20
deserving victims 21
disabled children
  life-story methods 36
  multiple/organised abuse 20
  oppression 24
disclosure 68–9, 128
dissociation
  see also memories
  abuse consequences 22
  memory blockages 132
  Ryan 65–6
  Sean 71
disturbed behaviours 26
domination 8–9
drawings 109
driving 101–2
drugs 102–3, 147

education 133, 145
emotions *see* feelings
empowerment 36, 119
enjoyment 91–2
environments, telling 46, 119
equality 34, 120
escapes 70
Etherington, K 26
ethnography 33
evidence, admissibility 130

facts, sexual abuse 16–31
false memory syndrome 21
families
  abuse consequences 103–4
  interactions 115
  therapeutic practices 129
  trying to tell 75–6
fears
  abusing others 93–5, 134
  rationalisations 58–9
  recovery 132–3
  sexuality 84–92
  telling 68–9, 74–5, 144–5
Feeling Safe and Being Safe (author) 126, 145,
  173–5
feelings
  abuse consequences 99–100

anger management 133
colours 138
Feeling Safe and Being Safe 126, 145, 173–5
Feelings and Colours 125
paintings 109, 137–8
research participation 106–9
Thoughts and Feelings Sort Cards 125, 128,
  141–2, 169–70
trying to tell 72–4
Feelings and Colours 125
feminism 9, 34–5
Finkelhor, D 21–2, 26, 131
flashbacks
  abuse consequences 97–9
  recovery 132–3
  sexual enjoyment 91–2
flexibility 126
flooding, memories 23
Foucault, M 7, 12, 83, 147
Four Preconditions to Sexual Abusing (Finkelhor)
  131
Four Traumagenic Dynamics Model (Finkelhor
  and Browne) 21–2, 26
Freud, S 13
friendships 83–96
  abuse 60
  recovery 134–5
  trying to tell 77

gay sexuality
  homophobia 11–12, 147
  queer theory 5–7
  sexual abuse 29, 147
  sexual fears 84–92
Gramsci, A 8

headmasters 55
heads of care 51, 59
hegemony 8–9, 11–13
  see also power issues
helpful services 121–3, 149
heterosexuality
  internalised oppression 85
  masculinities 10, 147
  patriarchal relations 5–7
  Paul 94
hierarchies 34–5
homophobia 11–12, 147
homosexuality *see* gay sexuality
Hooks, B 34

identity issues 28–30
impacts, child abuse 21–4
improvements, services 121–3
inappropriate sexual behaviours 27
Information About Child Sexual Abuse 126, 145,
    177
insights 120
institutions 20, 122, 149
interactive relationships 33, 115–16
internalised oppression 84–5, 122–3, 147
international dimensions, multiple/organised
    abuse 20–1
interviews 26, 45–7

Jubber, K 29
Justin's story 47–8
    see also multiple abuse
    abusing others 93–4
    adult power abuse 64
    being abused 55–6, 58–9
    butane gas 102–3
    emotional pain 99–100
    families 103–4
    nightmares 98
    peer groups 88
    research participation 107–8
    sexual enjoyment 91–2
    sexual fears 90–1
    trying to tell 70–1, 74–5, 77–81

Keeping Safe Plan 125, 127, 142–3
Kelly, L 21

language issues 114–15, 119
legal aspects
    Achieving Best Evidence in Criminal Proceedings
        130
    changes 149
    compensation 48, 53, 80, 131
    criminal justice system 113
    Criminal Records Bureau 122
    disclosure 68–9, 128
    evidence admissibility 130
    police involvements 77–9
    *Provision of Therapy for a Child Witness Prior to a
        Criminal Trial* 123, 130
    Sex Offenders Register 122
    support systems 129–30
    telling processes 79–81
    therapeutic practices 129–31

Liam's story 50
    adult power abuse 64–5
    being abused 60
    research participation 108
    sexual fears 85–6
    trying to tell 75
life stories 32–4, 36, 43–110

male-child sexual abuse 16–31, 118
manipulation 54, 63
masculinities
    behavioural issues 117
    heterosexuality 147
    power issues 56
    sexuality 117
    social contexts 10–14
    violence 12
medical examinations 78–9
memories
    see also dissociation
    flooding 23
    Justin 48
    PTSD 97
    recovery 132–3
    Ryan 138–9
Mendel, MP 26
men's practices *see* masculinities
mixed feelings painting 137–8
multiple abuse 20–1
myths
    abusing others 93
    child-centred practices 120
    gender 131–2
    male-child sexual abuse 16–31
    sexuality 84

nightmares 98–9
non-pathologising therapeutic practices 148–9
non-verbal contributions, research 46, 109, 125,
    137–40

oppression
    anti-oppression 35–7
    disabled children 24
    internalised oppression 84–5, 122–3, 147
    racism 23–4
    recovery 131–2
    therapeutic practices 120
    under-reporting 19
organised abuse 20–1

paintings 46, 109, 137–8
panic attacks 98
participants, research 106–10, 148
pathologising therapeutic practices 148–9
patriarchal relations 4–7
Paul's story 48–9
    abusing others 94–5
    adult power abuse 65
    anger 101
    being abused 56–8
    emotional pain 100
    families 104
    flashbacks 99
    research participation 107
    sexual fears 87–8, 90, 92
    trying to tell 72, 74–7
peer groups 83–96
    adolescence 114
    families 103
    interactions 115–16
    recovery 134–5
    sexual identity 29
perversions 6–7
physical pleasures 133–4
plans 125–35, 142–3
pleasures 133–4
poetry 46, 109, 125, 138–40
police involvements 77–9
possessions 5
Post Sexual Abuse Trauma (PSAT) 22
Post Traumatic Stress Disorder (PTSD) 22, 97
post-abuse services 123
post-interview phases 47
post-structuralism 114, 147
power issues
    adults 64–7, 121
    anti-oppression 35–7
    being abused 54–67
    empowerment 36, 119
    feminist research 35
    hegemony 8–9, 11–13
    language 114–15
    manipulation 54, 63
    masculinities 56
    powerlessness 119, 128–9
    racism 115
    relationships 54–67
    sexuality 12, 147
    therapy abuse 13
practice implications 113–49
practitioner research 37–9

prevalence, male-child sexual abuse 16–20
preventive programmes 121
protective behaviours 142
Provision of Therapy for a Child Witness Prior to a
    Criminal Trial (Home Office et al., 2001a)
    123, 130
PSAT see Post Sexual Abuse Trauma
psychological traumas 13
PTSD see Post Traumatic Stress Disorder

queer theory 5–7
quotation cards 141–2

racism 19, 23–4, 115
rationalisations 58–9
recovery issues 125–45
reflexivity 34
relationships
    families 103–4
    interactions 33, 115–16
    patriarchal relations 4–7
    peers 83–96
    power 54–67
    practitioner research 39
reporting 18–20
research issues
    benefits 106–10, 148
    effects 31
    feelings 106–9
    feminism 35
    participants 106–10, 148
    practitioner research 37–9
    researchers 33, 36–8, 109–10
    selection procedures 43–5
    sensitive areas 32–40
    studies 17–18
    techniques 125–6
residential care institutions 122, 149
resilience factors 24–5
resistance 8–9
responsibility issues 128–9, 148
retaliation responses 27
rituals 19, 21
Road to Recovery 125, 135–7
rules, safety 127
Ryan, G 27
Ryan's story 52–3
    adult power abuse 65–6
    families 104
    non-verbal contributions 109
    peer groups 88

research participation 108–9
research techniques 125
Ryan's Poetry 125, 138–40
sexual fears 86–7
trying to tell 71, 76

safety factors
  Feeling Safe and Being Safe 126, 145, 173–5
  Keeping Safe Plan 125, 142–3
  rules 127
  therapeutic practices 126–7
satanic ritual abuse 21
school escapes 70
Sean's story 50–1
  adult power abuse 66
  being abused 59–60
  driving fast 101–2
  research participation 108
  sexual fears 92
  trying to tell 71, 75, 77, 80
secrecy 18–20, 36
selection procedures, participants 43–5
self-reliance 19–20
sensitive areas
  equality 120
  participant selection 44
  research 32–40
  therapeutic practices 117–18
services, improvements 121–3, 149
Sex Offenders Register 122
sexual issues
  confusion 28–30
  enjoyment 91–2
  identity 28–30
  inappropriate behaviours 27
  perversions 6–7
  violence 14
sexuality 83–96
  see also gay sexuality: heterosexuality
  education 133, 145
  fears 84–92
  hegemony 8
  masculinities 117
  myths 84
  patriarchal relations 4
  power 12, 147
  sexuality and attraction diagram 6
  social contexts 83–4
  therapeutic practices 133–4
social contexts 3–15
  dissociation 22

male-child sexual abuse diagram 118
  oppression 147
  sexuality 83–4
social oppression *see* oppression
spell-breaking 128
staff, residential institutions 122, 149
stepfathers 48, 56–8
streetwise personalities 61
strengths, anti-oppressive research practices 35
stress 110
structuralism 113–14
studies 17–18
subordination 8–9
suicidal feelings 100
supervision 38
support systems
  abusing others 28
  legal issues 129–30
  post-interview phases 47
  practitioner research 37, 39
  researchers 38, 110
  resilience 25

telephone helplines 122
telling processes
  families 129
  life stories 68–82
  non-verbal contributions 46, 109, 125, 137–40
  recovery 143–5
  therapeutic practices 127–9
  *Why Young People Find It Hard to Tell about
    Sexual Abuse* 125
theoretical contexts 3–40
therapeutic practices 13, 113–24, 126–35, 148–9
Thoughts and Feelings Sort Cards 125, 128, 141–2,
  169–70
threats 19, 55
trade-offs 63
training issues 122, 149
traumas 13
trust 36, 38, 127

under-reporting 18–20

venues, interviews 45–6
violence
  Colin 61
  masculinities 12
  patriarchal relations 4

Paul's stepfather 48, 56–8
sexual violence 14
women 4

Why Young People Find It Hard to Tell about Sexual Abuse 125, 143–5

Women's Liberation Movement 9
word games 128
writing 109

young person-centred practices 117–21, 149